Race and Culture in *New Orleans Stories*

Race and Culture in *New Orleans Stories*

Kate Chopin, Grace King, Alice Dunbar-Nelson, and George Washington Cable

James Nagel

THE UNIVERSITY OF ALABAMA PRESS
Tuscaloosa

Tuscaloosa, Alabama 35487-0380

Manufactured in the United States of America

Typeface: Caslon
Cover illustration: *Portrait of Betsy*, François Fleischbeing, ca. 1837. Courtesy of the Historic New Orleans Collection, Acc. No. 1985.212
Cover design: Michele Myatt Quinn

∞

The paper on which this book is printed meets the minimum requirements of American National Standard for Information Sciences—Permanence of Paper for Printed Library Materials, ANSI Z39.48-1984.

Nagel, James.
Race and culture in New Orleans stories : Kate Chopin, Grace King, Alice Dunbar-Nelson, and George Washington Cable / James Nagel.
pages cm
Includes bibliographical references and index.
ISBN 978-0-8173-1338-8 (hardback) — ISBN 978-0-8173-8717-4 (e book)
1. American literature—Louisiana—New Orleans—History and criticism. 2. Chopin, Kate, 1850–1904—Criticism and interpretation. 3. King, Grace Elizabeth, 1852–1932—Criticism and interpretation. 4. Dunbar-Nelson, Alice Moore, 1875–1935—Criticism and interpretation. 5. Cable, George Washington, 1844–1925—Criticism and interpretation. 6. New Orleans (La.)—In literature. 7. Local color in literature. 8. Social structure in literature. 9. Social change in literature. 10. Social problems in literature. I. Title.
PS267.N49N34 2013
810.9'976335—dc23

2013019094

For Gwen

Contents

Preface

This book began in the classroom, in a graduate seminar I taught on Realism and Naturalism in which we were discussing George Washington Cable's story "Belles Demoiselles Plantation." In the process of dealing with the historical and racial aspects of the situation, a student asked how it could be that the mixed-race character owned a mansion in New Orleans and had sufficient financial resources to have lent $180,000 to his white relative over the years. Injin Charlie does not seem to work, and yet he is quite wealthy. Charles De Charleu, a white aristocrat with a plantation and seven beautiful daughters, seems impoverished in comparison. Why, the student asked, would the ancestor have married a Choctaw woman and then, without benefit of a divorce, a white woman in Paris? Would this be legal? Would the children from each of these marriages feel a kinship strong enough to warrant such enormous loans? These were reasonable inquiries, insightful, probing, significant, and I could not answer them with any degree of certainty.

This book, in a real sense, is an attempt to answer the questions raised on that day some four years ago in a seminar at the University of Georgia. It has taken me, rather late in my career, on a long and fascinating journey through time, geography, and cultural history, and along the way I have encountered French colonial history, the *Code Noir*, the *plaçage* tradition, the various flags that have flown over New Orleans, the complex racial stratification that guided social interaction in Louisiana, the Spanish introduction of the slave contract, the changing meanings of the word "Creole," the founding of one of the great cities in the world, and the reason why many traditional Creoles would not cross Canal Street. It was a challenging and intriguing journey, and it brought to life for me a region of the United States unlike any other.

I found the artistic expression of these ideas in the short stories of four important writers who lived in New Orleans in the second half of the nineteenth century, a period in American literary history that emphasized the Local-Color tradition of capturing the dialects, folkways, culture, and personalities of nearly every region of the United States. Although my own background is in northern Minnesota, originally another French settlement at the very origin of the Mississippi River, I found myself engrossed in the world at the other end of it, especially in the work of Kate Chopin, George Washington Cable, Grace King, and Alice Dunbar-Nelson. What these writers shared was not only that many of their stories take place in New Orleans but that they had all lived there, absorbed Louisiana culture on the bustling streets of the French Quarter, and derived their understanding of the people and social values of the lower Mississippi during their years in the Crescent City. Grace King spent her life there, but Alice Dunbar-Nelson and George Washington Cable eventually moved north, as did Kate Chopin, residing the last two decades of her life in her native St. Louis. Nonetheless, she wrote exclusively of Louisiana and New Orleans, the richest setting of her experience and the locus for the work of the other writers as well. In the course of her lifetime, Alice Dunbar-Nelson was born Alice Moore, married Paul Laurence Dunbar to become Alice Dunbar, and later married to become Alice Dunbar-Nelson, the manner in which she is consistently referred to in scholarship. I have followed that convention.

My specific focus became a story cycle by each of them, a collection of interrelated short fiction with continuing characters, settings, and themes. In a sense, my interest was an outgrowth of a decade of research for an earlier book, *The Contemporary American Short-Story Cycle: The Ethnic Resonance of Genre*, which discussed the long history of the genre and its popularity in the last decades of the twentieth century. In the course of my reading, I was delighted to find that this approach to literature was even more popular at the end of the nineteenth century in the heyday of the short stories that flooded the hundreds of new magazines that flourished with the expanding population of the country. Throughout this investigation, I have been aware that scholarly books share some common properties: they are essentially a formulation of tentative propositions representing the state of knowledge at a given point, a position awaiting new information, or a fresh interpretation of existing data. It is ever thus. Academic studies also are invariably the result of collaboration, interaction with previous scholars, colleagues, and students who have informed, challenged, inspired, and energized the thinking about a given subject. That is certainly the case with this study. After the enquiry began in the classroom, I have been aided in countless ways by the counsel of treasured colleagues who have guided my efforts and supplied me with valuable information. Although there have been far too many such contributions to attempt to acknowledge them all here, among those who have been especially helpful are Alfred Bendixen (Texas A&M University), Oliver Scheiding (University of Mainz), Gloria Cronin (Brigham Young University), and my colleagues at the University of Georgia, especially Hugh Ruppersburg, John Lowe, Hubert McAlexander, Mary Anne O'Neill, Robert Clark, Steven Florczyk, Nicole Camastra, and a host of graduate students who continue to inspire me virtually every day. Professors Donald Pizer (Tulane University) and Thomas Bonner (Louisiana State University) read the manuscript and made valuable suggestions for revision, and their generous comments are deeply appreciated. Over the last several years various research assistants have given generously of their time and energy to uncover obscure documents, previous scholarship, and photographs that have added to this study immeasurably. Among these are Katherine Barrow, Bradley Bazzle, and Kyli Lamar, all of whom will go on to write their own books. My life has been enriched by the generous assistance of all of these people and more.

Among earlier scholars of the story cycle, I have been especially aided by the work of Forrest L. Ingram, Rolf Lundén, J. Gerald Kennedy, Susan Garland Mann, and Robert M. Luscher, as well as by Maggie Dunn and Ann Morris. Our profession has been enlarged by their research. The contributions of Per Seyersted and Emily Toth to Chopin studies is beyond measure, and I have learned much from them. Arlin Turner's work on Cable established an intellectual platform upon which subsequent scholarship has rested, including the valuable studies by Louis Rubin and Alice Hall Petry, which have guided my own approach. No one has done more for understanding Alice Dunbar-Nelson than Gloria Hull, and I am indebted to her insight and wealth of knowledge. Robert Bush, David Kirby, and Helen Taylor informed my reading of Grace King, and they have made important contributions to the study of American literature. Everyone in the field owes an immense debt to Alfred Bendixen for his leadership of the American Literature Association, which has provided enormous stimulation and energy in literary studies through its international and regional conferences. The warm fellowship of that organization has demonstrated what is profoundly "human" about the Humanities. My editor at the University of Alabama Press, Dan Waterman, has provided cordial guidance and crucial support throughout the development of the manuscript. I am deeply indebted to the good judgment and cooperation of Jon Berry, project editor at the press, who resolved many important issues with grace and kindness. Finally, my wife, Gwen, has walked at my side through every step of this book and many others, and her knowledge, insight, and energy have been indispensable. I owe her more than I could ever express.

Race and Culture in *New Orleans Stories*

Introduction

The Historical Context

By the end of the nineteenth century, Realism flourished as a dominant force in American literature, depicting normative characters facing believable conflicts and speaking the vernacular of the various sections of the United States. Within that tradition, the Local-Color movement gave specificity to the regional representations of people and settings, capturing the underlying values and folkways of distinct locations throughout the nation and depicting the indigenous customs, conflicts, social strata, ethnic issues, and ways of life in virtually every geographic area. As the countries of national origin shifted from one place to another, so did the religions, languages, and traditions of a population that, having survived the vast upheaval of the Civil War, was embarked on a new adventure as an emerging nation that would quickly take its place as a powerful force in the Western world.

In fact, the Local-Color movement provided the most instructive and clarifying portrait of regional life in American literature, a vibrant and popular tradition in fiction that in a very few decades produced thousands of stories for roughly three-hundred new magazines that had recently appeared across the country. Before the Civil War there had been only a score of important literary periodicals, among them *Harper's Monthly* and the *Atlantic Monthly*. In the aftermath of the war, and with the continued westward expansion of the country, a host of vital new outlets for stories was launched, beginning with "the *Galaxy* in 1866, the *Overland Monthly* and *Lippincott's Magazine* in 1868, *Appleton's Journal* in 1869, and *Scribner's Monthly* in 1870."[1] Many of these publications quickly established sales of over a hundred thousand copies each month, and their foundation was in the new regional stories that were received with astonishing popularity. This interest was by no means restricted to the white, English-speaking audience. German immigrants could read fiction in the *Cincinnati Republikaner* and the *Philadelphishe Zei-*

tung. Scandinavians in Minneapolis were flooded with periodicals in virtually all of their languages. Japanese readers enjoyed the *Ensei*, begun in the 1890s, and new arrivals who were Spanish speakers could explore *La Revista Ilustrada de Nueva York*. Pauline Hopkins edited a magazine for African Americans, the *Colored American Magazine*, although black writers such as Charles Chesnutt increasingly published in the *Atlantic Monthly* and other leading outlets.[2] America had become a truly multicultural society, and readers across the spectrum enjoyed the new emphasis on sectional literature.

Historically, when the central elements of the humor traditions evolved into what became known as "Local Colorism," the short story emerged as a dominant literary form. America had its own literary genre, and it was succeeding beyond anything that had come before. However complex and subtle the origins of this movement, the central streams of influence upon it are clearly the oral and written traditions of storytelling from almost every immigrant group to arrive on the continent. The sharing of tales across the dinner table was a common form of entertainment throughout the country. When these brief narratives were written down, they evolved into the "yarn," a dramatized form that presumes a speaker, often a regionalized rustic who speaks in the vernacular, reciting a story to an unruly group gathered about him. The fun often derives more from the manner of telling than from the tale told. These yarns, prevalent throughout the first half of the nineteenth century, were wildly popular entertainment enjoyed by a broad spectrum of Americans.

Implicit in humor stories was the assumption of class condescension, that the narrator and the readership were more sophisticated, better educated, and more worldly wise than the ungrammatical and unwashed characters of the tale. However, other comic forms used common folk to tell the tale in their own dialect. Down East humor, deriving from Maine and the rest of New England, featured ironic understatement from laconic speakers using their regional language. Often they seemed not to understand there was anything funny in the portrait of ridiculous characters (the overdressed Yankee peddler, the long-suffering, rustic husband) engaged in absurd events, told in a clipped, restrained, ungrammatical speech. When outsiders appeared in such tales, sometimes as frame narrators, they were normally urban and educated, superior in assumptions but naïve about the world they were visiting, as the plot often reveals. Some tales were told by a crackerbox philosopher such as Jack Downing, introduced in the 1830s by Seba Smith. The humorous events are small and contained in this method, and the amusement is generally verbal rather than physical.

In contrast, in the even more popular Southwestern humor, the comic effects are based on hyperbole, implausible events, irony, and outrageous characters. These tall tales presented frontiersmen, great hunters, legendary fighters, or a "ring-tailed roarer" engaged in wrestling bears or crocodiles. Thomas Bangs Thorpe's "The Big Bear of Arkansas" falls in this tradition as does Davy Crockett's "Bear Hunting in Tennessee." Some tales featured athletes jumping the Mississippi River or prevailing in nature against impossible odds. Often an "Eastern," educated frame narrator introduced the scene, set the stage, and turned over the "telling" to a local character, speaking in dialect, who spun out an improbable tale. Mark Twain's "The Celebrated Jumping Frog of Calaveras County" exemplifies this genre. In Twain's story the urban narrator ultimately becomes the victim of the joke for listening, helplessly, to an interminable shaggy dog story. Bret Harte's "The Outcasts of Poker Flat" is told by a speaker with knowledge of the classics who nonetheless describes simple characters, even prostitutes, with great sympathy and understanding. James Kirke Paulding's "Nimrod's Wildfire Tall Talk" also exemplifies the tradition. Although some of these humorous tales seemed hastily constructed, they contributed much to literary history, especially in the implementation of a highly localized setting and the use of vernacular speech in the construction of a tale. The appeal of the humor traditions helped to inspire the growth of the magazine in America, a phenomenon that defined the literature culture of the last three decades of the nineteenth century. Short fiction had burst into view in these popular new periodicals, driven in part by the new concept of syndication, and the American public was fascinated to read about people from a broad range of traditions and ethnicities. The common folk generated broad interest in the superficial aspects of their lives as well as in the deeper conflicts that sprang from unique historical, social, and religious traditions.

Of all the regions of the country, New England furnished the settings for the most popular early works in the movement, particularly in the stories of Harriet Beecher Stowe, Sarah Orne Jewett, Rose Terry Cooke, Alice Brown, and Mary Wilkins Freeman. Their fiction depicted agrarian scenes in sometimes sentimental terms, but they could also write about gripping issues of life and death and searing moral dilemmas that served as the climactic moments of their fiction. Although the New England Local Colorists tended to be women writers, male authors played an equally important role in creating stories located in the rest of the country. Mark Twain and Bret Harte set many of their early works in California, which flourished after the discovery of gold in the 1840s. Owen Wister dealt with Wyoming, while Charles Chesnutt wrote about North Carolina, Alice Dunbar-Nelson, Grace King, and George Washington Cable about Louisiana, and Margaret Deland about Pennsylvania. Hamlin Garland depicted the upper Midwest, whereas Edward Eggleston and Maurice Thompson worked with settings in

Indiana. Constance Fenimore Woolson wrote two volumes of stories about Michigan before she moved south and addressed a new set of localized issues. For his part, Philander Deming featured upstate New York in his *Adirondack Stories*.

The old Confederacy became an area of special interest after the Civil War, and the *Nation* ran a series titled "The South as it is" that was so popular other Northern magazines quickly followed with similar coverage. After Augustus Baldwin Longstreet published *Georgia Scenes* in 1835 as part of the Southwest Humor tradition, featuring "uncouth backwoods folk," the region emerged as the focus of interest across the nation.[3] After the war, it quickly became a literary center, with Mary Murfree writing about Tennessee, Thomas Nelson Page about Virginia, James Lane Allen about Kentucky, Sherwood Bonner about Mississippi, and a host of authors, including Ruth McEnery Stuart, about Louisiana, in many ways the richest locus of complex ethnic, religious, and racial cultures in the country.

A multitude of factors merge to explain why the New Orleans area should have occasioned such a wealth of literature. As Louis D. Rubin Jr. has indicated, these writers had before them "almost two hundred years of Louisiana history and life, under five flags, two contrasting modes of civilization, with myriad gradations of caste, class, and race. Here were poverty and wealth, old loyalties and old hatreds, several varieties of lost cause, a provincial but thoroughly urban metropolis dependent for its livelihood upon a vast agricultural region around it; here were the Old World and the New, with their competing institutions and loyalties, Latin, Catholic Church and an Anglo-Saxon Protestant Establishment."[4] Beyond the general situation within the state, the Crescent City itself, as Arlin Turner maintains, offered much in that as "the most European city in the United States, it exhibited as no other city did the new world alongside the old world transplanted. It was bilingual; and besides French other languages of continental Europe clashed on its sidewalks, its *banquettes*. There were also varieties of patois compounded of half a dozen tongues. The Creoles, tracing their lineage to the best blood in France and Spain, maintained a proud aloofness, frequenting the opera and the theater, reading the newest books from Paris, and having no more than necessary to do with the pushing, commercial *Américains*."[5] The fictional portrayal of such a culture, flourishing in a robust and newly revitalized city in which there were still newspapers published in French and German,[6] was a perfect subject for the aesthetic of a burgeoning Local-Color fictional tradition, and writers after the war did not delay in utilizing it.

New Orleans and its surrounding bayous served as a complex setting because of its diverse population, its ownership by three different countries, its amalgam of languages and customs, its French legal system, ethnic codes, music and literature, marriage and courtship practices, and a legacy of slavery and racial stratification quite unlike any other area of the country. Indeed, in this sense, the literature of Louisiana fiction in the latter half of the nineteenth century, especially in the work of those writers most closely identified with New Orleans (Kate Chopin, George Washington Cable, Grace King, and Alice Dunbar-Nelson), cannot be fully understood without a grasp of the social and historical context from which it emerged.

Prior to the arrival of European adventurers in the sixteenth century, the southern Mississippi River region was home to a spectrum of Native American peoples, among them the Atakapa, the Bayougoula of the Choctaw nation, the Natchez, and the Natchitoches, and many of these names survive in locations throughout the area. At the same time, in the North, the French established New France, surrounding the upper and central Mississippi, a vast area incorporating much of Canada and the Midwest. In due course the expansion of the empire reached first to the Caribbean, where Santa Domingo was its most successful colony, and then into the Gulf of Mexico. In 1682 Robert Cavelier de La Salle claimed the Mississippi River area for France and named it "Louisiana" in honor of King Louis XIV, and in 1699 Pierre Le Moyne d'Iberville established the first permanent settlement near Biloxi, Mississippi. The French thus claimed land on both ends of the river from its origin in northern Minnesota to its mouth in New Orleans. The settlement of Natchitoches, which figures prominently in the work of Kate Chopin, was founded in 1714 to promote trade with the peoples of the Texas area and to deter further encroachment of the Spanish empire into the region. French settlers quickly came in significant numbers along with the Germans, who clung to the Mississippi shores in what was called the German Coast. In the early seventeenth century, slaves were brought from the Caribbean and Africa, and they arrived with their native languages and cultural traditions, including voodoo, stirring music, and sexually explicit dances, all of which gradually merged into the local social fabric. Over time, the French lost their territories to the east of the Mississippi in what Americans called the French and Indian War, but it retained its dominance over the New Orleans area, which was inherently Francophile. However, the war had weakened France's position as a major power in the West, and in 1763 it ceded Louisiana to Spain.

The Spanish interregnum (1763–1803) changed local society less than might have been expected, in part because French-speaking immigrants continued swarming into the territory, including the Acadians, who had been driven out of Nova Scotia by the British. Of course, Spanish-speaking immigrants arrived with increased frequency, expanding the reach of their empire, and territorial law and governance were temporarily changed, but the language of the area remained French for the vast preponderance of the population. The slave trade expanded dramatically during this period, so much so that the African population quickly became the majority. Most importantly, perhaps, the Spanish introduced the concept of *coartación* allowing for slaves to contract to purchase their manumission, greatly increasing the number of free people of color.[7] The French had earlier freed slaves who had served in the militia in various Indian wars, including two complete units of mixed-race soldiers in 1757.[8] Some owners, Governor Bienville among them, freed his slaves after twenty-six years of service, which he was allowed to do because he no longer needed the permission of government officials.[9] Other legal modifications also had an impact: under Spanish law slaves could own property, serve in the militia, and enjoy some of the other rights of free people, and life became easier for them during this period.[10]

However, after four decades, Napoleon purchased the territory back from Spain and quickly reestablished French law and culture throughout the area, only to sell Louisiana to the United States in 1803, a maneuver deeply resented by the local Creole citizenry, those white, wealthy, French and Spanish settlers who had been born in America. As Kjell Ekstrom has explained, "*Creole* is a term applied, especially in the former Spanish, French, and Portuguese colonies of America, Africa, and the East Indies, to natives of pure European blood (*sangre azul*), distinguished from immigrants themselves born in Europe, and from the offspring of mixed blood, as mulattoes, quadroons, Eurasians and the like."[11] The term "Creole" is used consistently in this sense by George Washington Cable, Kate Chopin, and Grace King.[12] In fact, Cable wrote a book on the subject, *The Creoles of Louisiana*, which Scribner's brought out in 1884.[13] King used the term in the same way in *A History of Louisiana* in 1893, *New Orleans: The Place and the People* in 1895, and the later *Creole Families of New Orleans* in 1921.[14] On the other hand, Alice Dunbar-Nelson, writing an extensive essay on "People of Color in Louisiana" in the *Journal of Negro History* in 1916, used the term to refer exclusively to persons with some portion of African blood who were born in the United States.[15] By then, the term had come to mean "racial mixture," not purity. The revision of the concept may derive from the fact that, as the nineteenth century progressed, an increasing number of children had both wealthy white fathers and quadroon mothers; since, under the Napoleonic Code, the children carried their father's name, they identified with his position in society and adopted the epithet he used. In any event, by the twentieth century, the general understanding of "Creole" had changed to include people of mixed race in Louisiana.

At the time of the Louisiana Purchase in 1803, however, people called "Creoles" were pure white, and the fact that they had been born in America, which distinguished them from French and Spanish immigrants, was the basis of their claim to land rights, which formed the core of their wealth.[16] The term indicated, in a sense, a new ethnic category, one with implications for racial identity, social stratification, property rights, and religious orientation.[17] The concept allowed Louisianans of colonial backgrounds to differentiate themselves from more recent immigrants from Europe, who represented a lower social segment of the population. With the sale of the Louisiana Territory to the United States, the official language of Louisiana suddenly became English, the currency the dollar, and the politics American democracy, although the territory clung tenaciously to the Napoleonic Code as the system of law. In the immediate years that followed, the slave rebellion in Haiti led to the influx of thousands of French-speaking new arrivals, some of them white plantation owners, many of them free people of color who had prospered on the island. Spanish-speaking people flooded into the region from Cuba even after the Louisiana Purchase, and Irish, Polish, and "American" businessmen arrived seeking opportunity in a burgeoning economy. Aiding this effort, Louisiana formally became a state in 1812, and its new status only increased the rapid change of the lower Mississippi.

The focal point for much of this social upheaval was New Orleans, founded in 1718 by Jean-Baptiste Le Moyne de Bienville and named for the Duke of Orleans, Regent of France. After 1803, spurred in part by vibrant financial activity brought by the "American" emphasis on free enterprise, the local economy grew rapidly, making the Crescent City one of the wealthiest in the country. Of course social mobility was a concept anathema to the traditional Creole elite, who, following European traditions, depended upon birthrights and landed income as the underpinning of positions of wealth and stature.

Thus, rather early in the nineteenth century, New Orleans aristocrats were behind in adapting to the new realities, clinging to an elegant past with silk gloves. They continued to think of Paris as their cultural axis, and they could afford to import fine wine, expensive clothing, and other luxuries from the Continent. In accord with their European background, they valued the arts and supported them lavishly. For example, the French Opera House, built in 1859, was the largest in America, and it featured imported French companies in major performances that attracted vast audiences from every level of society. The city was a major success, a marvel of multiethnic culture that was more complex in its origins and interactions than any other metropolitan population in America.

At the inception of the Civil War in 1861, Louisiana joined the Confederacy, in part because its economy was dependent in large measure on slavery for the growing of sugar and cotton crops. New Orleans was of strategic importance in that it controlled shipping on the Mississippi River and, equally important, to European destinations through its extensive port, one of the largest and most active in the world. As a result, Union forces quickly moved on the city, which could not resist the threat of a bombardment, and federal troops took command of the city in April of 1862. At the conclusion of the war, Union forces remained in Louisiana to protect the interests of the newly freed slaves, especially their ability to attend the numerous Freedmen's Bureau schools that the North had established to educate people of color. Many of them excelled in this new climate: some were elected to political offices, others succeeded in business ventures, more than a few rose in social prominence within the city. However, vestiges of the *Code Noir*, the French laws regarding the treatment of slaves, remained in force in the Louisiana Civil Codes, which were revised to account for abolition. But many of the racially restrictive provisions remained, although African Americans were granted some new rights: "Among their numerous provisions, the codes legalized Negro marriages, permitted Negroes to hold and dispose of property, to sue and be sued. They also took steps toward the establishment of racial segregation in public places. They prohibited inter-racial marriages, prohibited Negroes from serving on juries or testifying against white men, and reenacted many of the criminal provisions of the prewar slave codes."[18] Although the establishment of the Jim Crow laws later in the century reversed many of the gains black people had enjoyed during Reconstruction, there were new opportunities for the freedmen and their descendants, and Louisiana life was fundamentally changed.

The complex historical background of New Orleans and the surrounding bayous, and especially the rich cultural mix of the city, provided a perfect setting for the Local Colorists of the area, and Chopin, Cable, Dunbar-Nelson, and King devoted themselves to the depiction of the setting and the deeply significant ethical conflicts at the heart of such a dynamic society. Their work was informed by historical context and by the subtle modifications within the local ethic that had ensued from each of the political transformations of the territory. Indeed, the stories they produced rested upon issues unique to Louisiana, matters that often reflected complex international traditions.

For example, in 1685 the French established a set of regulations for slavery in the colonies, particularly in the Caribbean islands.[19] The *Code Noir*, the Old Black Code, migrated from there to Louisiana Territory, where it was signed into law in 1724 by Governor Bienville in the name of the King of France.[20] It was in force during the Louisiana Purchase and, slightly altered in 1825, persisted in law until 1870.[21] Although most of the regulations dealt with the treatment and, to a limited extent, the rights of African slaves, who outnumbered white people, the first provision of the code was the exclusion of all Jews from the colony of Louisiana. Most of the rest of the regulations dealt with racial issues involving African slaves, but some touched on religion. For example, Roman Catholicism was the only religion allowed in the territory, and all slaves had to receive instruction in that faith, although Africans retained their original beliefs in clandestine ways. But formally, only Catholics could own or control slaves, who were compelled to observe the Sabbath; indeed, they could not legally be forced to work on Sunday upon threat of confiscation from their owners by the local authorities.

Other regulations are of special relevance to Cable's fiction. There were harsh penalties for insurrection and disobedience on the part of slaves. One who struck his master and caused a bruise was to be executed, for example. A slave who ran away and was absent for more than a month was to have his ears cut off. On the second offense he could be hamstrung; on the third, he was put to death. However, as Shannon Lee Dawdy has pointed out, the most severe forms of punishment were carefully supervised by the legal authorities: "Beginning in 1738, the Superior Council required slaveowners to register a report any time one of their slaves died or ran away. . . . In these reports, owners carefully justified the 'natural' or 'accidental' causes of their slave's death."[22] But the family life of slaves was also protected under the Code. Husbands and wives were not to be separated, nor could their children be taken from them until they were fourteen. Masters aged twenty-five and older could grant manumission to their slaves, which happened frequently, and the Code established the designation of "free persons of color," which could not be abrogated. Any slave who served as a tutor to white children was declared to be free, and all manumitted slaves were to have the same rights as free persons. Freedman often prospered in Louisiana, growing in wealth and property, owning plantations and slaves, and they felt a loyalty to the society. In the War of 1812, for example, New Orleans contributed two regiments, with a thousand men each, made up entirely of free men of color. Andrew Jackson issued orders that allowed them to become officers, specifying that "due regard will be paid to the feelings of freeman and soldiers. You will not, by being associated with white men in the same corps, be exposed to improper comparisons, or unjust sarcasm. As a distinct, independent battalion or regiment, pursuing the path of glory, you will, undivided, receive the applause and gratitude of your country men."[23] At the conclusion of the war, the slaves who had served honorably in the defense of the city were granted their freedom. Five decades later, in the Civil War, a local regiment of one thousand four hundred free men of color fought for the Confederacy, the only such racial unit to serve the Southern cause.[24]

Of special pertinence to the fiction of New Orleans were the regulations concerning courtship and marriage. For example, white subjects were forbidden to marry black people or anyone of mixed race. Thus, they were prohibited from marrying slaves, as were free-born blacks, who could wed neither whites nor enslaved African Americans. Of special significance is the fact that white Creoles, under the Code, could not legally take a black woman as a mistress, although this regulation was outmoded from the day it was implemented. The fact that there were few French women in early Louisiana led to a rather predictable miscegenation with the local Native-American population. When the first African slaves arrived in 1719, the French settlers also produced children with them, leading to a mixed-race population from the very beginning.

This situation so startled the authorities in Paris that they rushed eighty-eight female prisoners to New Orleans, although, amazingly, in later years not a single citizen ever claimed lineage from these women. As Anna Shannon Elfenbein has explained, this event was "followed by the importation of more respectable girls in 1728, the famous 'casket-girls' who arrived with their belongings packed in small trunks provided by an alarmed French government, and the introduction of the *Code Noir*, proscribing interracial sexual activity between whites and slaves. . . . [But even that] could not alter the tacitly condoned facts of life in New Orleans."[25] As a result, there was a standard of behavior prescribed by law and a counter set of social traditions established by custom, the historic French practice of *plaçage*.

Plaçage was a custom among white French and Spanish Creole gentlemen throughout the colonies; it allowed for *marriages de la main gauche*, left-handed marriages, with women of African or Native-American descent. The practice was especially prevalent in Santa Domingo, where the reputation of these women for beauty caused them to be known as "the sirens." When the Creoles migrated to New Orleans, the *placées* were nearly always quadroon or octoroon young ladies. Known as plaçage, the "placement" of women, this widespread tradition in Louisiana led to the development of a relatively prosperous segment of free women of color who owned homes on the basis of a legal agreement with the gentlemen involved, who also provided a monthly check. These relationships represented long-term commitments, and many Creole gentlemen in such an arrangement never married a white women but devoted their lives, and fortunes, to their mixed-race families.[26] Some of these women owned their own slaves and set up thriving businesses renting rooms or property in the city. Their free-born children of mixed race carried the names of their father and the right to inherit a third of his estate. Often educated in France, sometimes including a university degree from the Sorbonne, these children enjoyed a social and economic mobility unknown among people of African descent in other sections of the United States.[27] Young quadroon men, educated in Paris, often stayed in the city for their careers, and there were so many of them that they constituted a definable population in the city known as the "Louisiana colony."[28] Many of them became quite prominent citizens. Norbert Rillieux, for example, was a chemical engineer who transformed the sugar industry throughout the world. He was the son of Constance Vivant, a plaçage mistress in New Orleans. Edgar Degas, who owned property in the Crescent City, was his distant cousin on the maternal side of the family.[29] Similarly, the plaçage offspring of Marie Thérèze Coincoin amassed a small fortune in the Cane River district of Louisiana, where they enjoyed respect and prestige among the free black population. They owned a great deal of property, numerous slaves, and enjoyed virtually all the rights of white people save for the capacity to vote.[30]

These relationships were not universally approved, of course. White women, especially wives, hated the concept, as did the authorities within the church. Many women of color refused to be subjected to an unwanted sexual union to an older man and a life of prostitution. Perhaps the most famous of these was Henriette Delille, a quadroon born in New Orleans in 1813. Her father was a French white man who had a plaçage marriage to her mother, who was a mulatto. Henriette was trained in the traditional manner for young quadroon girls, studying French literature, the arts, and music. An educated woman, she was preparing to be a companion to a wealthy Creole white man, and she attended the Quadroon Balls. But rather than replicate the life of her mother, she became a nun, taking vows in the Roman Catholic Church; most importantly, she went on to found the Sisters of the Holy Family, an order devoted to free women of color who cared for orphans in the city. They later opened a famous school for such children as well. She died in 1862 and was declared a saint by the Vatican in 2010.[31] A plaque in the French Quarter near St. Louis Cathedral now commemorates her service to the city. One of the ironies in this matter is that the key location for the Quadroon Balls, the Orleans Ballroom, was purchased in 1881 by her order, the Sisters of the Holy Family, and used as the assembly hall for the convent.[32]

No doubt there were many young women of color who felt the plaçage tradition degrading and a violation of Christian principles, as did George Washington Cable, who, in the manuscript "Foreword" to "'Tite Poulette," commented that "we must remember that at the time the scenes of this story were laid, the marriage between whites and colored was forbidden by law, [but] there was no law, legal or social, strong enough to prevent a quadroon from being the mistress of a white man. And among the quadroons this position was considered horrible in *every way*. The famous Quadroon Balls fed this custom."[33] The law to which Cable refers was the revision of the *Code Noir* into the Louisiana Civil Codes in 1825, one section of which stated clearly that "free persons and slaves are incapable of contracting marriage together. The celebration of such marriages is forbidden, and marriage is void; there is the same incapacity, and the same nullity, with respect to marriage contracted by free white persons with free persons of color."[34] Plaçage arrangements were nonetheless an important part of the fabric of New Orleans society. Such a "marriage" was much more complex than simple prostitution or concubinage and involved formalized commitments that traditionally lasted a lifetime. Indeed, as Alice Dunbar-Nelson has explained, most Creole men involved in such a liaison never wed a white woman and disdained traditional marriage, preferring family life with a woman of color.[35]

Universally described as being extraordinarily beautiful, these young ladies had been trained in social manners and the arts, and, often educated in Paris at the Sorbonne, they excelled at intelligent conversation. They were often sent to Europe for their schooling because under state law the education of people of color in Louisiana was difficult prior to the Civil War.[36] Since few white women attended college in the first half of the nineteenth century, young quadroon women seemed especially sophisticated. They exhibited elegant manners and social graces and attended the fashionable events of New Orleans cultural life, with special seating for them at the opera and theater. Raised to respect chastity and protected by their mothers until they entered a committed relationship,[37] they were invariably well dressed, soft spoken, and adorned with expensive jewels. When they established a "marriage," their mothers were present before a judge to ratify a formal contract involving a house and a monthly check, and they traditionally held a public reception to acknowledge the new domestic alliance.[38] In some cases, as Violet Harrington Bryan has pointed out, the arrangements were blessed by the church. These white men "cared for the children of these unions, often baptizing them in their name and educating them in France. Such unions were historically widely accepted."[39]

Children born of such liaisons were free persons of color who carried the name of their father and, under the Napoleonic Code, had the right to a third of his estate. As a result, many descendants of plaçage marriages had the names of the most prominent families. Some of them became quite wealthy, owning mansions, plantations, and slaves, and many of them rose to significant positions in society. Young quadroon women were forbidden by the Old Black Code to marry outside their precise caste, since people of differing races could not enter into wedlock in Louisiana, and as Alice Dunbar-Nelson found in her research, few such women ever married again after their gentleman died. That fact alone explains the long "widowhood" of Madame John in Cable's "'Tite Poulette," a matter that has puzzled generations of literary scholars.

Central to the process of establishing a plaçage arrangement were the Quadroon Balls, held in the major dance halls every Wednesday and Saturday evenings, originally at the Orleans Ballroom at 717 Orleans Street in the heart of the Vieux Carré, although such events were also held at the Globe, the Salle de Condé, and the Salle de Lafayette.[40] Protective mothers would bring their daughters to what constituted a debutante ball, with expensive gowns, gentlemen of means dressed in formal evening clothes, and mothers arrayed about the periphery serving as chaperones.[41] Only wealthy Creole men were allowed to attend; poor whites and those who were not of French or Spanish origin were excluded; black men were relegated to the role of servants at these events. The mothers attended to the dance cards of their daughters, selecting only suitable men for introductions. One quarter of New Orleans, largely along Rampart Street, was reserved for the homes of such domestic alliances, and the practice was open and common. After the Louisiana Purchase, wealthy American men also began attending the dances, although not with the same objective of long-term relationships.

The children of plaçage relationships occupied a unique place in society. Since their mothers had nearly always been emancipated (sexual contact with slaves was forbidden by the *Code Noir*), the children were also free people of color, with special rights within local social structures. They were acknowledged by their fathers before a notary and regarded as "natural" children, not illegitimate, and they were entitled to inheritance rights. These octoroon children were, however, forbidden to marry formally with either a white or a black person since such an act would promote miscegenation. (The fact that these women were the product of mixed-race romance seems never to have occurred to the authorities.) By the end of the eighteenth century, nearly two thousand such quadroons lived in New Orleans. When they became widows (the gentlemen were nearly always a good deal older), they and their children inherited a third of the gentleman's wealth under provisions of the Napoleonic Code, which explains why by the time of the Civil War roughly 30 percent of the property in New Orleans was owned by people of color, a situation Cable describes in his stories and novels. Indeed, by 1840, free people of color owned 40 percent of the property in two of the quarters of the city, the Faubourgs Marigny and Tremé, both of which were dominated by people of mixed race,[42] a situation Cable presented in "Belles Demoiselles Plantation" when the Colonel goes to visit Injin Charlie to borrow money. The Civil War, which brought emancipation and an end to the prevailing caste system, signaled an end to the plaçage tradition, leaving behind a huge population of people of mixed racial heritage who carried the names of the most distinguished families in Louisiana.[43]

These unique ethnic traditions inform much of the literary work of the period. For example, Cable's fiction touched on two elements of life in Louisiana that were extremely sensitive to his fellow New Orleans citizens: the conflict following the Louisiana Purchase between a historically Creole culture predominately Catholic, Latinate, and devoted to privileges of birth and social stratification and a new American population primarily protestant, Puritanical in sexual matters, and devoted to hard work, financial success, and unlimited social mobility. The place where several of these matters collided was the fate of the quadroons, a subject in literature from roughly 1830 onward in the "tragic mulatto" or "tragic quadroon" traditions. Such narratives usually featured a beautiful but innocent young woman of color who is cruelly forced into a horrible concubinage and prefers death to such degrading circumstances. There were variations on the theme but, in general, these works portray the defilement of purity by an unworthy and insensitive white villain, and they end tragically. The tradition of such tales has a Louisiana origin even in Europe.

Although the earliest literary representations of the plaçage arrangements came in French literature from the Continent and the Caribbean in the 1830s, there was a New Orleans connection, as Werner Sollors has explained.[44] One of the earliest was what may be the first story by a black American author, Victor Séjour's "La Mulâtre," published in the *Revue des colonies* in March of 1837.[45] The author's father was a free man of color from Santo Domingo; his mother was from New Orleans. Victor was born there in 1817 as a free quadroon; he grew up in the city but was sent to Paris in 1836 for his education, a standard practice for colored people of means. He stayed in France because of the open and accepting racial atmosphere, and he pursued a career as a writer.

"Le Mulâtre" is a complex story of slave life in Santo Domingo with a master attempting to force himself upon a beautiful, married slave woman, an act that would have violated the *Code Noir*. Her husband kills the master and then discovers that he is his son. He commits suicide, following which his wife is executed. This last event somewhat misrepresents the *Code Noir* in the Caribbean, which held that if a master had sex with a slave, she was immediately pronounced free and he was obligated to marry her.

A rather more complex variation on the subject by Madame Charles Reybaud was published as "Les Epaves" in February of 1838, a novella about the *Code Noir*. Significantly, it is narrated by a woman of mixed race, Zoe, described as a Creole woman. That story, set in Martinique in 1720, involved two white women in love with a handsome mulatto, and it became part of a novella cycle titled *Valdepeiras* (1839).[46] An illustration of how popular the theme had become is the fact that Hans Christian Andersen wrote a romantic play based on "Les Epaves" produced in Copenhagen in 1840 under the title *Mulatten*. It proved to be so popular that it was revived in 1868 and 1873. A Swedish version of it ran at the Royal Theater in Stockholm.[47] As Sollors has indicated, "the Mulatto theme is very specifically enacted, with reflections on the nature of black and white, the attitude of Creoles, and so forth, but it is also clustered with such general themes as romantic love vs. calculating coldness; spirit vs. form/body; entitlement of mind and valor vs. entitlement of inheritance. In this scheme of things, the handsome, Paris-educated Mulatto is a perfect human being, has nobility of soul, is well educated, yet retains Rousseauvian naturalness: in one word, he seems so eminently eligible that it is little wonder that two women would fall in love with him."[48] The tension within the plot derives from the looming threat that although free, the protagonist will be sold as a slave. Yet another adaptation of "Les Epaves" was Eugène Scribe's *Le Code Noir: Opera-comique en 3 actes*, which was performed at the Comic Opera in Paris on June 9, 1842.[49]

In the United States, New Orleans was the only area that institutionalized the plaçage tradition, drawing on French and Spanish practices in the Caribbean.[50] But since the theme had already become clichéd in literature when Cable began to write about the *Code Noir* and the plaçage tradition in the 1870s, he had to find an original approach to it. Indeed, by the end of the Civil War, the heroine of color caught in a fate worse than death had become a stock character in Romantic literature of race.[51] What Cable brought to the idea was a focus on those mixed-race relationships based on mutual attraction and devotion, those not uncommon instances in New Orleans in which the Creole gentleman never married but remained loyal to his quadroon "wife," leaving her his entire estate in his will. It was, to be sure, a "romantic" approach to a complex subject, but it was based on historical practices widely in evidence in the French Quarter. Cable was deeply against racial stratification and the caste system the *Code Noir* promulgated, as his essays and lectures demonstrate, and he wrote about the matter first in a brief newspaper sketch titled "A Life-Ebbing Monography" that appeared in the New Orleans *Picayune* on December 24, 1871. It recounts the situation in which a mulatto woman and a white man loved each other but were forbidden to marry because she carried mixed blood. They each cut open their arms, mingled their blood, and thus qualified to be wed. This simple account underscored the absurdity of family law based on racial lines and paved the way for some of Cable's most intriguing stories in *Old Creole Days*.

Such a subject was consistent with the central aesthetic of Local Colorism, which had at its core the portrayal of regional characters, values, folkways, dialects, and traditions. Although the humor traditions, and the very first stirrings of sectional stories, often employed a point of view that condescended to rustic characters, that device gave way to allowing a localized narrator with knowledge of indigenous customs to tell the story in dialect, thus capturing the personality of the teller as well as the characters within the narrative.[52] This strategy also promoted a focus on regional American characters and issues pertinent to the moment, a matter strongly advocated by Hamlin Garland.

In *Roadside Meetings*, for example, he recalls an address he delivered at the Columbia Exposition in Chicago in 1893 in which he maintained, somewhat famously, that "American literature cannot be built up out of romantic tales of medieval France, and stories of country life will be false if they deal only with June sunshine, roses, and strawberries. . . . We must base our fiction on reality."[53] A year later, in *Crumbling Idols*, he was even more forceful in advocating for the fundamental significance of regional fiction, maintaining that "every great moving literature today is full of local color." On a national level, he pointed out that for the United States, "its political freedom was won, not by its gentlemen and scholars, but by its yeomanry; and in the same way our national literature will come in its fullness when the common American rises spontaneously to the expression of his concept of life."[54] Garland was expressing a sentiment that had become widespread by the 1890s, the idea that a truly great literature was based on a portrayal of ordinary people speaking their genuine language and confronting the conflicts common to the life of their region. Such an aesthetic informed the Local-Color movement and generated much of the great fiction of America.

A literature that emphasizes distinct settings, regional folkways, and common, often rural, people can find expression in a variety of genres. Within the movement a strain of poetry proved to be notable, beginning with John Greenleaf Whittier's "Snow-Bound," Bret Harte's "Plain Language from Truthful James," Joaquin Miller's "Kit Carson's Ride," Sidney Lanier's poems of rural Georgia, James Whitcomb Riley's of Indiana, and nearly the entire body of work by Robert Frost. Dialect verse continued to exert an influence into the 1920s and the poems of the Harlem Renaissance. The Local-Color novel was not a major form in terms of magnitude, but it contributed much to literary history: Cable's *The Grandissimes*, Joseph Kirkland's *Zury: The Meanest Man in Spring County*, Chopin's *The Awakening*, Mark Twain's *Adventures of Huckleberry Finn*, and, in the twentieth century, nearly the entire corpus of work by one of the greatest American writers, William Faulkner.[55]

But the most successful genre was the short story. Such fiction featured a precise description of scene in the deepest sense, capturing values and traditions as well as topography. The characters were generally common folk with a depth of humanity that could resonate with readers from other regions. The local figures spoke in a dialect that was sometimes charming, occasionally amusing, and always interesting in that it suggested a foreign language or a blending of linguistic traditions in the melting pot of the new land. Early stories subordinated plot to character and setting, but by the 1890s the climactic moment, especially in Realistic stories, was often an ethical choice that drew on the deepest of underlying values, as when Sylvia must choose between the bird and the handsome young ornithologist in Jewett's "A White Heron." The decision point or climax became common by the end of the century, and the inherent moral dilemma in each case revealed the ethical structure of a given location. Such stories were popular in the major magazines and helped the genre become a literary force at the end of the century.

Of special significance were works that appeared as story cycles, those increasingly popular volumes in which individual stories were interrelated by a continuing setting, recurring characters, overarching themes, or some other system of unification.[56] Such volumes fall into a long tradition in literature, reaching back centuries and looking forward to some of the best work of the decades to come. Despite the fact that when Ernest Hemingway's *In Our Time* appeared in 1924 the reviews suggested that he had invented a new form,[57] the cycle actually has its roots in the narrative traditions of antiquity. In ancient Greece the "cyclic poets" supplemented Homer's portrayal of the Trojan War, and the *Odyssey* constituted linked tales as did Ovid's *Metamorphoses*, the Arabian *A Thousand and One Nights*, and, later, Chaucer's *The Canterbury Tales* and Boccaccio's *The Decameron*.

In America the concept of the story cycle was well established by the time the New Orleans writers utilized it in the late nineteenth century. Washington Irving's *The Sketch Book* (1820) was among the early volumes in the genre, as were Sarah Josepha Hale's *Sketches of American Character* (1829), Augustus Baldwin Longstreet's *Georgia Scenes* (1835), and Eliza Buckminster Lee's *Sketches of a New England Village, in the Last Century*. Nathaniel Hawthorne added *Twice-Told Tales* (1851) as did Herman Melville with *The Piazza Tales* (1856). The form proliferated with the appearance of the American Realists, and more than a hundred such volumes appeared before the First World War. Especially notable were Harriet Beecher Stowe's *Sam Lawson's Oldtown Fireside Stories* (1871), which captured Down East characters and locations. Garland's *Main-Travelled Roads* (1891) used the Midwest settings of his youth, and Margaret Deland did the same for Pennsylvania in *Old Chester Tales* (1898). James William Sullivan demonstrated that the cycle form could portray an urban setting in his *Tenement Tales of New York* (1895), and Stephen Crane moved the location upstate for his *Whilomville Stories* (1900). By late century, the cycle had an embarrassment of riches.

Within this growing form, the portrayal of the South was particularly popular: Frances E. W. Harper's tales of African Americans in *Sketches of Southern Life* (1872), Constance Fenimore Woolson's *Rodman the Keeper: Southern Sketches* (1880), Mary Noailles Murfree's *In the Tennessee Mountains* (1884), and Charles Chesnutt's *The Wife of His Youth and Other Stories of the Color Line* (1899) demonstrated the strength of the form. The appearance of important volumes of interrelated stories about New Orleans thus fits within a vibrant and burgeoning literary tradition, not an offshoot of the novel. George Washington Cable's *Old Creole Days* in 1879 initiated the use of the Crescent City as a subject for cyclic stories, and Grace King's *Balcony Stories* (1893), Kate Chopin's *Bayou Folk* (1894), and Alice Dunbar-Nelson's *The Goodness of St. Rocque and Other Stories* (1899) quickly followed. The complex ethnic population of the city, its mix of dialects, religions, and social traditions, made it a perfect setting for portraying the regional life of Louisiana.

These authors also came from suitable backgrounds to write about varying aspects of their city. For example, Cable, born in 1844, was of German descent, the original name being "Kobell," then "Kable," and then "Cable."[58] As Presbyterians, the family was out of place in a French Catholic city, and many of Cable's underlying values, especially regarding race, caste, and ethnic stratification, grated on the entrenched local society in the Annunciation Square area of the Garden District. Nonetheless, when the Civil War broke out, he enlisted in the Confederate Army and served in the Fourth Mississippi Cavalry until he was wounded in battle.[59] As was often the case with the American Realists, although he had an intellectual bent, he did not finish high school and was self-taught as a writer. Early in life he began collecting the songs of African Americans, singing them during his lectures throughout his career, and he was deeply concerned with their lives, especially the quadroon girls who were plaçage mistresses. In politics, he challenged the Democratic Party for its insistence on racial discrimination and endorsed Republican efforts to support civil rights for people of color, a matter he made central to the fundamental purpose of his life and work.[60] Indeed, his first lecture was in June of 1882 at commencement ceremonies at the University of Mississippi, where he said the South had to change its way of thinking about the plantation, slavery, and social caste system.[61] His career was launched when he was discovered by Edward King, who had been sent by *Scribner's Monthly Magazine* to do a series on "The Great South." King returned to New York with Cable's "'Sieur George," which led to the eventual publication of *Old Creole Days*. As Louis Rubin has maintained, "there can be no question of Cable's good fortune in having been born and raised in New Orleans; the lavish color, the romantic history, the exotic mixture of races and civilizations, provided him with a setting that was ideally suited to the growing interest in provincial life, and his own descriptive talents were precisely those best calculated to take advantage of the situation."[62] Cable's artistic gifts, his ear for the various dialects of Louisiana, his intimate knowledge of the culture of his home city, and his engagement with the dramatic social issues during Reconstruction made him one of the most important Southern writers of the period and *Old Creole Days* a central book for understanding the dynamic life of New Orleans.

Grace King had very different attitudes about life in the South. Born in 1852 to a wealthy Creole family, as a girl of ten she watched Union troops march into New Orleans and occupy the city, thus giving it the longest period of Reconstruction of any Southern metropolitan area.[63] An excellent student, she was educated at the Institut St. Louis, a French-speaking school she used as a setting in her stories. Her father, a prosperous lawyer, lost his wealth in the war, and during Reconstruction the family was reduced to renting a modest house in one of the less prestigious wards of the city. This situation provided her with one of the major themes of her literary career, the psychologically traumatic adjustment of women of stature to reduced circumstances, a humiliation that proved devastating on multiple levels. Often such women survived without the support of the men who had protected them in antebellum times, and it was up to the widows and spinsters to draw upon their inner strength to forge some kind of meaningful life within the new realities. That is precisely the situation in King's *Balcony Stories*, which was published in New York in 1893. Throughout that volume, women share a terrace in the evenings, after their children have been put to bed, and relate the stories of their lives, gripping tales of despair, strength, and perseverance. This volume, enthusiastically received in the North as well as the South, was reprinted in 1914 and again in 1925, testifying to the enduring appeal of King's brilliant achievement as an artist.

Kate Chopin was not from New Orleans but lived more than a decade in Louisiana, the exclusive setting of her fiction. Born in St. Louis in 1850, she grew up in a world strongly influenced by French society.[64] For one thing, Creoles from New Orleans founded the city in 1764, and their presence was still felt throughout local institutions, including the St. Louis Academy of the Sacred Heart, where young Katherine received all of her formal education. Her first language was French, which dominated conversation in her household because her great grandmother, a Creole from Louisiana, lived in the home. She had owned the shipping company on the Mississippi from St. Louis to New Orleans and, a natural raconteur, she shared countless stories of life along the river.[65] Young Kate also had the advantage of an early life in a vibrant urban environment. As Helen Taylor has pointed out, "the St. Louis in which the young Kate O'Flaherty grew up, and which she left in 1870 upon her marriage to Oscar Chopin, was a busy cosmopolitan city with a tight Creole community that gave its bourgeois and mercantile community a southern Gallic atmosphere."[66] At age twenty, Kate married Oscar Chopin, and the couple lived in New Orleans for nine years, during which she bore six children. A dedicated wife and mother, she wrote nothing during this period of her life. When their business failed in 1879, they moved to the Chopin plantations near Cloutierville, the setting for much of her fiction. Her husband died in 1882, and for two years she ran the family enterprises before moving back to St. Louis to live with her mother. It was there that she wrote the entire corpus of her fiction.

It is astonishing that she managed any writing at all, what with a household of children and servants and the relentless duties of a widow with children, especially after her own mother died in 1884. Part of the cultural life of the city, she and her family attended concerts regularly, and for many years she was active in a local literary society. Inspired by the intellectual companionship of Dr. Frederick Kolbenheyer, an agnostic from Austria, she became interested in progressive philosophy and less involved with the Roman Catholic Church.[67] Soon her stories were appearing in the major magazines, including the *Atlantic Monthly, Vogue*, and *Century*, and in 1894 twenty-three of her Louisiana stories appear in a tightly unified volume titled *Bayou Folk*. Despite the enormous later popularity of her sensational novel *The Awakening*, it was this story cycle that carried her creative reputation well into the 1970s, and it quickly won the admiration of an international body of readers.

Alice Ruth Moore was born on July 19, 1875, in New Orleans, the daughter of a white seaman and an African-American seamstress who had been born a slave in Opelousas, Louisiana. Her father, Joseph Moore, abandoned the family when Alice was young, and her mother reared her with an emphasis on education and a sense of social propriety.[68] A bright and talented young student, and a traditional Episcopalian, she enrolled at Straight University in 1890, where she excelled in the classroom and in music, playing the cello in the orchestra and the mandolin in an ensemble.[69] Upon graduation, she lived at 56½ Palmyra Street in New Orleans and began teaching at the Old Marigny Elementary School, remaining in the profession for the rest of her life. She moved freely within white society, forming important friendships and earning widespread respect and admiration. She later took a Master of Arts degree from Cornell University, making her by far the best educated of the Louisiana Local Colorists. Outside the classroom, she was also developing as a writer, and her first book, *Violets and Other Tales*, a collection of stories and poems, was published in 1895. In 1896 Moore moved to Massachusetts and taught for a year before taking a position in Brooklyn, where she served at the White Rose Mission. At this time, she began corresponding with the poet Paul Laurence Dunbar and in 1898 they married and moved to Washington, D.C. A disaster from the beginning, the union lasted only until 1902. Then she took a position as a teacher and administrator at Howard High School in Wilmington, Delaware, where she was also on the State Republican Committee of Delaware, an organization at the forefront of civil rights for people of color.

In her fiction, however, she was against the utilization of propaganda for the promotion of racial causes, commenting in a letter that "I haven't much liking for those writers that wedge the Negro problem and social equality and long dissertations on the Negro in general into their stories."[70] Nonetheless, her major volume of fiction, *The Goodness of St. Rocque and Other Stories*, published in 1899, is invested with two of the major concerns of her life: the role of women in American society and the lives of people of color in the vibrant cultural mix of New Orleans. She was especially skillful in capturing the spectrum of dialects across the city, the mixture of Roman Catholic faith with voodoo practices from the Caribbean, and the exotic urban culture of people of color in the decades after the Civil War. In 1916 she married a journalist, Robert J. Nelson, but she continued writing until the end of her life in 1935. Much of her later work remains unpublished.

There are many factors that unite these four important writers, all of whom have found a place in the literary canon of the late nineteenth century, but the most important are their experiences in the rich cultural diversity of New Orleans. Although they had differing relationships to the dominant culture, they all featured the city as a prominent physical and ideological setting in their fiction. They all utilized the central tenets of the Local-Color aesthetic, capturing regional customs and traditions, a range of dialects, and a spectrum of characters from the Creole elite to the Acadian poor, from recent immigrants to the descendants of former slaves. Furthermore, their most important volumes of short fiction are consistent with the ancient tradition of the story cycle: a continuing setting, recurring characters, and progressively developing themes. But an appreciation of the subtlety and complexity of *Balcony Stories, Old Creole Days, Bayou Folk*, and *The Goodness of St. Rocque and Other Stories* depends upon a detailed examination of the craft and intellectual depth of these four individual volumes.

1
George Washington Cable's *Old Creole Days*

George Washington Cable is often credited with being the first author after the Civil War to address the social and racial issues unique to the South, especially those relating to Louisiana and, more specifically, New Orleans. The Crescent City had long been an area of interest for American writers, but the richest aspects of this complex community were traditionally forbidden material: the multifaceted racial mixture of the society, the rigid caste system that had been in place for more than a century, the uneasy blend of Spanish, French, Caribbean, African, Native American, Irish, and American cultures into one communal system. Of the spectrum of possible subjects for his fiction, Cable chose to reach backward to the early nineteenth century, when the social issues revolved around the adjustment of a conservative Creole society to the Louisiana Purchase. He avoided dealing with contemporary social themes: the collapse of the aristocratic class of plantation owners, the position of newly freed slaves, and the Northern occupation of the city during Reconstruction, all of which were richly explored a decade later by Grace King. Focusing on 1803 allowed Cable to portray the arrival of the American Yankees and a vast spectrum of immigrants seeking financial opportunity in a newly structured economy. In the background were political and cultural traditions only dimly understood by the new arrivals, including Napoleonic law, the French aristocratic tradition of *plaçage* relationships, and the *Code Noir*, all institutions unique to Louisiana and central to understanding the background conflicts in *Old Creole Days*, a subtle and challenging collection of interrelated stories.

Of these concepts, only the *Code Noir* has even been mentioned in Cable scholarship and then with erroneous representations of its provisions and their role in the conflicts in the fiction. Perhaps this problem results from the fact that Cable's fiction touched on two elements of life in Louisiana that were extremely sensitive to his fellow New Orleans citizens: the conflict between a historically Creole culture (Catholic, Latinate, devoted to privileges of birth and social stratification) and a new American population that was protestant, Puritanical in sexual matters, and devoted to hard work, financial success, and unlimited social mobility. The place where several of these matters collided was the fate of the quadroons, long taken as plaçage mistresses by wealthy Creoles and forbidden to marry outside of their narrow caste.

Cable's career in fiction actually began when Edward King was commissioned by *Scribner's Magazine* to write a series of articles titled "The Great South," part of the Northern effort of regional reconciliation. King encouraged Cable to submit his stories for publication, and he did so. The first important writer to use New Orleans as the subject of serious fiction, he found his greatest theme in the complex cultural background laid out before him: a French Creole society with an overlay of American culture; the importation of the *Code Noir* from the Caribbean forbidding interracial relationships; the plaçage marriage as a widely accepted social tradition in New Orleans (and nowhere else in the United States); and the rich social, moral, and psychological conflicts that emerged from the confluence of these complex ideas in a single city.

Cable wrote about these matters first in a brief newspaper sketch titled "A Life-Ebbing Monography" that appeared in the New Orleans *Picayune* on December 24, 1871. It recounts the situation in which a mulatto and a white man loved each other but were forbidden to marry because she carried black blood in her veins. They each cut open their arms, mingled their blood, and thus qualified to be wed. This simple account underscored the absurdity of family law based on racial lines and paved the way for two of Cable's most intriguing stories in *Old Creole Days*.

The first short story was "'Tite Poulette," which appeared in *Scribner's Monthly* in October of 1874 before it was incorporated into the first edition of *Old Creole Days* in 1879.[1] Although on the surface it appears to present a sentimental romance plot, the cultural and racial background of the action is what gives depth and substance to the events. A young immigrant from Holland, Kristian Koppig, arrives in New Orleans seeking economic opportunity. A Protestant, he is out of place in Catholic Louisiana, the only sanctioned religion under the *Code Noir*. He is operating in a system of caste, race, and inherited wealth he does not comprehend, nor does he understand its Latin sexual practices. The dialects, assumptions, and values of Creole culture are as new to him as they were to the American reading public, which had never before been exposed to so intricate a social system. In short, Koppig is an alien arriving only two years after the Louisiana Purchase, which had greatly expanded business activity and international trade; he secures a job as a clerk in a German firm and takes a room overlooking an old house across the street.

He quickly learns that it is occupied by a handsome quadroon woman named Zalli and her beautiful daughter, whose name is not known but who is referred to as "'Tite Poulette" by everyone in the neighborhood. Zalli had a plaçage marriage with M. John, which provided her with a comfortable house, and when he died he left her his family home, which she sold, putting the money in a bank. In honor of her love for M. John, she now wears black, assumes the role of a widow, and becomes widely known as Madame John. In time, the bank failed, and she lost all her money, forcing her to begin dancing at the Salle de Condé to support her daughter. Cable may have based this situation on the celebrated historical legend of Jean Pascal, a sailor killed in 1729 leaving behind a plaçage widow who lived in the house and grieved for him in black clothing until her death in 1777, a poignant tribute to emotional devotion. After publication of "'Tite Poulette," a new building on the same location, erected by Don Manuel Lanzos in 1788, became known as Madame John's Legacy, an archetypal colonial French house and a modern tourist attraction.[2]

What is clear in terms of cultural background, and confirmed by the details of the story itself, is that Zalli's mother had presented her at the quadroon balls at the Salle de Condé to be chosen as a mistress by a Creole gentleman. Such a relationship was not scandalously rare, as is assumed by Alice Hall Petry,[3] but a standard plaçage arrangement. By 1805 there were nearly four thousand such "marriages" in New Orleans. Zalli would have been chosen by M. John under the supervision of her mother, who would have reviewed the living provisions and approved them, and the relationship would have been registered before a notary. The details normally included a monthly check and, in most cases, a house for her, in this case only one block from his own, where he lived with his parents. Their relationship would seem to have been based on mutual love: he left his entire estate to her with his dying breath; she remained loyal to him until death, a common event in the plaçage marriages of the early nineteenth century. Very few quadroon women went on to a second relationship, as Alice Dunbar-Nelson discovered to her surprise during her residence in the city.[4]

Zalli does not wish for such a relationship for her daughter, since, as is revealed later, 'Tite Poulette is actually white, so she boards the windows of the house and protects the young lady from all intrusions. Kristian sees both of them on several occasions, and the women have become an obsession, his principal connection to the world; he persistently watches out the window from his darkened rooms to catch a glimpse of them. He is a benign voyeur, however, and he envisions himself a defender rather than a threat to them, but he little understands the world before him. In a sense, he is a "helpless innocent when confronted with the complexity and dubious morality of a society locked in a racial caste system,"[5] the most complex stratification in America. In due course, his affection grows for the charming daughter.

This feeling ripens when he fights with the manager of the dance hall, thinking he is protecting Madam John, and he is stabbed and beaten. Having long served as a nurse, especially treating yellow fever, Madame John and her daughter care for him during a long convalescence, at the end of which he has fallen deeply in love with 'Tite Poulette and proposes marriage to her. Deeply concerned about both the law and the proprieties, she refuses: it is against the *Code Noir* for people of different races to wed, and it seems to her improper. At this juncture, Madame John reveals that the girl is not biologically her daughter but that of a Spanish couple who died under her care. Zalli raised the girl as her own but confesses the truth to allow her to find fulfillment in a marriage to Kristian. This deus ex machina device removes the conflict, and the story ends happily.

All of this is rendered with a good deal of artistic complexity and uncertainty. For example, the narrative perspective would seem to be in first person ("All of the features of the building lead me to guess" [213]) and thus limited to what someone on the scene could know about the events. The tone of the comments suggests a Creole gentleman is speaking, since he possesses an intimate knowledge of the topography and history of the city, and he is insightful and compassionate if somewhat judgmental about Kristian's naiveté. However, the narrative is told at a temporal remove of more than fifty years, as is clear when the narrator comments on the "loose New Orleans morals of over fifty years ago" (217) at the time of the action and when he comments that "now," at the time of the telling, Italians live in M. John's former home. Cable indicated in a letter to his publisher that the setting of the plot is in 1805, so the time of the telling is somewhat later than 1855, perhaps in the 1870s, the period of composition.[6] The speaker thus has limited knowledge of the action and dialogue, even allowing for poetic license, and he frequently comments on not knowing various details: he has to guess that Madame John lived in what had been the old Spanish barracks, but he is not certain (213). At other times the narrator possesses omniscient information, the contents of the letter Kristian wrote home to his mother, for example (216). He knows the details of the relationship between Zalli and M. John and who was present when they first met at the quadroon ball, information that further suggests the narrator is a man, since white women were not allowed to attend such functions. Indeed, the description of this dance in "'Tite Poulette" may be the earliest portrait of this event in American literature.

The narrator is intrusive in the manner of the aesthetics of Local Color:

each character is introduced with a long expository passage establishing appearance, age, disposition, and details that will play in the ensuing romance.[7] Zalli, a quadroon, is dark and attractive; she is intelligent, an engaging conversationalist, and a suitable companion to M. John, who never married a white woman. She has known internal struggle and emotional loss, but she loves her adoptive daughter and does not want to lose her. Thus she maintains the deception that she is the girl's biological mother despite the limitations that strategy will have for the young lady. Her stance in this matter is at best morally ambiguous, justified only by the deep emotional bond between them and a surrogate mother's desire to protect the child.

'Tite Poulette is known exclusively from the outside; the narrator presents only a superficial description of her as beautiful and "white," an aspect of her appearance that is repeated on several occasions and ultimately proves central to the resolution of the conflict: because her parents were Spanish, Kristian can marry her under the *Code Noir*. Koppig is a Dutch immigrant, an interloper in the process of discovering the folkways of a new society, a frequent stance for protagonists in Local-Color works. Because of geography, he is a social outsider; Zalli is one because of race and circumstance; 'Tite Poulette is one because of misrepresentation. Even as the situation is resolved at the end, they can never be fully accepted in aristocratic Creole society. Koppig's confrontation with local values is an essential element of the plot, and his innocence nearly costs him his life. He is isolated in New Orleans, with no discernable friends, and his chief recreation seems to be his preoccupation with the women across the street. In the course of events he gains little understanding of the culture before him, but he does become deeply involved in the lives of Zalli and 'Tite Poulette.

His historical innocence actually leads him to violence at the home of the quadroon balls, a place of historical fighting and stabbing. Interestingly, there are turbaned women in the hall, quadroon mothers following the Caribbean tradition of presenting their daughters for selection. When Koppig intervenes with the manager of the Salle de Condé, who is compared in imagery to a snake (219), he does so as a protector not of Zalli only but of her daughter, whom he presumes to be performing the *Danse de Chinois*. Kristian is not as innocent as when he first arrived in New Orleans; he is watching an erotic dance on a Sunday. But it is actually Madame John who appears before the Creole audience. When she danced there as a teenager, it was not for exhibition but as part of her "coming out" as a quadroon woman in society. No one was paid to attend in the late eighteenth century, and there was no disgrace. In a sense, Zalli is exploited by the manager, Monsieur de la Rue, but she is also employed by him. The threat is his desire to hire her daughter to perform in the same way, even though he strongly believes that she is fully white, as he clearly indicates (224, 225). Indeed, the "racial blending" motif is surprisingly simple in this case: all of the miscegenation has already taken place before the action begins. 'Tite Poulette is not the biological daughter of M. John and Zalli; it is her mother who was the product of an interracial mixture.

The story is built on top of a romance plot with several standard elements: a quick infatuation, an impediment to the fulfillment of love, and a resolution of the problem via deus ex machina. The conclusion also removes Madame John's concern about whether 'Tite Poulette should reveal her supposedly biracial heritage. With no need to continue as a voyeur, Kristian's loneliness has also been assuaged, although he will need to find another job. He is still a Dutch alien and a protestant who will marry a devout Catholic. Given that his French is awkward, and that his intended speaks only broken English, their communication will be stilted for some time. His physical conflict with Monsieur de la Rue is also unresolved, despite the assault by the manager and his thugs. Nor is the background social issue of the vulnerability of the quadroon mistress mitigated in any way, a problem compounded by the *Code Noir* proscription against interracial marriage. The injustice of this tradition, and the exploitation of women of mixed race, is perhaps the strongest social indictment in the story.

Shortly after "'Tite Poulette" was published, Cable received a letter from a quadroon woman in New Orleans complaining about the ending. She urged the writer to "tell the inmost truth of it. The girl was her own daughter; but like many and many a real quadroon mother, as you surely know, Madame John perjured her own soul to win for her child a legal and honorable alliance with the love-mate and life-mate of her choice."[8] As his daughter records, Cable's response was to write again about the quadroon caste in one of the great short stories of American literature, "Madame Delphine," which explores the same territory but with rather different thematic emphasis.[9] As several scholars have pointed out, the very name of the protagonist suggests that there may also have been a literary source for the story, "Madame de Staël's *Delphine*, the story of a woman who finds her passion for her lover more important than the world's condemnation of that love."[10] At the time of its publication, the mere subject attracted attention, as in the review by Edmond Gosse, who proclaimed that "Mr. Cable has already shown himself to be a master of a new field in fiction—namely, the curious Creole and quadroon population of the city and environs of New Orleans."[11] Subsequent reactions have been uniformly enthusiastic.

"Madame Delphine" first appeared in *Scribner's Monthly* from May through July of 1881 and was published as a volume later that year. Then, in 1883, it was incorporated into *Old Creole Days* in a new edition that has become standard for scholarly purposes. An obvious companion to "'Tite Poulette" on the issue of caste, Cable said it was the best fiction he had ever written, and he used it to begin the expanded volume.[12] However, the plot covers essentially the same ground as the earlier story in that the central figure is a quadroon "widow" left with a house, a small income, and a beautiful daughter. The Creole gentleman who established this plaçage marriage is long dead in each case. In both instances there seems to be an octoroon ingénue with whom a young white man falls in love, but the *Code Noir* presents an impediment to marriage. In "Madame Delphine" the obstacle is erased when the mother testifies that she is not Olive's biological parent, the true mother and father having died of yellow fever while in her care. Thus, the wedding proceeds, as in the earlier version. The tragic ending unfolds when Delphine confesses to her priest that she has lied to save her daughter's happiness, just as the letter to Cable suggested. Racked with guilt and a sense of betrayal of her daughter, she dies of grief.

Quite apart from plot manipulations, however, "Madame Delphine" has much richer character development, a deeper emotional conflict for the widowed mother, significant secondary issues, and a much more complex thematic structure. Indeed, it is in the subtle psychological transformations at its dramatic center that Cable exhibits his artistic skill. Delphine Carraze faces the responsibility of importing her daughter into New Orleans, where her racial status will be of paramount importance, rather than leaving her in France. Her daughter, Olive, has spent the first sixteen years of her life in Paris, where she was raised by her father's relatives as a white child. Now, she enters into a highly racialized society as a quadroon and encounters a complex psychological and social adjustment.[13] Olive's love interest, Ursin Lemaitre-Vignevielle, undergoes perhaps the deepest transformation when, in his role as a pirate and smuggler associated with the Lafitte brothers, he encounters Olive aboard a ship he is ransacking and she presents him with a Bible open to the Apostles' Creed. He gazes into her eyes and immediately orders his men off the ship. He rejects his adventurous ways and returns to New Orleans totally reborn as a banker who is soft spoken, concerned for others, and obsessed with finding Olive, with whom he has fallen deeply in love.

Behind these events resides a wealth of crucial historical information that every citizen of New Orleans would have understood but that was unknown in the rest of the country. After the United States assumed possession of New Orleans in 1803, trade negotiations with France became tenuous, leading to the Embargo Act of 1807 that blockaded ships coming from France and raised tariffs on goods imported from other countries. Creole society would collapse without trade with the home country, without shipments from the tailors and jewelers of Paris, to say nothing of the unthinkable deprivations made to the local cuisine.

The Lafitte brothers, Jean and Pierre, working out of the island of Barataria, smuggled huge quantities of goods through the barricades, sold them at reasonable prices, and established themselves as renegade heroes to the local population. Unimpressed, the United States government put a price on their heads. But Jean Lafitte was ultimately decorated by the federal authorities and made a citizen when he led his men against the British in the War of 1812, joining the forces of Andrew Jackson in defense of the city. Captain Lemaitre is said to have been similarly heroic, but he mysteriously disappears at the end of the war. His friends remember his contempt for government and law, but when he returns, surreptitiously, he has been changed into a banker not by war but by his deep love for Olive. It is the historical context that makes plausible his dramatic redemption and the respect the community could have for a former pirate.

Beyond the major characters, there is a rich cast of secondary figures with considerable depth. Pére Jerome, for example, is a goodly priest in a small parish, but he plays a large role in the events, struggling with his philosophical concepts of communal responsibility for sin and attempting to assist Madame Delphine in her plan to ensure her daughter's happiness. The priest believes the racial restrictions of the *Code Noir* to be evil and assists in undermining them. He was one of four friends who were deeply devoted to one another. Another was Ursin, in whom they never lost faith in his fundamental decency, piracy and smuggling being regarded as minor infractions against the blockade that had been placed on New Orleans. Evariste Varrillat is a physician who exhibits the habits of mind of a scientist: he thinks in terms of empirical investigation and logical conclusions. Jean Thompson, an attorney, reasons in accord with the law. Together they constitute a crucial support team for Ursin, standing by him when he is regarded as an outlaw, hiding him from the authorities, and even, in the case of the priest, performing a wedding ceremony that he knows to be illegal. In a sense, these seven characters constitute the collective protagonist, for they each deal with social, legal, and moral conflict.

The story opens not with any of the principal characters but with the city itself at the time of the telling in 1881. The narrator, a guide to the French Quarter, emphasizes the vestiges of the former beauty and grace of the district and its current architectural decrepitude and widespread decay, a circumstance, the implication seems to be, that is paralleled by Creole society as well. The time of the action is during the golden age of the quadroon tradition in 1821 and 1822, when Madame Delphine first appears as a plaçage widow, dressing in black, absorbed with loyalty for her "husband," and living quietly in the house he purchased for her. Her octoroon daughter, Olive, has recently returned from her education in Paris, and her mother protects her from the temptations of the city, particularly so because of the frightening adventure on her return to America.

Much of the action proceeds through indirection in the conversations of Lemaitre's closest friends, especially Pére Jerome, with whom the narrative perspective is often identified. He gives a sermon, attended by Delphine and Olive, in which he explains Ursin's adventurous past and recent salvation, which he knows to be motivated by love. In the scenes following Ursin directly, he manages his bank by day and spends his evenings searching for Olive throughout the city. When he ultimately finds her, they build on the mutual instantaneous infatuation kindled on the ship and fall deeply in love. They vow to wed, but there is a serious social restriction: the *Code Noir* forbids interracial marriages. Madame Delphine solves the problem by producing a photograph of an aunt, swearing that the white woman is Olive's mother, and the legal issue is solved. The moral dimension inherent in the situation persists, however, for Madame Delphine is not one to regard law and social custom lightly, and she is consumed with guilt. She confesses the truth to Pére Jerome and quickly dies; he believes the deeper sin is the racism of society, not the subterfuge of a loving mother, and the plot ends with his invocation to God to "lay not this sin to her charge" (81). The priest thus reiterates the philosophical premise he introduced earlier, that there is "a community of responsibility attaching to every misdeed" (13), one of the central themes of the story and the main thesis of the sermon he gives in the cathedral (17).

That concept is initially applied to a generalized consideration but would most directly pertain to Ursin Lemaitre's career as a pirate and smuggler. In that context, the judgment would be that the Embargo Act was sufficiently devastating and unjust so as to validate the careers of Ursin and the Lafitte brothers, and history had done so. Ursin's transformation into a banker assisting the poor is further confirmation that it was the law that was corrupt, not the man. To whatever extent there is "sin" in smuggling, therefore, the guilt must be borne by the society that imposed the regulations.[14]

That thinking applies in a more important sense to the life of Madame Delphine, for the restrictions placed on her as quadroon led to a plaçage marriage rather than a conventional one. Olive, as an octoroon, subsequently encounters the same prohibition in the *Code Noir*, which forbids her from legitimately marrying Ursin. She does not fully understand the nature of the code: having been raised in France, which formulated the regulations but did not apply them to the home country, she has been removed from their pernicious effects. Her mother must deal with the situation, as she does when she fabricates pseudo-parentage for her, signs a penurious document, and the wedding proceeds. The priest's reflections would implicate the whole of society in the sin of sustaining a corrupt system of racial stratification and caste limitation, the decrepitude implied by the decaying building in the opening of the story. Although the priest does not state it directly, his judgment would seem to be that Delphine acted properly, expressing the deep love of a mother, in ensuring that an unjust law not circumscribe the happiness of her daughter. The two issues would constitute the two major applications of Jerome's thinking.

Thus "'Tite Poulette" and "Madame Delphine" are unified by a New Orleans setting, a romance plot, central quadroon characters, the portrait of a fading Creole aristocracy after the Louisiana Purchase, and themes of civil rights for people of color, moral responsibility for a rigid social caste system, and the broader portrayal of life in the French Quarter in the early part of the nineteenth century. The Napoleonic Code is important in that it established the right of inheritance for children born of liaisons out of marriage; the *Code Noir* is fundamental in that it established rules of conduct for the caste system and expressly forbade sexual contact and marriage among the races; and the plaçage tradition instituted a contravening social convention allowing formalized relationships between Creole gentlemen and women of color. All of these traditions play crucial roles in *Old Creole Days*, including in the most famous of Cable's stories, "Belles Demoiselles Plantation."

First published in *Scribner's Monthly* in 1874, the story is set in New Orleans and on a Mississippi River plantation a short distance to the north.[15] Although Cable designated the dominant action as taking place in 1820,[16] the narrative opens with an omniscient narrator providing an expository background that reaches back four generations in the lives of the central characters. What is explained, however, is crucial to the rest of the action. In the background is Count De Charleu, the patriarch of the family, who obtained his land in a grant from the French government near the end of the seventeenth century. He ran the commissariat that supplied food and clothing to the French army in the colony, and the narrator implies that he may have embezzled money from the operation. In the midst of an investigation, the building mysteriously burned to the ground with the account books inside. The suggestion remains that the very foundation of familial wealth begins with corruption, a matter that, as in the biblical injunction, will come to rest on generations to come.

The earliest French settlers were entirely men, which perhaps explains why the count married a Choctaw woman, a member of the Native-American people who lived in the Mississippi Valley at the time of European arrival, and they had a child. Such a union was not, at the time, unusual. The Choctaws integrated quickly into French culture, and many of them married white settlers prior to the adoption of the *Code Noir* throughout Louisiana in 1724. The initial action thus must take place prior to this date since such a marriage would have been illegal after the ratification of the code. In the process of the investigation, the count journeyed to the French court, and when he returned to America he had with him a gentlewoman he wed in Paris in "a fit of forgetfulness" that he already had a bride. Meanwhile, his Choctaw wife had starved to death, leaving behind a family that was, under the provisions of the new *Code Noir*, represented in the count's will. His return to Louisiana was most likely shortly after 1724 because his first marriage would no longer have been a legal impediment to the second, and yet his will would, by law, contain provisions for a third of his wealth to go to his mixed-race progeny. Congruent with the Napoleonic Code, he thus had two families bearing his name and sharing in the disposition of his estate. As a result, three generations later Injin Charlie owns the property in the city, an entire block that includes a mansion and a number of business establishments that produce a great deal of income. His distant white relative, Colonel De Charleu, has inherited the plantation property, a mansion on the river surrounded by extensive fields of sugar cane.

The colonel has lived a dissolute life filled with the standard Creole vices: gambling, drinking, dancing, dueling, and quarreling at the quadroon balls at the St. Phillippe Street theatre (123). To support his extravagant lifestyle, he has borrowed a great deal of money from Injin Charlie, a total later indicated to be $180,000 (125). This sum needs to be understood in social context: far from the general assumption that people of color were impoverished because of law and custom, the Free Men of Color in this era owned roughly one-third of New Orleans, much of it inherited from their Creole fathers and quadroon mothers. Since Native-American women were sometimes part of a plaçage arrangement or, prior to 1724, a marriage, mixed-race children were often left with considerable wealth. Injin Charlie, in other words, is representative of a fairly sizeable economic phenomenon.

Central to the developing conflict are the colonel's seven daughters, sisters drawn from Greek mythology and the origin of the Pleiades. The daughters of Atlas and Pleione were said to have been extraordinarily beautiful. Although the many legends concerning them differ, in several they were pursued by ardent lovers and, to escape, were changed into birds and placed among the stars, thus forming the constellation. In some accounts, they were drowned, a circumstance related to the representation in the Greek poet Hesiod's *Works and Days* when the "Pleiades flee mighty Orion and plunge into the misty deep." In Europe they were traditionally associated with mourning and funerals, and the mythological structure of the reference foreshadows that the sisters will come to a tragic end, as is the case. In Cable's story, the sisters are consistently portrayed in relation to the plantation house; in fact, they are never shown outside of that context.[17] When the house collapses into the river with them inside, it is the logical conclusion of their mythological origin. This idea is further reinforced when the colonel is compared by the narrator to the Roman god Saturn, who, as the Greek deity Cronus, was made king of the Elysian Islands, the home of the dead. Both father and daughters are thus associated imagistically with death, and the trajectory of the plot leads inevitably to tragedy.

Beyond the expository setup of the introduction, the rest of the action is centered around negotiations for the purchase of the New Orleans house from Injin Charlie. That transaction is motivated not so much by the colonel's desires, although he would like to consolidate the familial holdings, as by the longings of his daughters, who manipulate their father with increasingly emotional pleas. The first negotiation (128–31) is simple: the colonel offers $10,000 for a property Injin Charlie says is worth $50,000. It is clear, however, that he is rich and that he places much value on the "blood" he shares with the colonel, a feeling that reaches to the core of Creole culture. Charlie then offers an even trade for the plantation that is immediately rejected, and the scene ends.

The second such discussion (132–34) follows the deprecation of the plantation by the seven daughters and their desire for the delights of an urban atmosphere. The colonel makes another unsuccessful offer, and Charlie again suggests trading his property for the plantation, which the colonel rejects emphatically. Charlie dwells on the significance of a familial bloodline, which his relative considers a "preposterous ancestral loyalty" (134). Before the next conversation in the series, however, spring arrives with the annual runoff from the north that swells the river for its entire length. Given the unhappiness of his daughters, it is clear that the colonel has lost much that he values: his land is mortgaged; gambling has cost him his inherited fortune; he owes his mixed-blood relative a great deal of money; his wife is dead; his daughters pine for the house he cannot buy for them; and he is essentially useless in the new American economy.

Walking about his property one day, he sees tons of land slide into the Mississippi, and he realizes that his mansion and surrounding property are vulnerable. He rushes into the city to accept the trade with Charlie, thus hoping to gain the urban home in exchange for a worthless plantation house. Charlie, not knowing about the collapsing property, responds with reluctance to take so fine a property from his own relative, and the colonel is conscience stricken to "betray his own blood" (141). He suggests they both inspect the estate. Walking the plantation, Charlie is trusting and generous, and the colonel says "you better not make the trade" (142). Just at that moment, the land and the house collapse "with one short, wild wail of terror—sunk, sunk, down, down, down, into the merciless, unfathomable flood of the Mississippi" (142). It is one of the most dramatically tragic scenes in American Realism, one with obvious echoes of Edgar Allan Poe's "The Fall of the House of Usher" in which the family and the dwelling are entwined psychically as well as physically. In this case the house itself has significance that reaches back four generations, and its collapse seems, as in the case of the Ushers, the logical disintegration of the family line. Injin Charlie has no offspring, so the lineage will end with him.[18]

The colonel is devastated by the loss of his daughters, the "seven goddesses of his only worship" (136), and he collapses, never to rise again. For an entire year he is lovingly attended to by Injin Charlie, who allows no one but a physician near his relative. On the final day, there is a fourth crucial negotiation about the trade for the house. Knowing that his plantation is now worth little, the colonel maintains, to his own disadvantage, "we didn't trade," certainly the apex of his moral growth (144). For his part, Charlie says that they did: "Oh yes, we did, it was a bonafide swap!" The colonel counters that the land will not "pay you out," by which he means it is not worth the $180,000 that is owed on it. Charlie's response is to say "dat makes not'in," and the colonel dies (145). Both men have, through tragedy, achieved a level of extraordinary decency, a moral rise driven by the call of common blood and by the benevolent stance Charlie has taken through four negotiations. Although of mixed blood, he has proven himself to be the true "gentleman" in the family, the person of greatest substance, and it is his moral stature that solidifies the central ethic of the conclusion. Cable notably developed the same racial situation in his brilliant novel *The Grandissimes*.

"Belles Demoiselles Plantation" is thus built on the same cultural foundation as "Madame Delphine" and "'Tite Poulette," a French Creole society that indulges in mixed-race liaisons that result in progeny that must make their way in a rigidly caste-ordered ethos. Injin Charlie is unique in that he thrives financially, free of the impoverishment that threatens the women in the other two stories. The corruption of Creole life is well in the past, and the crux of the action rests on the consequences of former behavior, not on current improprieties. The colonel's profligacy is not the focus of his life, which is preoccupied with his daughters. As in the other stories, there is a Local-Color underpinning in the representation of multiple dialects and in the importance of regional mores, but there is little detailed description of New Orleans, a limited range of characters, and a conflict born of unique family relationships.

Although there are universal issues involved, including the mutability of happiness and the vulnerability of the human condition, the central themes would seem to revolve around two concerns: the first is the extent to which the death of the sisters is the culmination of the sins of the fathers, and the second involves the theme of redemption. Alice Hall Petry argues that "it required decades of waiting, but the manifold crimes of the original Comte, and the personal sins of De Charleu, are punished in a moment with the destruction of the plantation and the drowning of the seven daughters."[19] Indeed, her interpretation is built on the assumptions of a religious allegory. But this view makes sense only in terms of a Protestant Christianity based on a vengeful God who wreaks punishment on innocent children, not the more relaxed religion of French Catholicism as practiced in New Orleans. More viable would seem to be John Cleman's approach emphasizing the "treatment of social themes—race, caste, ancestral pride, and ancestral guilt."[20]

Unlike the other stories in *Old Creole Days*, this one has a redemptive outcome in two senses. At the end, the colonel sends for the priest, reaffirming his commitment to at least the ritualistic form of his religion, which is absent from the rest of the action. But more important is the humanistic commitment of the two men to one another, neither one wishing to cheat the other in their final negotiation, both of them acknowledging the deep connection of the family line. Quite apart from the frivolous social ambitions of the seven daughters, the two men bond in the concluding scenes. Their redemption is humanistic, a matter of love and loyalty, not fundamentally religious, an issue of spiritual salvation. As Arlin Turner formulates it, "they discover in the presence of calamity the loyalty each owes the other."[21] It is perhaps the twining of these themes with an artful structure, a more sophisticated narrative technique, and the allusive significance of Greek mythology that led Hjalmar Hjorth Boyesen to proclaim that "the whole plan & execution of the story have always seemed to me excellent above the need of praise."[22] The Norwegian immigrant was, of course, a great admirer of Cable's work, risking his personal fortune to ensure the publication of *Old Creole Days*.

Of all the stories in the volume, the most popular during Cable's lifetime was "Posson Jone'," perhaps because it is a tour de force of dialect manipulation; the author was a consummate performer on the lecture circuit.[23] Arlin Turner emphasizes this point, maintaining that the story had the "widest and most distinguished commendation in his lifetime."[24] Despite its eventual celebrity, it was originally turned down by four periodicals (*Scribner's Monthly*, the *New York Times*, *Galaxy*, and *Harper's Magazine*) before it appeared in *Appleton's Journal*.[25] In general, the editors were wary of offending the readership with the portrayal of a drunk parson from West Florida who wrestles with a tiger in Congo Square and is thrown into jail. The irony is that Cable did not invent this plot but found the inspiration for it in the archives of New Orleans newspapers.[26] But the audience of the day found enormous humor in a ribald tale of an innocent, trusting preacher set upon by a Creole confidence man who gets his mark drunk and attempts to steal his money. The deflation of stature for the minister, the riotous action at the circus, and the wise and caring slave who proves smarter than his master were all elements that had enormous appeal to a nineteenth-century audience. In fact, "Posson Jone'" was so popular that as late as 1901 Cable was working on a dramatic adaptation for the stage.[27]

Beneath the surface of riotous action and gross humor, however, there are masterful artistic touches in historical allusions, the subtle manipulation of point of view, the representation of dialect, and a spectrum of characterizations in what is essentially a comic narrative. As is common in Cable's stories, the narrative method is retrospective and inconsistent: it purports to look back seventy years to the action, and yet at times the narrator seems to comment in the present, as when reporting conversations, and yet is sometimes unable to hear when two people move out of earshot (156). A speaker seven decades distant from the events being related does not have problems hearing anything. Furthermore, since Cable explained that the action takes place in 1815, and the story was first published in 1876, the temporal distance is too great.[28] Yet the representation of a variety of dialects is masterful, capturing the linguistic distinctions between French and Spanish speakers of English, the language of a minister from West Florida, and the dialect of the parson's slave, Colossus, as opposed to that of the Creole's servant, Baptiste. On the lecture circuit, Cable was said to have been the consummate entertainer, enthralling the audience with his skill in presenting these dialects, even while sharing the stage with the most famous of the Chautauqua lecturers, Mark Twain.

The first character to be introduced is Jules St.-Ange, a profligate Creole miscreant who has frittered away his inheritance. This fact is all the more ironic because he was educated by a Capuchin priest in a Catholic school. The Capuchin order was dedicated to extreme austerity and poverty; they were not allowed to touch money, and they lived entirely by begging. It was primarily a European order, but the Capuchin Franciscan Fathers had a church on Erato Street in New Orleans. St.-Ange's extravagance in frittering away an inheritance is thus in contravention of the central theme of his childhood instruction. Given his total lack of income, he is faced with lamentable choices: the first is going to work ("they shuddered"), and the second is to join "Major Innerarity's filibustering expedition" (149).

Audiences in Cable's time would have remembered that John Innerarity was rumored to be John Lafitte himself, for both were privateers who were declared outlaws and redeemed themselves in the War of 1812 by coming to the defense of New Orleans by aiding Andrew Jackson in fending off the invading British army. More likely, his career paralleled that of Lafitte because a fair amount is known about his background. He came to New Orleans in 1802 when his grandfather moved his trading company away from St. Augustine and located in western Florida. John grew up in the area, learning multiple languages, including several Native-American dialects, which made him useful in trade negotiations with the indigenous people. But he abandoned trading for privateering when the English instituted the blockade. Bereft of produce to market, Innerarity joined Lafitte in running the lines of the British attempting to prevent trade with France, with whom England was at war. Jean Lafitte had ten ships he could use as pirate vessels or for filibustering, and Innerarity was in command of one of them. That is what is at issue for young Jules St.-Ange. There would be risk in joining such an adventurous enterprise, so he opts for another option, becoming a confidence man. He is clever, quick, resourceful, manipulative, and without scruples, the perfect combination for either politics or con games, and he selects Parson Jones as his first easy mark.

Baptiste, Jules's "yellow" body servant, undoubtedly a man of mixed blood, is an accomplice in the confidence game, but he plays a stock character role in the drama, including the clichéd indication that he is wiser than his master. In fact, Jules owes him money. There is a possible allusive irony in his name because Jean-Baptiste Say was the most celebrated economist in New Orleans at the time. In *A Treatise on Political Economy* (1803), widely taught throughout the United States, he argued that supply creates its own demand. The pertinence here would be that when the parson reveals that he is carrying $500 he inspires Jules's determination to acquire it by getting the minister drunk.

The parson's servant, Colossus of Rhodes, also has an allusive name. The original Colossus was the statue of the Greek god Helios on the island of Rhodes, and it was constructed about 280 BC. One of the seven wonders of the ancient world, it commemorated the successful defense of the city when Demetrius attempted to invade. He had built enormous scaffolding equipment that was left behind in the failed siege. Rhodes had the materials sold and erected a statue over one hundred feet high at the entrance to the harbor. In contrast, Cable's Colossus is ironically small, a "short, square, old negro, very black and grotesque" (154), but he nevertheless serves as the protector of his master. He warns against gambling and drink, and, when that fails, he steals the money from the minister and keeps it for him as long as they are in New Orleans, where it is vulnerable. As soon as they are on board ship, he returns it, but he does so not directly but by allowing the parson to believe it comes as an answer to his prayers (174). Jules observes the strategy of all of this, and he is profoundly moved by the character of the slave.

The plot is standard in Local Colorism: a country bumpkin arrives in the city where worldly wise con men take his money and leave him broke and bewildered. From the time he first appears, the threats to his money are essentially his naiveté buttressed by the traditional Creole habits of drinking and gambling. When Jules pretends to befriend him, the product is a tour of some of the rowdy sections of the city, including gambling dens, saloons, and, most notably, Congo Square, where the famous Cayetano Mariotini had established his circus a decade earlier. Lafcadio Hearn, in fact, dates the establishment of Cayetano's circus as 1816, but that would place it a year after the action of the story.[29] The facility was constructed in Congo Square just outside the ramparts of the city, an area where slaves and Free Men of Color could celebrate on a Saturday night and all day Sunday, when, by the *Code Noir*, they were forbidden to work. It was a riotous venue filled with drink, voodoo practitioners, erotic dancing, and ceremonies derived from African and Caribbean traditions. That the parson goes there is a comic intrusion of innocence entering the den of iniquity, and the outrageous consequences greatly entertained a nineteenth-century audience.[30]

Jules succeeds in getting the minister drunk and induces him to see a bullfight at the circus. Four decades of Spanish rule in Louisiana had introduced the practice to the area, and it had become very popular. However, a storm the night before has delayed the corrida, so a fight between a buffalo and a tiger has been substituted. The crowd is drunken and raucous, but it is also representative of the uniquely diverse population of the city. French and Spanish Creoles abound, of course, but in the mélange are Gascons (the Basques from southern France), "Sicilian fruiters," "Portuguese sailors," "mariners of England, Germany, and Holland," "Canadian *voyageurs*," "drinking and singing *Américains*, too—more's the shame," Mexicans, and, in addition to the parson and Jules, Baptiste and Colossus as part of the riotous crowd (165). Predictably, the parson flies totally out of control, preaching in his inebriation to a laughing and shouting mob that attacks the buffalo, pulling him into the square. The massive parson suddenly appears carrying the tiger from his pen, and he throws the cat onto the back of the buffalo, and the crowd kills both animals. The Americans lift him on their shoulders and parade him about while he shouts about "Daniel in the 'buffler's' den" (167). The minister is quickly thrown in jail, where he sleeps off his intoxication.

The concluding events are simple but thematically rich. Jules bails out the minister, hoping somehow to steal the missing money, but the minister still believes in the goodness of his new friend and praises him continuously for his generosity. The parson feels obligated to return to the calaboza to serve out a just sentence, but Jules argues, falsely, that the judge forbade him to come back (169). Jules cannot cheat him as long as he is in jail. He suggests that Colossus stole the cash, but his owner believes in his servant absolutely: "No, Jools, I never will believe he taken that money" (170). Jules is shaken by the trusting heart of the parson, and he offers to replace the $500 with money of his own, but the minister will not accept it. It is only Colossus's ruse of pretending that prayer returned the church treasury that sets things right, and Jules realizes the truth of what has transpired. He is transformed by the decency of the people before him, and he resolves to pay his debts and lead an honest life.

In the spectrum of themes that arise from the events, central is the transformative power of virtue, even in the most profligate of men. Alice Hall Petry argues that the story rests on a conflict between Christian and "heathen" perspectives: "New Orleans in 1815 was a heterogeneous, non-Americanized, and fundamentally irreligious society that would not accommodate someone like Parson Jones."[31] But the plot has little to do with theology, for the only religious comments are absurd observations by Jules that everyone should have the religion they like best (159) and his account of how his father created the sweetest barrel of sugar on the market by sprinkling holy water on it, not realizing that a protestant minister would have little regard for the sacred font. Rather, Jules's alteration is moral and humanistic, a psychological transformation that has ethical consequences for the rest of his life. In contrast, Parson Jones is static, impervious to experience, learning nothing from what has just happened to him. He returns home the same country bumpkin as when he left, a perpetual innocent.

The central theme is thus not spiritual redemption nor "mutual Christian love" between the two men but humanistic growth,[32] and the character with the internal transformations is Jules, not the minister. The secondary themes are also vital, with important social and cultural implications, as is often the case in *Old Creole Days*. As Louis Rubin Jr. contends, despite the comedic tone, the story presents a dramatic contrast between Anglo-Saxon and Creole morality and, despite the naïveté of the preacher, the country ethic proves superior to the urban.[33] Furthermore, the two men of color, Colossus and Baptiste, both servants, are wiser, and better, than the men they assist. It is Colossus who saves the money, and the day, and he does so selflessly, with no remuneration for himself. The crowd at Congo Square presents the persistent motif of cultural variety, the social richness of New Orleans, and it is buttressed with a "linguistic smorgasbord" demonstrating the vast range of backgrounds of the people assembled.[34]

On the other hand, "Posson Jone'" lacks some of the continuing themes in the volume: there is little of the deterioration of Creole culture in this case, although Jules, the prototypical representative, has no marketable skills in the new, American, entrepreneurial society. The buildings are not collapsing, both physically and metaphorically, as is often the case, and the central issue is not the exploitation of the quadroon caste. Indeed, there are no important women characters at all. In place of these ideas Cable presented a broader portrait of New Orleans culture that includes virtually every component group and within that context the possibility of two men from differing social and religious backgrounds who grow closer together on the basis of humorously dramatic events.

"Café des Exilés" is also set in New Orleans, but unlike "Posson Jone'," which has no significant female characters, it features a standard love triangle at the center of its romance plot.[35] The characters are not indigenous French Creoles but recent Spanish-speaking refugees from Cuba, San Domingo, Barbados,[36] and Martinique, each fleeing the consequences of international wars and cultural transitions. Cuba, for example, belonged to France from 1791 to 1809, but the loss of the war with Spain in 1808 forced French citizens to leave the country. As was common throughout the Caribbean, they fled to New Orleans as did a spectrum of other nationality groups. Major Galahad Shaughnessy, for example, is Irish, part of a large population of dock workers in the early part of the century. He is innocent, idealistic, trustworthy, and habitually utters his key comments twice. Although a worthy suitor of a beloved ingénue, Pauline, he is described continuously in terms of his "boyishness" (88). His competitor in this quest is Manuel Mazaro, of Cuban blood mixed with Indian (89), the clear villain of the melodrama. He is always described in feminine terms, with a "girlish face" and locks that "curled so prettily," and he has the "hands of a woman," apparently traits that indicate abnormality and corruption in a man (87–88).

Pauline is a saintly innocent compared favorably to the Virgin Mary (91), and men have reverence for her, sublimating sexual desire in favor of spirituality and genteel manners.[37] Lust is never suggested at any point in the action. At one juncture she is described as Rebecca, who was possessed of profound beauty, the biblical wife of Isaac, son of Abraham (93). She knows Galahad's character, trusts him, and never doubts him even when her father is told that the Irishman is insincere in his attentions to her. The father, M. D'Hemecourt, was born in Martinique, lived in San Domingo in his adolescence, moved to Cuba as an adult, and fled to New Orleans when the Spanish seized control of the country. His speech is an amalgam of dialects. These four characters are at the heart of the action, but the first-person narrator is an additional presence throughout.

Indeed, the story is entirely verbal in the sense that it is told many years after the action by a man who observed none of it. At the time of the telling, the narrator has just dined with the Shaughnessy family, where Galahad recited his memory of the events, conceding that, as is the case in his accounts of the history of various houses in the French Quarter, "if he happens not to know a true one, he can make one up as he goes along" (117). Similarly, the narrator suggests that, in the main, he has related what he heard accurately, "though here and there my enthusiasm may have taken liberties." The entire recitation is thus conceded to be uncertain and unreliable, although it is given a putative sincerity in the speaker's confessions of his limited knowledge of things he cannot quite remember or does not know for certain (85, 94). The emphasis is on building conflict and drama, and there is a theatrical structure to the plot.

Actually a double plot energizes the center story. The romance drama is focused on Manuel's attempt to win Pauline through his representation of his rival as callous and disrespectful of the young lady. He is disclosed through a device common in eighteenth-century British melodrama: Galahad and Pauline are hidden in a closet and overhear the conversation between the Cuban and M. D'Hemecourt. Right on cue, they emerge amid Manuel's lies and the truth is evident. That line of action concludes not in the revelation that the pair has wed but with the comments by the narrator at the time of the telling that they have been happily married and have had many children. The second plot involves the refugees from Cuba who plan revolution against Spanish control of their country, an effort that, historically, continued through the Spanish-American War of 1898 and culminated in Cuban independence in 1902. This activity in 1835 must be seen as an embryonic expression of the desire for national sovereignty that had not been realized even in 1879, when *Old Creole Days* first appeared.

This revolutionary activity is presented as a burial society meeting in New Orleans for the purpose of smuggling guns to Cuba hidden in coffins. Lafcadio Hearn records that there were indeed meetings of this kind in the Café des Réfugiés during this period, but the restaurant was on Rampart Street, not the Rue Burgundy.[38] Alice Dunbar-Nelson comments on the number of exiles from the Caribbean in New Orleans, saying that there were "ten thousand white, yellow, and black West Indian islanders, some with means, most of them destitute, all of them desperate."[39] Galahad and Manuel are on the same side of that effort, even though the Cuban is eventually drowned in a canal, probably as the result of his conflict with the Irishman. These characters are unique in *Old Creole Days* in that they have no historical connection to New Orleans, do not intend to remain there, and perceive it only as a transient base for their smuggling activities.[40] Cable is skillful in intertwining the two lines of action, which are presented as a seamless flow of activity.

The handling of time is problematic, however. The narrator places the action in 1835 with gentle equivocation, "I think he said thirty-five" (85), but later, in a letter to his publisher, Cable placed the events in 1845.[41] With regard to historical events, both dates seem to provide a frame of reference. For example, in the key scene in the Café des Réfugiés the exiles discuss the issues of the day, among them the annexation of Texas, which declared itself a republic in 1836. It became a state in 1845, an act that resulted in war with Mexico in 1846, a conflict that has not yet begun in the story. This conversation would thus make best sense in 1845. But there is another event that clearly helps establish the action in that year: Galahad has been to a concert by the great Norwegian violinist Ole Bull, and he regales the group at the café with an account of it. Bull's first visit to the United States was in 1843, and he performed a series of concerts at the Great Armory Hall in New Orleans in early 1844, ending on January 23.[42] In terms of historical accuracy, the action is thus impossible in 1835. That date is either a simple fictional construct with no reference to history or a corollary of the unreliable narrative stance in which the speaker misremembers what was said to him or was misinformed.

Although the romance plot was a staple of popular fiction by the 1870s, Cable's introduction of a diverse cast of ethnic characters into a New Orleans setting is historically important. It was the first such portrayal of a Southern city, and it is handled with realistic details ranging from the presentation of dialects to the grimly serious conflicts between the two men. "Café des Exilés" also expands the human spectrum of characters portrayed in the book to include a transient population not directly involved in the Creole issues central to most of the stories in the volume.

"'Sieur George" plays a unique role in the publication history of *Old Creole Days*. It was the first of the stories to see print, appearing in *Scribner's Monthly* in October of 1873, and Cable used it as the opening story for the 1879 edition of the volume.[43] It thus played a prominent role as an introduction to the world of New Orleans, and Cable made many changes in the text as it moved from the magazine to the book and from the 1879 edition to that in 1883. Primarily, he deepened the role of the landlord, Kookoo, as a voyeur by extending his obsession with the tenant to over five decades and emphasizing the themes of decay and moral degeneration. Significantly, the protagonist is not a French Creole but an outsider who observes society and does not fully understand its established codes. But rather than reveal social weakness, this story depicts, as Alice Hall Petry formulates it, "the title character's moral, emotional, and physical degeneration in an alien environment."[44] In the magazine, the subtitle, entirely missing from the collected volume, read "A Story of New Orleans," as though this grim tale of corrosion represented the generic situation in New Orleans in mid-century.[45] Cable made other revisions to his manuscript, as well, including an entirely different conclusion and many that established greater thematic depth, a richness of historical texture, and a delicacy of style that astonished his editors at Scribners. As Turner has commented, "they expected a plot with definite complication, suspense, and resolution, and so were hardly prepared for a story achieving its effects through lightness of touch, half-revelation, and suggestion."[46]

"'Sieur George" begins, as do many of Cable's works, with a detailed description of the building in which George resides, a genteel, four-story structure in a state of advancing deterioration emblematic of the decaying Creole world around it. The introduction is handled skillfully, as Petry maintains: "Cable progressively narrows the focus of his story—from New Orleans, to 'the heart' of the city, to a particular building, to a courtyard of that building, to a two-room apartment off that courtyard, and finally to a mysterious trunk inside that apartment."[47] Similar to the people living around it, the tenement suggests "gentility in rags," nobility amid decay, vestigial glimpses of the once proud culture that produced it. Into that society comes the titular character, an American, apparently a retired army officer who originally came to New Orleans to serve in Fort St. Charles, since the soldiers there know him and drink with him into the night. When the Mexican War breaks out in 1846, he re-enlists to serve in the conflict, and he is wounded, taken prisoner by the Mexicans, and released well after the end of the war. Up to this point in his life, he is guilty of only common vices, most of which he shares with his Creole companions: he drinks, but not compulsively; he abhors common labor; he is willing to duel to avenge a slight; and he gambles, which fact changes the entire course of his life.

These background details are told from a non-dramatized and otherwise unexplained first-person perspective that is nonetheless omniscient, providing details of the history of New Orleans, the transitions in the buildings of the city, and the events in the life of the man who becomes known as 'Sieur George, although there is no confirmation that is actually his name. Given the assumptions of the point of view, other facts are strangely missing, vaguely suggested, or reported as speculation, leaving a tense uncertainty in the "telling." The narration is primarily identified with the mind of George's landlord, a "small square" Creole reputed to be of mixed blood, which would make it possible that he is the child of a plaçage arrangement. That suggestion is further underscored by the fact that he inherited the building and a sum of money from his father, which would have been standard Civil Code procedure. For more than five decades, Kookoo is obsessed with learning more about George and with discovering the contents of an old hair trunk he moved into his apartment. His driving urge to look into the chest creates an aura of suspense that is relieved in the final scenes.

The rest of the plot presents, largely in suggestion and speculation, a series of "probable" events beginning with the revelation that George was an American soldier, an interloper into Louisiana society; he may or may not have won a small fortune gambling when he was a young man; he may have fought a duel with his opponent, wounded him mortally, and, in the final moments, promised to care for his family (248). All of these assumptions are made more probable by confirming details: George is on intimate terms with the federal soldiers in the fort, with whom he frequently drinks. When the Mexican War erupts in 1846, he appears in full regimentals, rejoins his unit, and serves with it for at least two years. During this time a striking Lady in Black, presumably the French-speaking widow of the man he killed, lives quietly in his rooms, explaining nothing of her life to her landlord. It is he who admires her beauty and finds her slave women, a mulattress, handsome (251). Kookoo's fascination is temporarily shifted to her, and he hopes to use her presence in the apartment as an occasion to open the trunk, but time passes without the opportunity. She remains a mysterious presence even after the end of the war, since George fails to return with the rest. When he does arrive, he has been wounded and carries a long scar, and with him is a tall, charming stranger who speaks Creole French (255). Kookoo, in his imaginings, has guessed that George intends to marry the widow, but instead she is wed to the tall stranger, who proves to be a drunkard. Both of them die soon after, leaving an infant daughter, who is raised by George. He adopts her, at least informally, and his role of surrogate father continues through her adolescence until she emerges as a mature young lady of sixteen, "very beautiful, with very black hair and eyes" (261). At this juncture, there is a crucial scene in which Kookoo peeks through the keyhole into the room and the narrator records what he can see and hear.

It is from this voyeuristic perspective that the most crucial details emerge: that George was responsible for the death of the girl's grandfather, although the specifics are not clarified; that George frittered away the fortune he had won by drinking and gambling; that he had promised to care for the man's family, which he has done. Finally, the most shocking revelation is that George proposes marriage to the "daughter" he has raised, and she is horrified. Kookoo, alternately hearing and observing small pieces of this scene, hears the word "fortune" and, given his preoccupation, assumes it refers to the money he believes is in the trunk, but he later finds it filled with worthless Havana lottery tickets (264). Later, from his window, he sees the girl pause on the corner before she disappears.

The original conclusion in *Scribner's Monthly* deals with her, with her apparent disillusionment as she escapes to Mother Nativity's asylum driven by her lack of alternatives; weeping, she kneels at the altar.[48] Her actions suggest that she was horrified that the man she had known as a father would think of her as a possible mate and lover. The trajectory of the plot, in this version, is thus toward her painful sense of betrayal as a result of her surrogate father's moral failings. His corruption has been complete, and she is left to carry the emotional burden. However, Cable changed the ending for book publication. Now, the conclusion places the girl in the convent looking outward, observing a destitute George wandering through the peripheral fields looking for a grassy place to bed down for the night. He has searched for the girl at the convent, but Mother Nativity has denied any knowledge of her. It is clear that he seeks not a reconciliation with his daughter but someone to loan him ten dollars to play the lottery again because he is confident he has the winning combination of numbers. This conclusion thus shifts the weight of the degeneration back to George, with the girl simply observing him rather than bearing the consequences herself.

What is significant about this tale of economic collapse and moral decay is that it features a protagonist who is not a Creole but an American interloper who cannot cope with a world of genteel idleness, drinking, and gambling. George follows a path that begins with fascination with this culture, moves to an enthusiastic entry into it, and ultimately ends with his corruption. Around him is the decline of the Creoles; what was once grand in their world is now degraded and crumbling, as are the pretensions of this once exalted class. As Arlin Turner has commented, "the Creole nature of the society is abundantly clear in the language as well as in the setting. The flavor of the dialect is unobtrusive but unmistakable in its effect. Through the simple French phrases and the occasional Gallicized pronunciations the reader is reminded that the people are French and talk in French."[49] Other than his military service, George develops no marketable skills, no discipline, no commitment to a set of ideals, no self-respect. His surrogate parenting is the most commendable thing about him, but he tarnishes even that at the end with his inappropriate proposal. Exposed to the most laudable aspects of New Orleans culture, the sophistication of the Creoles, their taste for art and music, their commitment to honor and proper decorum, George has endorsed the most lamentable dimensions of their collapsing world: an aversion to productive labor, an attempt to acquire wealth through gambling, and a lack of respect for the sexual codes of behavior that have guided social interactions for centuries. These issues were matters Cable had criticized in other venues, in particular by writing two editorials directly attacking the Louisiana Lottery Company.[50]

Another work with its origins in Cable's personal experience is "Jean-ah

Poquelin," first published in *Scribner's Monthly* in May of 1875.[51] In his youth, the author had witnessed the growth of New Orleans, especially the pushing of the low hills into the swamps to create land for streets and new homes.[52] Of course the reason for doing so was the rapid expansion of the city, the very circumstance at the beginning of this story when, just after the Louisiana Purchase, the migration of lower-class immigrants from Europe and the northern United States fueled a rapid growth of the population. The narrator places the events in the "first decade" of the nineteenth century, but Cable himself was more specific, placing the action in 1805, the same year as "'Tite Poulette."

Two years after the Louisiana Purchase, the Creoles of New Orleans were deeply resentful of the audacity of the American government in presuming to control a culture far more cultivated educationally and artistically than the United States, especially the ragtag riverboat ruffians who came down the Mississippi and drank and fought on the wharves of New Orleans. In the opening, the narrator enumerates the points of resentment for the local population. They despise the legal modifications, which substituted the English trial by jury for the French proceedings before a tribunal of judges; they resist the changes in popular dancing; they resent the new "anti-smuggling" laws since New Orleans culture had for many years been sustained by material carried into the city at night to escape the heavy tariffs levied upon imports; and they are especially offended by the use of English as the language of government. Although there are personal issues at the center of the conflicts in "Jean-Ah Poquelin," this undercurrent of cultural resentment surfaces in the protagonist's resistance to urban expansion.

Many of Cable's works begin with the description of a building, in this case the ancestral home of the Poquelins, which is "half in ruin," a house that is "grim, solid, and spiritless" (179). In contrast to the verdant nature that invests much of Cable's work, the imagery of the landscape surrounding the house underscores decay, with the "dead cypresses" standing in the swamps amid "coarse and spiritless flowers" and "big, ravening fish and alligators," a scene to "make one shudder to the end of his days" (180). The narrative stance is observant of the scene but, in a sense, outside of it. The Poquelin house is described only from a distance. As Turner has observed, the perspective "stays outside Jean's padlocked grounds, maintains that point of view, avoids speculations by secondary characters."[53] The same is true for the description of Jean Poquelin, who is presented only as the surrounding community would know him, creating mystery and suspicion. This remoteness also engenders a pervasive irony as the narrator reports generalized negative assumptions about Jean, nearly all of which later prove to be untrue.

In fact, the details that slowly emerge from the narrative comments describe a deeply sensitive and loving man who is grossly misunderstood by society. Jean is taunted in the neighborhood as he walks into town each day, for example, but his journey is to St. Louis Cathedral to pray at the graves of his parents. He is regarded as a "hermit alike shunned by and shunning all who had ever known him" (180), but his isolation is for the purpose of caring for his leprous younger brother, Jacques. His evasiveness derives from his desire to limit the spread of the disease. Unequivocally, he cannot explain his situation because Jacques would be taken away and isolated on Terre aux Lépreux. As Petry explains, "friendless and misunderstood, Poquelin must endure verbal and physical abuse at a time when he most needs compassion. He must deal with the guilt of having taken his beloved brother Jacques to the leprous Guinea Coast on a slave-trading junket, and he must face the simple, cruel fact that, being thirty years Jacques's senior, he will probably predecease him—and the dear brother, no longer protected and loved, will be forced to spend the remainder of his hideous life in a leper colony."[54] Although as a youth Jean was a wastrel who gambled away a fortune, in his adult life he proves capable of assuming the most awesome responsibilities, even at the cost of his own freedom and happiness.

The mystery of the plot is thus not the solution of a crime or the revelation of hidden guilt but the incremental disclosure of small pieces of information that coalesce to explain the situation. The structure moves relentlessly toward epiphany even as the narrative appears to wander through peripheral information. The Gothic setting, a decaying house in a dark and threatening swamp, is ultimately revealed to be a place of supreme caring and devotion, as Jean and an elderly slave risk themselves to assist Jacques. The historical backdrop of familial wealth squandered in riotous youth is a standard Creole motif, as is Jean's adventurous early life. His descent into slave trading on the Guinea Coast from 1796 to 1798 is driven by desperation, but it initiates the mystery since Jacques accompanies his older brother and is not heard of again until the conclusion in 1805 when he appears as a ghastly white leper. His concealment in an isolated house is misinterpreted by the rabble, as rumors of "witchery, devilish crime, and hideous nursery fictions" abound (183). Reports circulate of windows that glow "blood-red" at night and of owls that speak with human voices, all fueled by malignant speculation. But Jean perseveres. Indeed, the imagery associated with him is that of strength and resolve: he has a "bronzed leonine face" above his "Herculean breast, hard and grizzled," yet he projects, from within, a "peaceful and peaceable fearlessness" (185). The rhetorical figures throughout suggest a man who is worthy of respect.

He lives in a society experiencing rapid change resulting from immigration, and the new residents, especially the despised *Américains*, bring with them a new cultural ethic based on hard work, discipline, and a desire for social and economic rise. Their values rest on industriousness and entrepreneurship, not on inherited wealth and social stature, as in Creole society. The broad influx of ethnic groups also inspires rapid change, something deeply resented by the established French population. As John Cleman has observed, the Creoles are "mindlessly resistant to even the most trivial change, upholding traditions of dubious value, mostly fearful at losing their 'footing' in the coming 'crevasse of immigration'."[55] The specific manifestation of these ideas in Jean's life comes with the Irish immigrant workers digging ditches, filling in swampland, and building a new street to run by his house. Frustrated by futile efforts to stop the construction, which is motivated by his desire to preserve the delicate status of his brother, Jean goes to see the governor.

The visits with the governor and a subsequent conversation with a "city official" are often overlooked scenes that are crucial to the structure of the entire story. For one thing, they are sections in which the narrative perspective identifies with the minds of characters other than Jean, thus revealing how he appears to them. Given the rapid influx of outsiders, the officials are Americans in each case, uneasy in their French, unaware of local traditions. Jean speaks English in heavy dialect, revealing his linguistic limitations: "'My 'ouse is yond'; *dans le marais lá-bas*'" (186). He beseeches the governor to prohibit the completion of the street, but, of course, wishing for Jacques to remain under his care, he cannot explain why. His position is simply "strit can't pass dare." He does not recognize the new laws or the unfamiliar governor, but he gets a letter to carry to the city official, who employs an interpreter as an intermediary to the French-speaking population.

It is a classic encounter. For example, Jean says the street must not pass his house (188). The interpreter repeats the threat to the official, who replies that "such impudence was refreshing," which the intermediary translates as "why you don't want?" The conversation continues in this misinterpretive vein, with Jean making no progress in his request. When he leaves, the narrative intelligence stays in the official's office, recording a conversation in which the official considers the matter in monetary terms, observing that the value of the property will increase with the new road. The interpreter, recalling the rumors about the mysterious house, concludes that Jean is a witch. What he relates is an instance when, on a hunting trip, he passed by Jean's house and saw a man who was startlingly white. Of course, what he saw was the leprous Jacques out walking in the evening. The narrative method thus reveals the extent to which the community misunderstands Jean, judges him harshly, and congratulates itself on its superior morality. The deep vein of social and moral irony becomes increasingly acute in the concluding scenes of the plot.

Despite Jean's protest, the street is built, "progress" continues, and he becomes increasingly the focus of the opprobrium of the community. Local people refer to him as the "old pirate," "the old tyrant," the "old kidnapper," not understanding in the slightest the moral depth of his life. In time, the local folkways begin to change with German, Irish, and Sicilian immigrants joining the "swarming Americans" who are becoming part of city life. Indeed, their values of economic advancement and social change quickly dominate the situation, as embodied in the Building and Improvement Company, which plans to construct a market house where the Poquelin house has stood for decades.

The embodiment of this organization, an intrepid secretary known as Little White, proposes to investigate whether Jean keeps his brother as a prisoner in the house. Little White's surreptitious surveillance and response constitute the deepest and most dramatic psychological transformation in the story. Interestingly, it is not the protagonist who is altered by the epiphany, as in most fiction, but an initially antagonistic observer who is shaken by the discovery of a leper under the tender care of a loving brother. The secretary returns home unwilling to discuss what he has seen, and he becomes Jean's principal defender in the community. Jean is the object of continued scorn, even being struck by a clod thrown by an Irish urchin, but he does not retaliate, waving off the children who shout insults at him. As a drunken mob initiates a charivari planned for Jean, Little White is initially able to forestall them, but eventually, as the mob whips up ever greater frenzy, it swarms toward the property. The conclusion is simply the discovery of the truth, which occurs only after Jean has died and the mute slave, carrying a coffin on his back, is leading poor Jacques to the leper island. Little White extols Jean's misunderstood virtues as "a man of more self-forgetful goodness—than all of you put together will ever dare to be" (208). Meanwhile, the small funeral party vanishes into the jungle.

A plot that began with the wastrel youth of Jean Poquelin ends with his moral reclamation. The cultural clash between an established Creole order and the new American push for progress and economic development is a poignant but hopeless struggle for the indigenous population. In the process, the ethical diminution of not only local Creoles but the broader society enlarged with recent immigrants is shown to be nearly complete. The narrative method creates suspense by remaining outside the mind of the protagonist. It reports the thoughts and actions of the surrounding neighborhood, not his internal struggles and emotions. The subtle structure moves seamlessly outward into the world of cruel speculation and heartless judgment only to have that assessment shattered in a dramatic revelation of the truth. The horror is not only the appearance of the ghostly white leper but the hideous morality of the populace that has judged Jean so heartlessly. As Rubin has observed, "with its stark outlines, its sense of tragedy, its playing off of the commercialism of the Americans and the callousness of the Creole mob against the lonely dignity of Jean-ah Poquelin, faithful to his terrible burden, the story is one of Cable's best."[56] It also extends the social criticism of *Old Creole Days*, however grim, to a broader spectrum of society than the traditional French culture that is so often found wanting.

The concluding story of the 1883 edition of *Old Creole Days* is "Madame Délicieuse,"[57] which Cable indicated he set in 1830 New Orleans.[58] In this period, still within a generation of the Louisiana Purchase, and fifteen years after the Battle of New Orleans, there are conflicts raging within Creole society, which is where the drama of this story lies, not in external contact with American culture. The plot, however, is the stuff of pedestrian melodrama: a love triangle generated by a misunderstanding that is resolved in the concluding scene. What gives interest to the situation is that a father and son compete for the hand of a beautiful widow. The social dimension is that the father is aligned with conservative values and traditions, whereas his son is representative of a new spirit in Louisiana, the intellectual drive that inspires him to study in Europe and become a scientific researcher. Indeed, unknown to his father, he has earned widespread reputation in learned circles. The conflicts are thus multigenerational and played out on domestic, professional, and cultural levels. As Petry has commented, "far from being a slight love story, 'Madame Délicieuse' is a rich political and social document that is vital for an understanding of the complex world of antebellum Louisiana that Cable presents in all eight stories of *Old Creole Days*."[59] Both artistically and thematically, the story is suitably complex to serve as a concluding work in a intricate volume of short fiction.

"Madame Délicieuse" has a theatrical structure: it consists of a series of discreet scenes in a limited number of settings, all but a balcony scene indoors. The narrative is carried not by exposition but almost entirely by dialogue. In each scene there is a conflict and an advance toward a resolution, with complications that lead to a further incident. As on the stage, character rules the day. The principals in the drama are all well-drawn individuals who nevertheless represent pervasive attitudes of the time.

The traditional Creole, resistant to the Louisiana Purchase and determined to restore French culture in Louisiana, is General Hercule Mossy de Villivicencio, a veteran of the War of 1812, which concluded with the Battle of New Orleans on January 8, 1815. Since then he has led a grand commemorative parade each year, but he has been a warrior without a war, an empty uniform sitting upon a horse. A widower well past his prime, his proposal of marriage to Madame Délicieuse is a paradigm for all his ambitions, whether military, romantic, political, social, or familial. As Turner formulates it, "the General personifies archaic Creole pride and imperiousness."[60] His quest for public office is based on a "restoration" platform attempting to reestablish French culture as the foundation of Louisiana society. He hates everything American: the language, the government, the ragtag boatmen who come down the Mississippi. He is free of the standard Creole corruptions of gaming and idleness, but his social ambitions are shown to be "anachronistic and parochial," manifesting in "most pompous strutting."[61] He has the impeccable breeding, elegant manners, bravery, resistance to change, and devotion to hopeless causes characteristic of his fading social class.[62]

If the general is a creature of the past, his son, Dr. Mossy, is a man of the future, a research scientist in his thirties so engrossed in his endeavors that he is largely oblivious to the mundane world around him. Since he is devoted to the preservation of life, rather than its destruction, he refused to become a soldier, and he has been rejected and disinherited as a coward by his father. He studied medicine in Europe, and, unknown to the general, earned admiration as one of the leading scientists, although the text is vague on the details. The narrator's initial observations about the son, that he is negligent of his medical practice, are largely negative. As the narration moves forward, however, he is progressively described more positively until he is ultimately portrayed as a bastion of human virtues: brilliant but humble; devoted to his work but mindful of his place in society; generous to the poor, although impoverished himself; a respectful son who wishes only to receive the unqualified love of a father; steadfast to the woman he loves, Madame Délicieuse, but unwilling to marry her until he is financially secure and fully worthy of her devotion.

Madame Délicieuse herself would seem to represent a new character in literature, a virginal widow. She was married at noon one summer, celebrated with her husband throughout the afternoon, and at sundown the "tipsy bridegroom" was killed by the accidental firing of his own gun (273). At the "present" time of the action, she is attractive, socially charming, and sufficiently aware of psychology to direct and manipulate the people around her. Indeed, the last half of the plot runs entirely on one of her stratagems.

Cable's stories nearly always begin with a description of a building in a neighborhood, the protagonist's home or office indicating social status; the maintenance of the structure denoting cultural resilience or decline; the location representing ethnic and racial identity. In this case, the action begins with Dr. Mossy's office in a tenement located next to a café, suggesting a working-class neighborhood that, indeed, is home to most of the physician's patients. That his office is "dusty and disorderly" reveals not so much a slovenly character as one totally absorbed in his research, as illustrated by the jars of specimens crowding the room (271). Dr. Mossy is a professional person devoted to intellectual pursuits. On the other hand, the "mansion" of Madame Délicieuse, whose name is later revealed to be Clarisse, is described in positive terms with "luxurious light from the lace-curtained windows of the second-story balconies," a clear indication of wealth and stature. In fact, Lafcadio Hearn identified her house as 253 Royal Street in New Orleans, accurately described, complete with its verandas.[63]

Although she has been known to stretch the truth a bit, she has easy access to a confessional from which she can emerge cleansed of sin. While most often her prevarications are benevolent, aimed at reconciling father and son, she also has her own self-interest in mind: a marriage with Dr. Mossy. Indeed, there, in two buildings, is the heart of the romantic conflict: Dr. Mossy, although from an established family, is poor with few prospects; Clarisse, from a historic family, is wealthy and graceful, intelligent and quick, but not educated, since Creole women were thought to have no need of such mundane matters (274). She is also in love with the disinherited doctor, engaged to him, in fact, but his pride will not allow a marriage between two such discrete economic levels. Even the description of the buildings underscores one of the central conflicts, testimony to the artistic congruence of Cable's fiction. Clarisse must, somehow, remove this impediment to her wedding, and the rest of the action revolves around that objective.

The first scene beyond the expository introduction takes place on Clarisse's balcony, a vantage point that overlooks both Dr. Mossy's office and the street below, on which there is a massive parade. The occasion is the annual celebration of January 8, commemorating the glorious victory over the British in 1815 (276). The narrative perspective is briefly identified with General Villivicencio, who glances up as he nears the building and sees his beloved Madame and his son on a secondary terrace: "There he saw Madame and one other person only. A small blue-eyed man whom the arch lady had lured from his pen by means of a mock professional summons, and who now stood beside her, a smile of pleasure playing on his lips and about his eyes" (277). The suggestion is that he sees a son who loves his father and takes pleasure in his adulation. In an enigmatic gesture, the general, who has not spoken to the doctor in fifteen years, throws a kiss to the balcony. It might be a gesture of reconciliation with his son, but the general's later conversations reveal a judgmental condescension toward him indicating that the gesture must have been meant for Clarisse, to whom the elderly general will soon propose.

That the general leads the January 8 parade underscores his stature in local society, for this celebration was an annual event of considerable magnitude; indeed, Grace King devoted an entire chapter to it in *New Orleans: The Place and the People*, in which she elaborates on the significance of the victory over the British in the wake of Napoleon's defeat at Fontainebleau the year before.[64] There was some concern in New Orleans that England would demand the retrocession of the city to Spain, nullifying the Purchase of 1803. Such speculations gave rise to intense Francophile sentiments widespread in the local population.[65] The general is the embodiment of such ideas, and he hates everything American, even the bilingual newspaper, and desires a "purging out of Yankee ideas." He fervently seeks the restoration of traditional Bourbon culture in Louisiana, and he is running for office on that platform.

Later that day the general meets Clarisse alone, and their extensive conversation reveals that he is no match for this small woman, whose wit and quick apprehensions allow her to manipulate the aging man. Of course, their purposes are quite different: she wishes to reconcile father and son so that she can marry Dr. Mossy; he wishes to marry Madame himself. Thus they speak at cross-purposes. True to her reputation, she is quick to lie when it serves her objectives, manipulating him with the report that there is community gossip about his ill treatment of his son, who is "noble, gentle, kind, and brave." Remembering Dr. Mossy's refusal to enter the military, the general questions the attribution of "bravery" to him. Clarisse answers by saying that the doctor is "braver than *any soldier*, in tending the small-pox, the cholera, the fevers, and all those horrible things" (281). She does not win this encounter, but she shows that she is "typical of Cable's heroines, who often have more intelligence and strength of character than their male counterparts."[66] This scene ends on a startling note: the general proposes marriage to Clarisse, and he is flatly rejected. He does not know she is engaged to his son.

The next scene is played out in Dr. Mossy's office, where the general, spurred by Clarisse's comments, pays a rare visit to his son (285–88). Dr. Mossy greets him enthusiastically and "lifting his lips like a little wife, kissed him" (285), one of a persistent pattern of feminine images for Mossy, suggesting that within a Creole framework he plays a woman's role in society. But the conversation is awkward and stilted and no reconciliation ensues, although the son offers to be of service to his father as a writer, which the general rejects. When he is attacked politically in the newspaper as someone "antiquated," a "fossil" running for office, he comes to Mossy for assistance, by which he means a champion to fight a duel for him in the manner of a Creole gentleman.

What the general does not realize, of course, is that it is Clarisse who has written the attacks, knowing that they presented the occasion for a familial reconciliation. The conversation between father and son goes badly, revealing the gulf between them. Dr. Mossy writes a brief rejoinder to the newspaper article, but he does so in English, which angers the father. The letter, in its stilted and overly formal construction, exhibits Mossy's education in French and his aptitudes as scientific rather than verbal. He writes to say that "who is the author or writer of the above said editorial article your correspondent does at present ignore, but doubts not he is one who, hasty to form an opinion, will yet, however, make his assent to the correction of some errors and mistakes which, . . ." at which point the quotation ends. The general dismisses this draft as "nonsent" and responds, in wonderful dialect, "Hall you 'ave to say is: 'Sieur Editeurs! I want you s'all give de nem of de indignan' scoundrel who meck some lies on you' paper about mon père et se amis!" (295). The general wants his son to fight to defend the family honor, and the son refuses, although he promises to settle the quarrel.

He goes to the newspaper office and quickly learns that Clarisse wrote the editorial. In the meantime, there is a rich scene when Madame comes to the office to see Mossy and discovers the general there (296–303). Now, more pointedly than ever before, she assails the father with the revelation that his son is regarded as a great man in the major scientific schools in Europe, a leader in research, a widely respected scholar. Then, the conversation turns delicate as she asserts that Mossy has met the writer of the article and then reveals that she was the author of it. At last the general grasps the situation: he has disinherited his son, leaving him impoverished. Too proud to marry without means, Dr. Mossy has been betrothed for a decade to Clarisse. He returns from the newspaper office at that moment, and father and son embrace. All is set right: the general abandons his political campaign, reconciles with his son, and Mossy and Clarisse are free to marry.

Such a fortunate resolution of complex events is atypical of Cable's fiction, but in all other respects "Madame Délicieuse" exemplifies the essence of his fictional accomplishment. In his own day, his editor, Richard Watson Gilder, chose it as his favorite story, and Hjalmar Hjorth Boyesen, instrumental in the publication of *Old Creole Days*, could recite it nearly verbatim to his students at Cornell.[67] More recent scholars have also responded with enthusiasm, Petry maintaining that the book is remarkable "as a study of the social, political, cultural, and intellectual changes attendant upon New Orleans's painful transition from a discrete, static community with a prominent Creole element, to its submergence within the burgeoning, technically oriented entity known as America—changes that are insistent in every story in *Old Creole Days*."[68] In this case that conflict is embodied within father and son, the militaristic general basking in the faded glory of his youthful battles and the elegance of his privileged French culture as opposed to his scientific son, part of the advancing world of intellectual inquiry, who is moving in accord with the rhythms of the new world. A fitting conclusion to the volume, it dramatizes the central social conflict of the book, the intricate linguistic, cultural, and political changes in the wake of the Louisiana Purchase. The portrait of Creole New Orleans clinging to the past is only one element of this struggle, but in a very few skillful scenes, complete with local dialect and folkways, Cable was able to express the emotional and intellectual aspects of a profoundly American drama.

In the context of literary history, *Old Creole Days* constitutes a significant achievement in fiction. It demonstrates that the central elements of the Local-Color movement could be employed not only for comic effect and the portrayal of quaint regional folkways but for the serious depiction of the racial, ethnic, linguistic, and religious conflicts at the heart of Southern society. In selecting Louisiana as the focus of his stories, Cable became a pioneer in the regional mode, the first writer to portray the characters and dialects of his home city as well as its most intractable social problems. His portrayal of the plight of the quadroon caste is both poignant and insightful, and it opened the door to a frank depiction of racial issues among a host of subsequent writers, many of them African American. Cable's utilization of New Orleans showed that historic city to be fascinating and complex, worthy of sober consideration. As Pattee observed, "the mark of the old city was broad upon him: an exotic strangeness, a Gallic predilection to artistry, a tropic efflorescence in style and diction, an unhurried lingering over the amenities of life, a patrician fastidiousness that avoided as by instinct the unlovely and the coarse."[69] But his achievement is not simply localized, for his humor and pathos both rest on a compelling ability to draw comic and tragic personalities that touch on basic human issues.

As a literary construct, Cable's volume is not simply a collection of random stories, whatever their individual achievement. It is fundamentally a story cycle, a book of integrated works of short fiction unified by a continuing setting, ongoing character types, and progressively enriching themes. As a collective unit, it presents a record of conflict and change in New Orleans, and Cable's original intention was to arrange the contents chronologically to reflect local history, although that idea was rejected by his publisher.[70] Nonetheless, as a total volume, the book does account for historical events, beginning with the arrival of 'Sieur George with his American regiment at roughly the time of the Louisiana Purchase in 1803 and his moral degeneration over the next five decades. Another early arrival during this transformative period is Kristian Koppig, a Dutch immigrant whose involvement in the quadroon drama of 'Tite Poulette reveals the caste restrictions traditional in New Orleans society. The gross misunderstandings surrounding Jean Poquelin occur in 1805, early enough so that he was involved briefly in the slave trade. Reflecting the language of his youth, Jean speaks French, living on the periphery of society while taking care of his leprous brother. The intrusion of American culture transforms the city, and its growth encroaches on the ancestral home; Jean is powerless to forestall the "progress" the new social ethic has brought. That same year Posson Jone' arrives in Louisiana on his visit in 1815, a country bumpkin ripe for the confidence schemes of Jules St.-Ange, but the ultimate themes are those of moral growth rather than corruption. The complex racial interaction in "Belles Demoiselles Plantation" takes place in 1820, but it is possible because of earlier intermarriage, miscegenation, and racial mixing in contravention of the *Code Noir*. That is why Injin Charlie has inherited wealth from his white ancestors. Free of the self-indulgent hedonism of the colonel and his daughters, Charlie has preserved his fortune and his mansion in the French Quarter. Consistent with the overarching motif of multifaceted personal and social decay, the familial plantation house collapses into the Mississippi, and an era of grand pretense is nearing its end.

The tragedy of Madame Delphine occurs the following year, in 1821, and it reflects the intrusive damage racial codes had on the lives of innocent people in this era. "Madame Délicieuse" is built on the conflict of a father in 1830 clinging to French culture and the military glories of the past as opposed to the "modern" scientific orientation of a son who emerges as an internationally recognized scholar. By 1835, the ethnic mixture of the "Café des Exilés" reflects the continuing immigration into the city and the impact international conquests in the Caribbean are having on local culture. In all, the volume deals with cultural collisions wrought by the Louisiana Purchase and the transformations in commerce, language, social ethics, law, religion, and courtship that followed. William Faulkner depicted grand social transitions in the South based on the disruptions brought by the American Civil War; Cable's work presents a transformation of similar proportions following the acquisition of new territory by the burgeoning United States.

Volumes of integrated stories normally have definable elements of coherence in setting and character, and most of them gain further depth through thematic congruence, the progressive enhancement of central ideas as each subsequent story enriches the basic conflicts. Given the Creole background of the characters, most of the action takes place in the French Quarter of the city in precisely identifiable sections and individual buildings, as Lafcadio Hearn demonstrated. Within that sector there is the elegant historic address of Madame Délicieuse but also the more modest quadroon quarters of Madame Delphine and 'Tite Poulette. *Old Creole Days* does not present the continuity of ongoing individual characters, but it is tightly unified by the presence of continuing "types" of figures: the retrograde conservative resisting any alteration of traditional Creole culture, as in "Madame

Délicieuse," "Jean-ah Poquelin," and "Belles Demoiselles Plantation." Many stories introduce social conflict with the arrival of an outsider who does not understand the folkways of New Orleans, as is the case in "'Tite Poulette" and "Posson Jone'." In "Café des Exilés" the intrusion is not by an individual but revolutionaries from the Caribbean bent on fomenting armed rebellion. In a patriarchal culture that subordinates women, it is notable that many stories revolve around female characters who manipulate men for their own purposes, as in "Belles Demoiselles Plantation" and "Madame Délicieuse." The theme of caste consciousness invests "Madame Delphine" and "'Tite Poulette" most directly, but the familial interactions in "Belles Demoiselles Plantation" are the result of miscegenation in earlier generations. These are intricate and complex issues, both in literary and social terms, but they emerge from one of the great early story cycles in American literature, *Old Creole Days*.

2
Grace King and the Cultural Background of *Balcony Stories*

Grace King's career began as an answer to the negative representation of the Creoles of New Orleans in George Washington Cable's *Old Creole Days* and his celebrated novel *The Grandissimes*, in which some of the aristocratic class is depicted as dissolute gamblers incapable of conducting the family business and dependent upon inherited wealth for their survival. Although, as Presbyterians, both King and Cable were alike in being alien to the Catholic world of Louisiana, their works present dramatically different portrayals of life in the Crescent City. Cable fought for the Confederacy in the Civil War, but his fiction reveals the inhumanity of slavery and racial bigotry and the pretensions of the ruling caste. In contrast, King's stories depict a noble and benevolent portrait of the same society, one in which slaves had been loved and protected by their masters and then devoted their lives to serving them faithfully, even after they had been emancipated. Indeed, King's first important publication, the story "Monsieur Motte," involves just such a situation.

"Monsieur Motte" appeared in the *New Princeton Review* in January of 1886, the first issue under the editorship of William M. Sloane.[1] In a letter to Sloane's friend Charles Dudley Warner, who first advised her to write fiction to counter Cable's presentation of Creole life, King suggested that her objective was to focus on relationships derived from slavery and to bring the races together, an interesting goal in the context of the frequent complaints in modern scholarship about her racial insensitivity.[2] The story covers a few days in June of 1874 in the life of Marie Modeste, an orphan student at the prestigious Institut St. Denis in New Orleans, which featured a historical emphasis on French education. King had attended a similar school, the Institut St. Louis, and she took two characters from her experience for the story, a quadroon hairdresser and the headmistress of the institution.[3] As she explained in *Memories of a Southern Woman of Letters*, "the story shaped itself through the description of our annual Commencement Day with its great concert and distribution of prizes. The quadroon woman, Marcélite, I took from life, as also the head of the *Institut*, Madame la Reveillière, who was the old beloved and respected Madame Lavillebeuvre."[4] Given her disposition to work from life whenever possible, she set "Pupasse" in the same location.

The titular reference to a Monsieur Motte is ultimately revealed to be ironic in that there is no such person. A former servant in the Motte family, Marcélite, a woman of color, created a fictional uncle when Marie's parents died leaving her an orphan. Marcélite had been raised by the girl's grandmother and treated as a member of the white family, a sister to Marie's mother, and her loyalty and affection for the young girl are unbounded. This idea is a recurring situation in King's work in her depiction of "many instances of loyalty and even sacrifice to their former masters on the part of black or quadroon women in the period of Reconstruction."[5] Earning a meager living as a coiffeuse, the woman secretly sacrifices her own standard of living to support the girl at an exclusive institution. All of this is revealed in a melodramatic conclusion, and the girl is taken in by the head of the school, Madame Laraveillére, and her attorney, Monsieur Goupilleau, who agree to supervise her young adulthood.

In critical terms, the true protagonist is Marcélite: she struggles with the key internal conflicts, suffers emotional turmoil, and exhibits emotional and psychological growth, serving as a surrogate mother for Marie for thirteen years. The first extended character description is of her and emphasizes her positive qualities: "Her features were regular and handsome according to the African type, with a strong, sensuous expression, subdued but not obliterated. Her soft black eyes showed in their voluptuous depths intelligence and strength and protecting tenderness" (94). The narrative perspective is identified with her mind more than with any other character, and her activities are the main focus. However, two other women also serve as central concerns: Marie and Madame Laraveillére. Both become the center of consciousness for crucial passages, and their emotional investments in the plot deepen the psychological context.

The ruse of the nonexistent Monsieur Motte comes to a crisis with the completion of Marie's secondary education, which involves a French history examination followed the next day by graduation ceremonies, after which the students go home with their parents to begin their adult lives. Of course the uncle cannot appear, and Marie is devastated, thinking he must care little for her. Although the effect of his absence is focused on Marie, the psychological struggle is within Marcélite, and she is tortured with her deceit and aghast at the need to reveal that her bébé will be humiliated by having been supported by a person of color.

From the first description of her to the end, Marie is described in images of infantilization. Although she now has the body of a woman of seventeen, her mind and emotions are those of a child, and she requires protection, comforting, and nearly constant mothering. It is Marcélite who supplies it in expressions of deep love, even though the girl believes her graduation dress and shoes came from her rich uncle (100). The hairdresser devotes fourteen years of her life to Marie, and she does so without asking or receiving anything in return apart from the satisfactions of surrogate parenting. Marcélite is described at one point as having the impulse to "destroy, to surround herself with ruins, to annihilate the miserable, little, weak devices of intelligence, and reassert the proud supremacy of brute force," an assertion by the narrator that would seem to align the black woman with primitive instincts in the midst of her most loving sacrifice. It is those kinds of passages that have inspired some scholars to accuse King of "confident white supremacist assumptions."[6] It is plainly evident, however, that Marcélite is a character of selfless nobility and dignity of spirit, and she attains heroic stature. Although it is true that she sacrifices herself for the young white girl, which is sometimes perceived as a racist expectation, her actions replicate those of the white grandmother who raised her.

There is a third woman whose internal conflicts are explored the morning after graduation, Madame Laraveillére, who knows that Marie has spent the night alone in the dormitory and is also by herself for breakfast. Indeed, without Monsieur Motte, it is not clear where the child is to live nor who will support her. Sensitive to what Marie is experiencing, Madame Laraveillére realizes that her own life has been emotionally empty, and she begins to play mother to Marie, holding and comforting her. The girl responds to her in a way she has not to Marcélite: "This was it; this was what she had longed for all her life" (124). The introduction of Madame Laraveillére's attorney, the effeminate Monsieur Goupilleau, who has the "eyes of a poet and the smile of a woman," completes the familial circle and the story with them as a domestic unit, Marie at last having the parents that were denied her through childhood. Marcélite confesses her subterfuge but explains the circumstances of the death of Marie's parents. In the racial context of the time, however, the assumption is that it is out of the question for the girl to go home with a black woman, despite her enormous sacrifices, which are finally acknowledged. Marie will leave with her new white family.

There are implications in all of this that are unsettling to contemplate in another age, foremost among them the idea that race precludes Marcélite from continuing to parent the girl she so clearly loves. That assumption, of racial caste and separation, is a continuing reality in King's later fiction, as are the circumstances of families destroyed or collapsed by war or Reconstruction. The war disrupted Southern economic, cultural, and racial order, and the aftermath inverted the established social hierarchy. That a black woman should support a white girl was an expression of how dramatically things had changed, as Helen Taylor has explained: "This fear of a breakdown of relations between the races and thus of the social order, because of the rising power and resistance of freed blacks in New Orleans, was a common nightmare of Reconstruction and the early 1880s, when racial tension was high."[7] But it should not be overlooked that Marcélite is portrayed as having moral agency, emotional depth, inner strength, and a generous heart. Having been raised by a white woman, it is not simply an act of subservience that she should reciprocate by caring for that woman's granddaughter. King did not resort to simple stereotypes in her portrait of the races in her earliest fiction but drew characters of considerable depth and inner resources. This story proved to be so popular that King was encouraged to go on to write three more about Marie and Marcélite, concluding with the girl's wedding, at which she allowed only her former hairdresser to attend her, expressing her love for the quadroon woman and her sense of indebtedness to her.

As this story established, King wrote within the tradition of the Local-Color movement, capturing the dialect and mores of an indigenous population, presenting an accurate description of the streets and buildings of the city, and delineating the tone of life peculiar to New Orleans during Reconstruction. The fact that she added three additional stories to "Monsieur Motte," all covering further adventures in the young girl's life, demonstrates that she was aware of the genre of the story cycle, which was becoming popular in the early 1890s. As she moved to a series of new stories, all of them published in *Century Magazine* between December of 1892 and October of 1893, she continued that literary form, creating an introductory frame for thirteen stories of New Orleans. She also sustained the spectrum of themes and ideas she had earlier introduced.

In King's subsequent fiction, the major characters are women who find the strength to survive in difficult times. Their men have either been killed in the war or left destitute and ineffectual, and the protagonists develop "female strength in the face of despair" and rely upon the solidarity of women "in a world of unreliable men."[8] The characters are placed in especially vulnerable situations: often they are widows or orphans, the wife of an insensitive husband, or, in one case, a spinster who longed for marriage and children.[9] As was the case for King's family, which suffered a substantial financial and social decline after the war, these characters, once the privileged elite of society, have been impoverished during Reconstruction. Meanwhile, aided by the occupation of Union forces, freed slaves and poor whites have taken advantage of the situation, moving into mansions they now claim as their own, stealing from the open houses, and enriching themselves in the new economic order.[10] The psychological impact on the previously entitled class is a major unifying subject of *Balcony Stories*, published in New York by the Century Company in 1893.[11]

As is often the case with story cycles in American Realism, Grace King began *Balcony Stories* with a lyrical sketch, this one titled "The Balcony." Originally published in *Century Illustrated Magazine* in December of 1892,[12] where it served as an introduction to "A Drama of Three," it establishes a poetic frame for the stories to follow, the background setting, the narrative context, the people portrayed, the social and economic circumstances, and the essential issues for virtually all the action that follows (1–4). The location is the American South in summer, more specifically New Orleans and the surrounding Louisiana bayou. It is a place of quiet natural beauty where the mothers in an apartment building can sit out of an evening, after the children are safely tucked away, and share reminiscences with their friends. The doors and windows are open so the mothers can hear cries of distress; their children, on the other hand, can hear what is conveyed: the accounts of dignified Creoles who must deal with diminished fortunes, lost love, and psychological and emotional adjustments to reduced social stature, all of which alter their lives forever. What is discussed is primarily the world of women, especially young orphans, lonely widows, and aging spinsters, all of them facing tragedy and disappointment. One episode involves a blind boy, another an elderly general, but the emphasis is on female characters and the conflicts at the center of their lives.

What is nowhere stated explicitly is the precipitating event that has caused the enormous transformations in Southern culture: the Civil War and the period of Reconstruction that followed it. Not only did the South suffer the loss of lives and property, but the freeing of the slaves and the resultant social and economic changes initiated a period of inversion in which the aristocrats were reduced to indigence and their former servants often rose to positions of wealth and stature. The freedmen found new opportunity in the occupied South, and during Reconstruction many of them were elected to office, elevated to management positions in business, entered the professional classes, and occupied the residences of their antebellum masters.

In representing this matter, as in some others, King employs what Ernest Hemingway was later to call the "iceberg principle," the idea that there can be important elements in fiction that are nowhere stated or explained. So, in "Big Two-Hearted River," the most significant aspect of the story is never mentioned, that the main character is Nick Adams, home from World War I where he was wounded and traumatized. He is now on a therapeutic fishing trip as an attempt at recovery. That fact clarifies the tension behind the simple act of pitching a tent, starting a fire, and catching a trout, and it explains why it is crucial that he is able to sleep: in surrounding stories he is a chronic insomniac. Similarly, in "Hills Like White Elephants," a man and a woman waiting for a train engage in tense dialogue, but the true subject is never revealed. The man wants the woman to do something; she is resistant. By the end, it seems clear that the issue is an abortion; she wishes for a stable life and a family; he wants his freedom and transitory adventure.[13] Hemingway was skilled in the use of the unspoken issue, and it gives an element of tension to nearly all of his fiction.

In *Balcony Stories*, published three decades before Hemingway's work, King is remarkably subtle in instilling a similar unexplained background beneath the surface of her fiction, a crucial element that is never stated but only implied in context. The women who sit out of an evening are in diminished circumstances because of the Civil War, as are the characters they describe. When the slaves were freed, the economic base of wealthy families was reduced to nothing, and they lost not only their plantations but, often, their mansions in New Orleans as well. The characters in the tales have suffered a similar fate. In some stories their fathers or husbands were killed in the fighting, as in "La Grande Demoiselle," but in all cases the quality of their lives has been altered irrevocably, as it has for a disabled black woman in "A Crippled Hope." A direct analysis of what has brought such dramatic alterations is never proffered.

In "The Balcony" the emphasis is on the circumstances of the initial telling of the narratives that follow. Their subsequent appearance may constitute yet another rendition, perhaps by one of the children who overheard the original tales. This sketch concludes with a child, "wakeful and precocious," who listens "while memory makes stores for the future" with which to "decorate or hide, as it may be, the structure or ruins of life" (3–4). The passage suggests that this child is the source of the "experiences, reminiscences, episodes" that were heard in the "low, soft mother-voices on the balcony" (2). This narrative circumstance controls the entire volume.

The first formal work of short fiction, "A Drama of Three," is illustrative of King's skill in interweaving background, setting, character, and theme (7–20).[14] Since it also begins the series of stories, it is important artistically, thematically, and in terms of subject. As Mary Anne O'Neal points out, it presents "the effects of the war on a Creole patriarch. Fittingly, King starts with the psychological impact of loss on a white, aristocratic male; the subsequent stories that explore women's responses to loss follow in the wake of the collapse of traditional male authority."[15] The protagonist is an aging general, now in his seventies, who descends from the Creole elite of Louisiana. He was educated in the traditional way, in Paris, and acquired not only knowledge but elegant manners, good form, and the proper attitudes attendant to his station. Prone to excessive self-indulgence, he reveals himself to be condescending to those he considers beneath him, and he is especially contemptuous of the black servant Pompey despite the fact that the young man offers his assistance without compensation. Blindly imperious, the general cannot perceive that Pompey is kind to him. In the supreme irony, one based on a false sense of superiority, he is arch with his landlord, Journel, who comes to collect the rent the first of every month, money the general pays out of funds from an unknown benefactor who turns out to be Journel himself (15).

The entire drama is the result of the social transformations of Reconstruction, and yet it and the Civil War are never mentioned. The beneficent Journel is the grandson of the former overseer on the general's family plantation, a fact that makes any tone of equality quite impossible for the old man and his wife, Honorine. These postwar changes were nowhere so severe as in Louisiana, with its complex ethnic heritage of French and Spanish Creoles, Native Americans, African slaves, bayou Cajuns, immigrants from the Caribbean, and white Americans who flooded into the city after the Louisiana Purchase. The general speaks French, the language of his training, but the lexicon of the day is English, even in New Orleans, revealing how dramatically he is out of place and time. In his poverty, he dresses as a gentleman to receive his landlord the beginning of each month, concealing the humiliation of living in a rented apartment. The past clings to him, and only his wife grasps the full meaning of what they have lost. The general, aloof in his dreams of what used to be, is psychologically detached from reality, a condition that arises frequently in King's work. He lives in a Parisian fantasy that determines what he wears, eats, and speaks. When his wife mentions that Pompey assists them merely to "oblige" them, rather than feeling gratitude he suspects the young man of thievery. Nor does he even consider that it might be Journel who supports them. His friends deserted him when he lost his fortune, and he cannot acknowledge kindness from his social inferiors. The fundamental themes of the story thus embrace economic loss, social inversion, and psychological pathology all resulting from a war that is never mentioned.

The story that follows "A Drama of Three" derives from the same historical background but features a female protagonist, the normative case in King's fiction.[16] Also standard is the retrospective narrative stance, a woman on a balcony talking about things that happened many years ago, how "in those days, the days of '59, New Orleans was not, as it is now, a one-heiress place" (23). The "now" of the time of the telling is never explicit, but it would seem to be near the end of Reconstruction, since Freedmen's Bureau schools figure in the plot. As is true throughout *Balcony Stories*, much of what is reported is uncertain, the product of gossip and speculation: "But it must be remembered that this is all hearsay. When one has not been present, one knows nothing of one's own knowledge; one can only repeat" (30). That methodology introduces the same level of unreliability that faces the community of spectators, who never peak behind the veil. As Robert Bush has said, "by relating the information about La Grande Demoiselle through the eyes and ear of rumor, the author-narrator maintains an appropriate distance. Some of the details told about the great lady seem strained and incredible—all presented as the growth of a legend told either by the Negroes of the plantation or the ladies on their galleries. The story is replete with suggestiveness, with emotional possibilities left untold, which the reader's aroused imagination may complete."[17] In "La Grande Demoiselle" (23–35), Idalie Sainte Foy Mortemart des Islets descends from French Creole society in Louisiana, with all the excesses unearned wealth provides. At age sixteen, she writes a simple message to her clothier in Paris ("I make my début in November") and the finest silk dresses and lace and ribbons flood into her mansion. However, it is clear that despite her wealth, she suffers deficits of character, beginning with the fact that "her birth exceeded her education" (24). Imperious without substance, she lacks beauty, discipline, and grace, but given her wealth, her many suitors propose marriage upon her coming out into society.

There is also a fundamental corruption behind her social station, one revealed through an emphasis on the tainted source of familial wealth: "Stately walls, acres of roses, miles of oranges, unmeasured fields of cane, colossal sugar-houses—they were all there, and all the rest of it with the slaves, slaves, slaves everywhere, whole villages of negro cabins" (24). Despite the pervasive imagery of verdant natural production, the description of the country property compromises its elegance in that "it was a plantation, the Reine Sainte Foy, the richness and luxury of which are really well described in those perfervid pictures of tropical life, at one time the passion of philanthropic imaginations, excited and exciting over the horrors of slavery" (24). This historic background becomes ironic when, after the war has destroyed the wealth of her plantation and her face is scarred in the burning of the family mansion, Idalie supports herself by teaching black children in a Freedmen's Bureau school.

The communal perspective of the women on the balcony reveals the humiliating descent from grandeur endured by the protagonist and the level of her penury. Her father was killed in the war; the family mansion was pillaged; the economic foundation of her life depleted. The community offers not so much sympathy as understanding. The young woman whose family owned "slaves everywhere" would have been educated in French, as was

Grace King, in an exclusive private institution for Creole children of privilege. During Reconstruction, the federal government established the Freedmen's Bureau in March of 1865 to educate freed slaves, especially the children. These schools were bitterly resented in Louisiana, where they were under the direction of General Nathaniel P. Banks, who controlled the Department of the Gulf. In New Orleans, the largest program for black students was at the Abraham Lincoln School for Freedmen, which had some eight hundred students. Within the broader area of the gulf region, there were nearly ten thousand such pupils enrolled, most of them taught by women from both the South and the North.[18] Teachers in the system found social approbation a major problem; some of them were stoned, some schools were vandalized, and many educators of black children found it difficult to find a place to live.[19] White Southerners working in the Freedmen's Bureau institutions suffered social disgrace and estrangement, the situation at issue in "La Grande Demoiselle."

King wrote about these women not only in *Balcony Stories* but later in a series of essays, one of which was titled "A Southern Educator: Mrs. Mary Humphreys Stamps," who was the daughter-in-law of Jefferson Davis.[20] King emphasizes from the beginning that in postwar society what was lacking was very clear: "What the South needed most conspicuously at the close of the war was teachers—teachers who knew the capacity of the young and could forecast what their mental needs would be to meet the changed future before them." The essay extols the work of Southern educators, and, although her own training was entirely private, she calls for an expansion of public schools. King praises Mrs. Stamps for recognizing that the termination of the war signaled the inception of a new effort, the "common" education of formerly wealthy children:

> For into the rooms of the public schools then came a new element, a hitherto unknown class in the community, and on the benches, alongside of the children of the Irish, French, German, and Italian immigrants—the daughters of mechanics, domestics, fruit-sellers—there now sat also the daughters of the *ci-devants* of the war—children of another kind of immigrants, shipped from their fatherland of ease to a strange country of poverty, with no baggage except the clothes on their backs, and no capital except what lay literally in their heads, but provided plentifully with pride, prejudice, and the super-refined sensibilities of an exclusive hereditary caste.

This awareness, which also transcended issues of ethnicity, eventually led Mrs. Stamps to become the principal of a high school for young girls in New

Orleans. All efforts at the racial integration of such institutions were stymied, however, when the state legislature in Louisiana passed a law on February 15, 1865, forbidding it.[21]

In another essay, "An Old French Teacher of New Orleans," published in the *Yale Review* in 1922, King discussed the career of her own French teacher, Madame Girard, a delicate woman who invariably wore a barège veil out of doors, a detail King used for Idalie.[22] She had experienced the abolition of slavery in Sainte Lucie in 1848, with the result that plantation owners were reduced to penury. Fleeing from the incessant poverty of their island, Girard's family moved to New Orleans, where she became a teacher, parallel to the circumstance of Idalie Sainte Foy Mortemart des Islets. King emphasizes that "she did not live among the rich and influential families in which she taught, but among her humble neighbors, who she would help, not according to her means or her strength, but according to her sympathy." For the plot of her story, King would seem to have drawn from Girard's life, a fallen debutante driven to teaching, melding that situation with the career of Mrs. Stamps. Later in her career, King published *Memories of a Southern Woman of Letters*, in which she reflected on the postwar situation in the South: "Ah, the children who came through the war, and battles, and defeat! There are no monuments raised to them, no medals struck in their honor. Education was their need, and by the blessings of Providence education could be given them. Impoverished ladies throughout the city, dressed in mourning, most of them, were making their bread and meat by teaching."[23] In "La Grande Demoiselle," Idalie teaches African Americans in a school established after the war by the Freedmen's Bureau. She has lost all vestiges of stature; her students are the descendents of the slaves who served her family in its previous luxury. During the fighting, her home was occupied by a company of "colored" troops before it was looted and destroyed. Lacking beauty even in her salad days, she has been burned in the fire that destroyed the family mansion, and she hides her scarred face behind a veil. The elegant suitors who once swarmed her with proposals are long gone. Indeed, she is reduced to marriage with the old *célibataire* Champigny, disparagingly called "Champignon" (mushroom) by the local wags. The woman who once threw away silk gowns having worn them once now wears coarse cotton dresses, and she endures a marriage devoid of affection, "and as for love, gratitude!" (35).

It is a masterful story that in technique anticipates some of William Faulkner's best stories, such as "A Rose for Emily," in its use of unreliable information, rumor, and speculation as a basis for narration.[24] Counter to the genteel expectations of courtly Southern romance, there is no beautiful maiden to be wooed, no handsome cavalier who comes to her rescue, no triumphant conclusion that sets the world back in order. The rough, realistic substance of the plot is the depiction of crushing change and the need to find a way to endure new circumstances, a metaphor for the South during Reconstruction. The emotional dimension of the transition is unexpressed; Idalie does not speak at any point, so she is revealed only through indirection; the narrator expresses no opinion about the righteousness or injustice of the situation. Yet the lack of direct emotional explanation only heightens the sense of the psychological burden of having so fallen in social stature, to have had to adjust her sense of self so dramatically: "The negro women about her were better dressed than she" (35). She lost not only her familial wealth but herself as well, the person she was, the Southern lady she was becoming. Her veil may conceal her disfigured skin, but nothing obscures the internal damage she must live with every day.

Another story of economic loss and social adjustment in the postwar South is "The Old Lady's Restoration" (177–90), a narrative with a simple plot and a complex narrative method.[25] The action covers the opulent life of a wealthy New Orleans Creole widow who lives a life of luxury and ease until her dramatic change of fortune during Reconstruction. Her decline is representative of the general situation among the privileged classes, who transferred their wealth into Confederate currency with the outbreak of the war and lost their stream of income from their plantations with emancipation. In New Orleans the used furniture stores and pawn shops on Royal and Chartres streets swell with family heirlooms as the aristocrats sell their possessions to support a progressively diminishing lifestyle: "Old furniture, cut glass, pictures, books, jewelry, lace, china—the fleece (sometimes the flesh still sticking to it) left on the brambles by the driven herd. If there should someday be a trump of resurrection for defunct fortunes, those shops would be emptied in the same twinkling of the eye allowed to tombs for their rendition of property" (180). The protagonist's personal wealth recedes step by step as she relinquishes her carriage, her box at the opera, her servants, and then her residence, forcing her to rent a room in a poor neighborhood.

The women in her former social set, who provide the narrative point of view, drift away and have no contact with her for fifteen years. However, when the rumor surfaces that her wealth is somehow to be restored, her friends emerge to welcome her back and return her to a position of respect: "The old residence was to be rebought, and refurnished from France; the *avant scène* at the opera had been engaged; the old cook was to be hired back from the club at a fabulous price; the old balls and the old dinners were to gladden the city—so said they who seemed to know" (183–84). The upper crust of society act as though these rumors are true. They seek her out with difficulty: "Provided with congratulatory bouquets, they set forth. It is very hard to find a dweller on the very sea-bottom of poverty" (187). They intend to declare their undying loyalty only to find her bitter about her earlier abandonment. She declares that her friends are now the working-class seamstresses and carpenters in her courtyard, which abounds in vigorous life: "Opening her door, pointing to an opposite gallery, to the yard, her own gallery; to the washing, ironing, sewing women, the cobbling, chair-making, carpentering men; to the screaming, laughing, crying, quarreling, swarming children" (189–90). The women are incredulous and declare that the old lady has become an "imbecile" and should be placed in an institution. From their point of view, her economic decline has taken her mind; from the old woman's perspective, it has revealed the true nature of her earlier "friendships."

What is complex about the narrative is the source of the information related since it is not based on observed events, personal conversations, or first-hand accounts but rather on gossip, rumor, and communal supposition. As was the case in "La Grande Demoiselle," there is no solid basis for the telling on the balcony, which can only provide the "many versions" of the account, the gossip that fills in the "lapses of memory," and there is no avenue to the "truth," which the narrative intelligence reveals to be unattainable. Even the restoration of the fortune is not certain since no one knows the basis for the report even though it quickly becomes accepted as fact. The uncertainty of information provides for speculative interpretation, leaving open the possibility that the reestablished wealth is a social fantasy, that the attribution of mental illness is in fact true, or that the woman has genuinely come to prefer her new society to the old, believing it to be based on genuine feelings instead of social pretense. As Mary Anne O'Neal maintains, "the old lady's restoration is not just a financial restitution; her true restoration came years earlier as she was saved from the superficial lifestyle of the idle rich and became a woman of character."[26] In this sense her moral substance has been enriched by poverty, a concept her former friends cannot grasp.

"Mimi's Marriage" (39–53) begins with the same thematic concerns but uses a quite different narrative strategy.[27] It is the first story in the collection with an introductory frame by a narrator who introduces a character on the balcony who then tells her story. After the opening paragraph, however, it is only Mimi who speaks, a first-person narrator in the Local-Color tradition. She is clearly on the veranda telling her narrative to her close friend Louise, whom she calls Loulou at one point. The telling is dramatized, with interruptions and asides as people shift about, and Mimi speaks in the vernacular, mingling English and French, getting lost in her own thoughts. As in "La Grande Demoiselle," the romance plot is unconventional.

Mimi is another ingénue fallen from social stature after the war, which is mentioned once. Her father was a haughty aristocrat who "thought himself better than everybody in the world" and was especially condescending to the upstart middle-class "Americans" who became part of New Orleans life. He would certainly not have countenanced any social involvement between his family and the great unwashed. However, the wartime economy takes the family fortune, and they are left destitute. Mimi's idealistic dreams of romance with a handsome French "brun" with a "moustache and a fine baritone voice" are no longer viable, leaving only her father's arrogance and memories of their former glory. Penurious, humiliated by living in an apartment next to an American, the family must find a way to live, especially with Papa's second wife and eight children. Papa dies, and Mimi has no marketable skills save the least remunerative, the darning of stockings. Desperate, she accepts the marriage proposal of the American out of economic necessity, but he is "not good-looking" and is short, not the elegant gentleman of her fantasies. The ironic twist, unexpected in King's fiction, is that he is a good husband and Mimi quickly grows to "adore" him and seems pleased with the marriage. Unlike the situation in "La Grande Demoiselle," Mimi's humiliating descent from social stature in the Creole community, and her marriage to an American to support the family, leave her happy and fulfilled. However, even in her contentment, as Helen Taylor maintains, Mimi will "have to learn that the old social codes no longer apply in a more fluid, less class-conscious commercial society."[28] The nature of her psychological adjustment is clear only against the historical transformations brought by Reconstruction.

The next several stories are comparatively weaker in thematic substance, but each makes a unique contribution to the volume as a whole. For example, "The Miracle Chapel" introduces the nineteenth-century conflict between traditional religious faith and the growing emphasis on reason and science as a means for human progress (57–66).[29] The plot centers on a blind boy who has come to a chapel where he has heard that a child was healed by the blessed virgin. He is poor, and the third-person narrator observes that it is the impoverished who need divine intervention: "The poor, the miserable, the unhappy, they can show their miracles by the score; that is why God is called the poor man's friend. He does not mind going in the face of logic and reason to relieve them" (58). The boy explains his situation to a passing woman, and he relates the account of the baby who was cured, an event he did not witness but has heard in the general gossip: "That was what they told me" (62). Rumor and unreliable reports once again form the basis for narrative. The woman takes the boy to the chapel to pray for the restoration of his sight, but his solicitations are futile: "He was crying, and past the shame of showing it—crying helplessly, hopelessly" (66). So the woman brings him to a hospital where a physician restores vision to the boy.

The narrator contends, in the illogical conclusion, that it was the blessed virgin who helped the boy: "To her be the credit." Robert Bush seems to concur with this judgment in saying that the story is told "from the point of view of the thinking person who sees miracles as a sign of God's veering from the rules of logic and reason so as to help the poor in their distress. . . . The final authorial comment implies that the virgin did indeed hear his prayer and helped him."[30] But of course a benevolent deity could have performed a preventative miracle and the boy would never have been blind at all; indeed, such a supernatural intervention could easily have cured poverty at the same time and a great many social and moral issues would have been solved. Historically, New Orleans, a bastion of Catholicism, came late to modern medicine, clinging instead to the powers of folk healing, voodoo, and miracles for the cure of serious illness. As was true for King herself, Creole society clung to the glories of the past, shunned the new, and valued tradition above all else. Here those values come in conflict with an extremely threatening new wave of thought, one based not on faith but on reason, science, empirical investigation, and logical inquiry as a means to knowledge.

"The Story of a Day" (69–88) is a somewhat anomalous part of *Balcony Stories* in that although it takes place in the Louisiana bayou country, it does not involve the central unifying themes of social and economic loss in Reconstruction.[31] Rather it is a frame narrative that presents a lyrical evocation of a verdant nature in the beginning and conclusion with a tale of lost love in the middle. David Kirby maintains that it is "the most beautifully written piece in the collection. As do several of the other stories, this one looks at the past from the viewpoint of the present; in technical terms, the story proper, which is set in the past, is framed by introductory and concluding paragraphs set in the present."[32] The narrative stance is first-person plural, clearly the perspective of a group of city women, presumably those of the evening conversations on the veranda.

The account that is related involves a journey at dawn into the bayou, where the women observe extraordinary vitality in the birds and alligators and beauty in the lilies blooming everywhere. This section offers King's most lyrical prose, and the visual imagery is stunningly beautiful. As Bush has explained, the story "consists of two apparently unrelated parts placed in juxtaposition. In the first the narrator is proceeding with others by small boat to a remote Cajun farm at dawn in the spring of the year. Her poetic word picture is one of lyric exultation as the dawn gradually reveals the natural magnificence of the bright blue and white water lilies that lie upon the water in profusion."[33] Within this Edenic wonderland, however, there lurks deadly danger: the muck of the bayou is like quicksand, inescapable, relentless, and the narrator recounts how first a heifer and then a cow thrashed in the ooze until they disappeared beneath the water (73). This account, tragically, foreshadows the events of the internal narrative that the group hears from an Acadian woman who lives in the swamp.

The flashback concerns Adorine, a young Cajun of thirteen who falls in love with Zepherin, named for the Greek god of the west wind. His life is fittingly transient in that a week before they are to be wed he so longs for her that in the night he paddles through the water in his pirogue, leaves the boat for inexplicable reasons, and walks to his death in the bayou, as did the cattle. In this environment, the suggestion is, human beings are part of the natural order, struggling to survive in the same world of triumph and tragedy as the rest of living creatures. That motif is emphasized in this account of an event that occurred twelve years before. Adorine is now the woman of twenty-five who greets them. What is memorable is that she tells them how her young man was coming to be with her and was trapped in the quicksand of the swamp. At the very time he was dying, she was awakened by the sound of singing, the voices of angels, and one that sounded like her lover. This narrative is not related directly but is the product of inference, hearsay, speculation, and summary by the group of visitors. It is they who reflect, at the time of the telling, on what was lost that night, not only the romance and wedding but the marriage and the children Adorine will never have. The conclusion is rich in pathos and empathy, but the tragedy derives not from the war and its aftermath but from the inexorable danger inherent in nature, a matter inaccessible to human intervention.

"Anne Marie and Jeanne Marie" (91–101) explores yet another cultural dimension within the Louisiana bayou country, the Gascon community, those immigrants of French Basque ancestry who lived in the countryside surrounding New Orleans.[34] The issue in this case is personal, a case of betrayal and distrust between twin sisters. It begins with the pain and disillusionment Jeanne Marie feels for an incident that distresses her. Her life has been filled with loss after the death of her husband and all three of her children in the yellow fever epidemic, but now some new calamity has struck since the narrator says "she had not wept since she buried her last child" (91). She and her sister Anne Marie have lived together in a small cabin since the death of Jeanne's family fifty years before. Now, in their poverty and dotage, their only pleasure is playing the lottery each week hoping to win a small fortune, a standard vice in a French population that has gambling in their blood. Anne Marie has become disabled and remains in bed while her sister walks to town and buys tickets. One week she did so, winning $40.00 on her own ticket, but she allows her sister to believe that it was she who was so fortunate: "In a flash all Anne Marie's ill luck ran through Jeanne Marie's mind; how her promised husband had proved unfaithful, and Jeanne Marie's faithful; and how, ever since, even to the coming out of her lottery numbers, even to the selling of vegetables, even to the catching of the rheumatism, she had been the loser. But above all, as she looked at Anne Marie in the bed, all the misery came over Jeanne Marie of her sister's not being able, in all her poor old seventy-five years of life, to remember the pressure of the arms of a husband about her waist, nor the mouth of a child on her breast" (96). But despite the loving and compassionate motivation behind her misrepresentation, it is not repaid in kind.

The two sisters had always shared their meager resources, but now Jeanne Marie, looking into the cabin through a knot hole, sees her sister hiding the money. The method of impressionistic restriction of perspective is crucial here for it heightens the suspense of this excruciating discovery: "She put her eye to the hole. Anne Marie was not in the bed, she who had not left her bed for two months! Jeanne Marie looked through the dim light of the room until she found her" (100). She sees her sister concealing the money beneath a plank in the floor, and she is shocked, realizing that she has never truly known her, never enjoyed the trust she had assumed to be unqualified between them. It is a painful moment: "She could understand death, but she could not understand this" (91).[35] The conclusion features not psychological growth but poignant disillusionment, explaining her grief in the opening paragraph of the story: "And this was why Jeanne Marie leaned her head against the side of the house and wept" (101). This conclusion adds a dimension to the general theme of the degradations of penury by showing the effects on the poor as well as on declining aristocrats, and the consequences are similarly devastating.

Although the characters in King's work are often of uncertain racial identification, revealing themselves only through dialect, community, or custom, in "A Crippled Hope" the protagonist is clearly African American (105–23).[36] "Little Mammy," as she is known, was born in the barn for slave auctions, but she is regarded as unacceptable for sale because she cannot walk. The slave trader attempts to pair her with healthy slaves, but the trick does not work: "Nothing equaled a negro-trader's will and power for fraud, except the hereditary distrust and watchfulness which it bred and maintained" (108–09). Since she is never sold, she lacks the slave relationships the narrator seems to regard as benevolent, and she is described as longing for "some master whom she could have loved, some mistress whom she could have adored" (117). Such passages established Grace King's reputation as the unconvincing apologist for the most pernicious aspects of the Old South, despite the tenderness of her portrait of Little Mammy. Unsold, and worthless for ordinary work, the disabled protagonist follows her natural instincts and cares for sick or hurt slaves, crawling to them and administering treatment with extraordinary tenderness. As a result, the trader in human beings comes to regard her as a preserver of the goods he has to sell, a nurse of little intrinsic value but important in her capacity to improve the sales price of other slaves by helping them get well.

The narrative perspective is complex. The time of action begins long before the Civil War with the childhood of the protagonist and the injury of her hip. The telling on the balcony, however, is during Reconstruction, or later, for time has brought dramatic changes in the circumstances of the protagonist's life. The speaker is a disembodied member of the community, one of the women on the balcony, who adds rumor and speculation to what Little Mammy has revealed. To these accounts are added what "tradition" has accepted or what was said by a janitor (110). The narrator is apparently white, since she frequently comments on the peculiarities of life in black culture; she also makes reference to mythological concepts such as Jacob's ladder or to historical issues, such as the appointment of Philip Sheridan as the governor of the Fifth Military District, which included Louisiana (119, 123). The narrator also displays a majority perspective, lamenting that Little Mammy had no white people to serve. The protagonist never speaks directly, nor is dialect emphasized.[37] She is still alive at the time of the telling on the balcony, living with a white family as a nurse.

The central themes derive from life on the other end of the social spectrum from the fallen Creole aristocrats, whose poverty has generated not only misery but various forms of psychological pathology. Little Mammy was on the bottom of the economic spectrum before and after the war, but she had a function in society before liberation. It is a curious situation in that her freedom becomes a curse to her, leaving her with nowhere to turn. She laments her autonomy: "More than ever she grieved, as she crept down the street, that she had never mounted the auctioneer's block. An ownerless free negro!" (121). She longs for her earlier status. Now, without a slave trader to market her skill, she has no place in society: "She tried to find a place for herself, but she had no endorsers, no recommenders" (122). She runs away from the city and finds a place in a small town caring for the infirm, and, at the time of the telling, she is still there taking care of husbands who have worked too long in the fields, mothers with troubles, children who need comforting. This is the account Little Mammy is telling to the narrator even at the conclusion, when the listener gets tired, "one gets confused—one sleeps—one dreams" (123).

In the final analysis, the telling of the story is deceptively complex in that the truth of the events is indeterminate; rumor, "tradition," recollections, and thirdhand accounts serve in place of empirical data as a means to knowledge. The comments presented are similarly questionable. Surely the suggestion of loving relationships between slaves and masters is a judgment from the white narrator's perspective, for example, not from the long-suffering slave. Linda Coleman's observations are that "King's white characters are expected to sacrifice their lives for their families, Little Mammy's role in King's hierarchy of care is to serve white women."[38] Coleman's analysis here is somewhat inaccurate since Little Mammy spends most of her life treating black slaves, not white women. It is only on the last page that she serves a white family, establishing a surrogate maternity by raising the children. Further, there is little biographical evidence to suggest that this is the author's personal "hierarchy," although it is clear that the protagonist has an unusual status in New Orleans. Her disability makes difficult a normal courtship and marriage and the family that comes with them. Counter to Coleman, Bush regards the story as "the most moving portrayal of a black person" in all of King's stories.[39] However Little Mammy's portrayal is assessed, the presentation of New Orleans life from an African-American protagonist provides an insightful additional dimension to the total picture of Louisiana culture just before and after the Civil War.

"One of Us" (127–39) has occasioned surprisingly little critical commentary, but it is one of King's most subtle and poignant works of short fiction.[40] In many respects, in narrative method and the development of theme, it resembles Herman Melville's "Bartleby, the Scrivener" in that the psychological growth and transformation is on the part of the narrator, not the protagonist. The plot is simple: a former opera singer appears at an orphanage (called an "asylum" in the story) seeking a position supervising young girls. She asks for little by way of compensation; her interest is purely in being close to the children. Much of the narration is in first person by the singer; the rest is in first person by the narrator, reflecting and responding to what she hears. The singer had a disappointing career, never winning major roles but performing the *dugazon* parts of confidante or attendant to the lead soprano. Neither beautiful nor possessed of a strong voice, she resigned herself to this life, but when the company went on tour in France, they did not take her along. Now unemployed, she looks back on what she has sacrificed for her career: a home and marriage, the tenderness of children, the depth of love that family life can bring. At the orphanage, she hopes to reclaim some of that relationship by being close to the young girls under her tutelage.

The unnamed singer's account is straightforward and relatively simple; the narrator's response is not. The speaker reflects on a life lived in the false world of the opera, "the gulf between the real and the ideal," the makeup and costumes and scenery that create illusion on stage. The narrator appears to be a woman in charge of the orphanage, perhaps a nun, who is sensitive to what has been relinquished and what is now to be gained. She is aware that the singer has been dismissed and discarded in the manner of "dilapidated stage property" (132). The narrator's assessment of her is that she "would have blossomed love and children as a fig-tree does figs" (135).

The protagonist's recitation is dramatized so that she speaks directly, reflecting that she has never "held a child in my arms more than a moment, never . . . felt a child's arms about my neck!" (136). She offers to bring not only songs for the children but genuine love. The narrator is clearly overwhelmed by what she has heard, for her mind wanders to a fantasy of the life of the singer, to what she could become in the orphanage. There she could have reality instead of artifice; there true love, not theatrical romance, could fill her life; there the children could find the mother they would never have under other circumstances. Given these reflections, it is clear that the narrator finds a position for her. As Kirby maintains, "the narrator is able to give her a position caring for the children in an orphans' asylum. In other words, a woman-without-a-family is brought together with children-without-parents through the good offices of a second woman. Thus do women and children survive, through mutual support, in a world without men."[41] Kirby is perceptive on this point, but he misses the corollary gain for the narrator, who experiences a significant birth of compassion, deepens her capacity for altruistic identification with another person, and feels the need to tell others about the experience.

Yet another dimension of Southern culture is explored in "The Little Convent Girl" (143–61), which first appeared in 1893, after Kate Chopin first published "Désirée's Baby" in *Vogue* in January.[42] Chopin's story may very well have been an influence in that both works feature a young woman who discovers (or thinks she discovers) her mixed-race background and commits suicide by drowning. But even if King invented the plot totally, the fact remains that racial identity was still a complex and compelling social and psychological issue in the early 1890s, and the discovery of an African-American bloodline would require intense personal adjustment, something the protagonist in this case is incapable of doing.

The convent girl is a vague, repressed figure behind a veil who never utters a word, a not uncommon circumstance in King's stories; she joins the protagonists in "La Grande Demoiselle" and "A Crippled Hope" in that regard. The narrator must have been aboard the boat that brought the girl from Cincinnati to New Orleans since he relates details of events along the way. He can describe only her timidity and silence, and her reserved demeanor would seem to be the result of severe training by the nuns who took care of her education.[43] As O'Neal has said, "her convent education has not only removed any color she may have had but also any traces of vitality and youth."[44] She is entirely passive throughout the events until the conclusion, when she throws herself into the river. Her white father has died; she has no memories of her black mother, who was sent away upon the birth of the child. The unstated implication is that the father sent the mother away so that the daughter would not have to live with a multiracial designation. She apparently has passed for white since there are only a few descriptions about her appearance that suggest she might be of mixed blood: her black hair is said to have a tendency to curl; her complexion is "sallow" (146–47). She is reserved throughout the trip down the river, and she does not respond to the shocking discovery of her mother's race when the ship docks in New Orleans, despite the universal gasp by the members of the crew. The veil thus was placed upon her not only for mourning the death of her father but also to obscure her ethnicity during her journey. The nuns who cared for her certainly must have known.

The mother's identity is apparent both by her complexion and her dialect, and the convent girl seems to realize the truth since when she again visits the captain a month later to thank him for his kindness, her face has changed, her lips have tightened, her color has, rather ironically, turned pale (160). The final event, when the girl leaps into the Mississippi to her death, has been foreshadowed by earlier descriptions of the deadly potential of the deep water, replete with whirlpools and swift currents, and her body is never found. Her drowning would seem to suggest a rejection of the mother of color and an embrace of the eternal maternal force that flows beneath the Mississippi, a myth the pilot relates to her on the trip to New Orleans. He says that "deep under the earth, hurrying toward the subterranean stream, were other streams, small and great, but all deep, hurrying to and from that great mother-stream underneath, just as the small and great overground streams hurry to and from their mother Mississippi. It was almost more than the little convent girl could take in: at least such was the expression of her eyes; for they opened as all eyes have to open at pilot stories" (155). In one sense, her death is an affirmative act in that she has had almost no existence while she was alive: her personality was erased by the sternness of her childhood; her identity was concealed, even from her, out of racial prejudice and moral blindness. There is no epiphany acknowledging the destructiveness of these attitudes, as there is in Chopin's story, but the implications are dramatically clear in the understated conclusion.[45] The rigid caste system based on racial classification has once again proved a destructive force, tearing apart families and estranging a daughter from her mother, resulting in death.

The most anomalous episode in *Balcony Stories* is "Grandmother's Grandmother" (165–73) in that it is temporally and geographically removed from the central concerns of the volume.[46] It takes place in eighteenth-century colonial Georgia, and it concerns the great-great-grandmother of the narrator, who is presumably telling this retrospective narrative to the other women on the veranda. King here was drawing on family legends, since her people had moved to New Orleans from Georgia in 1829, and her mother used to tell stories based on the experience.[47] But whereas the other tales involve personal tragedy in the war or in Reconstruction, here the issues are personal and emotional. In its first telling, when the great-great-grandmother of the narrator told it to the great-grandmother, from whom it was passed down through the generations, it was a simple memory explaining the painful discovery of the death of a young husband who was murdered by a highwayman. The young wife, the great-great-grandmother, both discovered the body and, grieving, brought it into town. The most powerful dimension is emotion, for the widow expresses a "love which, if ever love could do so, would have effected a resurrection" (173). Remote in time and space from New Orleans, which is nevertheless the place of narration, this powerfully tragic event fits thematically with the renditions of more recent heartbreak that invests the surrounding works, especially "The Story of a Day." As Kirby formulates it, "there is no crueler fate in King's fiction than the loss of a father or husband; on the other hand, there is no right recourse for a woman except the active exercise of her love."[48] It universalizes both love and loss; it adds an increment to the growing series of deaths in a violent South; it resonates thematically in its portrayal of romantic affection and death in youth.

"A Delicate Affair" (193–219) is an apt title for one of King's most subtle and exquisite stories, a psychological study in the mode of some of Henry James's best short fiction, such as "The Real Thing" or "The Beast in the Jungle."[49] There is virtually no physical action, aside from people calling upon the protagonist, a woman of eighty who is still feisty and in whom an old grudge against a rival still smolders. There are five active characters, although the narrator, the niece, is never described. The protagonist is Josephine, a wealthy Creole widow who lost her husband many years before. She is attended by a black servant, Jules, who knows how to deal with her imperiousness and manipulates her with his clever anticipation of her habits and preferences. He is not well developed as a character but serves to reveal her cruelty and insensitivity in her treatment of him. She is a person of privilege who inherited everything, earned nothing, and who is willing to deceive to succeed, which she reveals in her playing of cards. She cheated as a youth as well, winning her husband away from the woman he truly loved, her best friend, known as Myosotis. She realized her husband's true affection on the day of their wedding, standing in the living room with the wedding party, and since that moment of epiphany sixty years before she has never spoken to the other woman, shutting her totally out of her life. Her husband's best companion was Mr. Horace, who comes every Wednesday evening to give Josephine the news of New Orleans, and it is his fellowship that has kept her alive. Also in the action is the narrator, a niece, who is referred to only once and even then obliquely. Speaking to Horace, Josephine says "she (nodding toward me) goes out, but she never learns anything. She is as stupid tonight as an empty bottle" (195). The speaker on the balcony is thus self-deprecating, revealing that the aunt regarded her as inferior, never realizing the perceptiveness of her niece. What is related, however, is how sensitive she truly is, how she understands human emotion and motivation and records the salient transformations among the three older characters.

What the speaker presents are transitional moments in the life of her aunt, a progression from pride to humiliation and bitterness, to compassion and forgiveness. In the context of the entire volume, however, this psychological movement is unique in that it is motivated not by the Civil War and its aftermath but by purely domestic concerns, beginning with the aunt's pride in her beauty when a young ingénue. The description of her house reveals her wealth and her old-fashioned French taste, perhaps understandable in an elderly woman but also suggests that Josephine's life has been arrested in the past, that she has never moved beyond that startling wedding day when she became aware of the emotional betrayal. Pertinent to this motif is the painting on the wall of her as a bride, a "portrait of Madame in her youth, and in the partial nudity in which innocence was limned in Madame's youth" (196–97). The suggestion is that Josephine used her sexuality to attract her handsome husband away from Myosotis, although the precise strategy is never outlined. However, the narrator implies that it was parallel to the way she now cheats at cards: "In short, Madame had played then to gain at love, as she played now to gain at solitaire; and hearts were no more than cards to her" (211). The narrator compares her to Atalanta, the mythic female who was suckled by a bear and grew to be a fierce hunter, and she is both ruthless and determined.

Her strength is also her weakness, since it leaves her impervious to the feelings of others, the way she did not sense until after the wedding that her husband loved another. Now, at eighty, she is unaware of the love and devotion that Horace brings to the relationship, has brought to it for over sixty years. Referring to their youth, he compliments her by saying that "the men used to say that your beauty was irresistible. None ever withstood you. None ever could" (208). He means himself, of course, which Josephine does not perceive, although her niece observes and records it. That is the hidden truth he refers to when he says to Josephine "what secrets can there be at our age?" (203). His feelings have persisted all these years, but even in her concluding epiphany, she remains oblivious to his quiet dedication.

In this sense the heart of the story is about love, the affection she felt for her husband, his fascination for his wife's best friend, the devotion of the two friends for one another, and Horace's long-suffering dedication to Josephine. His selfless fidelity is what leads to the conclusion, since he has come that evening to tell Josephine that her old friend, whom she has not seen for sixty years, is now dying. He manipulates her into the realization that all can be forgiven now and that a truly great person would be eager for a reconciliation. Even before his arrival that evening he had arranged for a carriage to take her to Myosotis, the forget-me-not, knowing what he was determined to do. When it succeeds, and the two old women are reconciled in their friendship, he is selfless and unobtrusive, slipping silently out the door, leaving them to revel in their renewed devotion. As Robert Bush has observed, "the point of 'A Delicate Affair' lies in the ironic contrast between the imperious Josephine of the early pages, especially in her irascibility with her servant, and her softness and sentimentality in reconciling with the rival who was once her bosom friend."[50] Almost entirely neglected in King scholarship, this story is one of the most skillfully crafted pieces of short fiction in American Realism.

Balcony Stories concludes with an unusual story in subject and theme but one that is subtle in narrative method and in the secondary motif of the growth of compassion. "Pupasse" (223–45) is yet another instance in which the time of the telling is at some remove from the action.[51] The suggestion is that the narrator is speaking on the balcony, looking back on an earlier event in her school years and relating an aspect of it that lingers. In this case what persists is the memory of the life of a hopeless young retarded girl named Pupasse in grammar school, an odd child who, for her ugliness as well as her limitations, was mocked and excluded by the other children. She is unable to learn French irregular verbs, and the teacher, Madame Joubert, suspends her from school until she can master them. Decades later, the narrator discovers, Pupasse is still studying the book, impervious to the paradigms that her fellow students had absorbed many years ago. Her parents are dead; her grandmother, who raised her, has also passed away. Alone in the world, incapable of comprehending the complexity of everyday life, Pupasse presents a pathetic portrait that still haunts the narrator.

The setting is the Institut St. Denis, the same school at issue in "Monsieur Motte," and Marcélite is there once again as the hairdresser. In contrast to the theme of self-sacrifice in that story, in this harsh school environment there was no sympathy whatever for the unfortunate child, she with her "black eyes" and "sharp-pointed teeth planted very far apart" beneath her "rat-tail" coiffure (225). Madame Joubert is particularly cruel and condescending, forcing the girl to wear a dunce cap and sit in the corner on a stool, humiliating her before the other children. When Marie Pupasse cannot learn her lessons, the teacher, knowing that the girl is several years behind the other students, sends her home despite the fact that her grandmother has died and there is no one there to help her. The school was the girl's true home, and Madame Joubert forbids it to her. However, reflecting on the emotional impact of the suspension, the teacher suddenly realizes how empty life will be for Pupasse, and she promises to come every evening to hear the girl's lessons.

It is an extraordinary commitment, a generous act that obligates her for years, since the narration is long after this event and "Madame Joubert was never known to break her word; that is all one knows about her part of the bargain" (244). The teacher thus grows, sympathy and compassion replacing the judgmental tone of her imperious pedagogy. This point is lost on Kirby, who concludes that "if 'Monsieur Motte' celebrates explicitly the indispensable love that one woman may give to another, 'Pupasse' mourns implicitly the absence of that love."[52] This is not so, as the teacher is profoundly transformed, and the narrator, once one of Pupasse's fellow students, is sufficiently moved by the events to recite them of an evening on the balcony. It is she, the teller, who is also altered by the events, who internalizes the emotional depth of an incident from school days.

In *The Development of the American Short Story*, published in 1923, Fred Lewis Pattee commented that King's "power lay in her lightness of touch, her dialogue—French in its rapidity and brilliancy, her restraint, her ability by touches of suggestion to do in a sentence what a heavier hand might do in a page, and finally in her characterization, her Creole femininities with their shrinking timidity, their tropic passion and intensity, their piquancy, their simplicity and folly, their innate gentility." Helen Taylor has more recently commented on somewhat the same idea, observing that "Grace King's white women characters tend to be loyal to their class, race, family, husbands, slaves, and servants, and especially to each other; they are courageous, independent, and infinitely adaptable."[53] Fundamental to this point is the fact that King writes about the world of women. Although the Civil War and the subsequent period of Reconstruction are the salient transformational events in the background of her stories, no military action is ever presented. Although in actual life New Orleans was filled with the vestigial consequences of battle, with the usual number of amputees or blind veterans as part of daily life, such persons do not figure in King's stories. Rather, her focus is on widows and orphans, on the domestic consequences of military conflict.

King demonstrated, as her stories appeared in *Century*, that she could handle the artistic fundamentals of fiction. She is subtle in point of view, graceful in style, complex in structural organization, and brilliant in her portrayal of New Orleans and the surrounding bayous. Her depiction of the psychological impact on aristocratic Creoles of diminished circumstances after the war is unique, sensitive, and, in some cases, profound, as in "La Grande Demoiselle." However, it is also a selective picture of society, leaving out crucial dimensions. As O'Neal comments, "King, speaking on behalf of white Southerners, failed to consider the divergent responses towards historical events. The story of a belle who lost her fortune has little resonance for a freed slave, nor does King's own account of the horrors of Reconstruction hold true for the many black people in the city who prospered during that decade."[54] She does not touch the world that Alice Dunbar-Nelson presents in *The Goodness of St. Rocque and Other Stories*, for example, nor do her characters ever feel regret for the horrors of slavery, for the attack on the North that started the war, or the rigid racial caste system that dominated life in Louisiana for more than a century. Of course Southern women were not in a position to dictate broad social and political policies, and their concerns were with immediate local issues, and that is the world her work portrays. At their best, King's stories are brilliant evocations of the lives of a fallen privileged class, and they are handled with considerable artistic sophistication, much more so than is generally acknowledged in literary history. But the fourteen short works in *Balcony Stories* are not only individual pieces of fiction, they are part of an overarching aesthetic construct as a story cycle, a book with shape, resonance among its constituent parts, and an artistic integrity that any one part of it cannot have.

A story cycle, by its very nature, presents an overarching narrative more expansive than any of its individual tales. Each episode can focus on an individual protagonist and the conflicts and resolutions that confront a family or small group. *Balcony Stories*, as an entire volume, captures the life of a culture, a vibrant New Orleans society struggling from the effects of the Civil War and Reconstruction. The book reveals the communal sense of the humiliation of defeat and the ensuing adjustment to the enormous changes brought by the collapse of the aristocratic Creole elite and alterations in the social hierarchy as poor whites and freed blacks find new roles in the local economy. King focuses on the psychological dimensions wrought by such enormous modifications, and she does so with considerable insight and sensitivity.

The volume as a whole also has an artistic unity beyond the reach of any one story, principles of juxtaposition, contrast, or continuity that give emphasis to central subjects and themes. For example, the setting in all but one instance is southern Louisiana, most often New Orleans itself, and the unique laws and traditions of that region invest the action with a meaning it would not have in another location. The privileged stature that is lost in "La Grande Demoiselle," for example, is also at issue in "The Old Lady's Restoration" and "A Delicate Affair." The same theme informs "A Drama of Three," although for an aged man rather than a woman, and the cultural transition has yet a different effect for Little Mammy in "A Crippled Hope." The restrictions on courtship and marriage established by the *Code Noir*, the subsequent Louisiana Civil Code, and by tradition are in the background of "The Little Convent Girl" and "Mimi's Marriage." The pain of lost love resonates throughout "The Story of a Day," "Anne Marie and Jeanne Marie," "One of Us," and "A Delicate Affair." The racial issues of "La Grande Demoiselle" take a contrasting form in "A Crippled Hope," as a disabled young black woman longs for a relationship with a white family. Elementary and high school education was a dynamic issue after the war in a state with no previous public institutions, and the privileged lost their exclusive private institutes based on French culture. "La Grande Demoiselle" captures one dimension of this transition, the Freedmen's Bureau schools, whereas "Pupasse" takes place in the antebellum world of private instruction. The meaning of race in this society is crucial to "A Crippled Hope," "La Grande Demoiselle," and "The Little Convent Girl," binding those works into a pattern of significance.

On a more subtle level, the book also documents the internal transformations in the way characters must think about themselves. The once elegant general in "A Drama of Three" must accept his poverty and economic dependence, as does the protagonist of "The Old Lady's Restoration." The growth of compassion is central to a group of stories, as it is for the visiting ladies who discover the woman who lost her lover in "The Story of a Day," the director of the school who interviews the retired soprano in "One of Us," and the teacher who visits Pupasse every evening. The narrative situation common to all of the stories is that they are all told by women on a veranda in the evening with the other mothers gathered before them. They have experienced the war and its aftermath, and they share a knowledge of the past of the Crescent City, its vernacular, historic French values, rigid racial and gender restrictions, and disorienting transformation. The volume, as a whole, relates something that any one story does not, a lament for the Romantic elegance and orderliness of the past and a resentment of the new. It is a saga of an idealized lost culture and the birth of a new one, a longing for what was lost, and a reluctant resignation to the world that has replaced it. It is powerful material, and no one explored it with more cultural understanding and artistic sensitivity than did Grace King.

1. George Washington Cable. George Washington Cable papers, Louisiana Research Collection, Tulane University. Courtesy of Tulane University.

2. Kate Chopin. Kate O'Flaherty in 1869 just prior to her marriage to Oscar Chopin. Courtesy of the Missouri History Museum, St. Louis.

3. Grace King and her sisters Flora Ann King and Nina King. Grace (left) lived with her two sisters the last thirty years of her life in the family residence. Courtesy of the State Library of Louisiana.

4. Alice Dunbar-Nelson, 1900. Courtesy of the University of Delaware Library.

5. George Washington Cable House. Cable had this Italian style home built on 1313 Eighth Street, New Orleans, in 1874. Photograph courtesy of Gwen Nagel.

6. Kate Chopin House. Kate and her family lived at 1413 Louisiana Avenue in New Orleans. Two other residences, one on Magazine Street and the other on Constantinople, no longer exist. Photograph courtesy of Gwen Nagel.

7. Grace King Home. Banker Frederick Rodewald originally built Grace King's home at 1749 Coliseum Street in the Garden District of New Orleans. She lived here with her two sisters. Photograph courtesy of Gwen Nagel.

8. Jackson Square. Originally known as the *Place d'Armes*, the square was renamed in 1851 in honor of the hero of the Battle of New Orleans in the War of 1812, Andrew Jackson. St. Louis Cathedral serves as the backdrop, and the equestrian statue of General Jackson stands dramatically in the center. Photograph courtesy of Gwen Nagel.

9. The Orleans Ballroom in the Bourdon Orleans Hotel at 717 Orleans Street. One of the prime locations for the famous Quadroon Balls, the building was later purchased by the Sisters of the Holy Family Convent. In recent years it has once again become a hotel. Photograph courtesy of Gwen Nagel.

10. Madame John's Legacy at 632 Dumaine Street. This historic house is typical of those provided to plaçage mistresses and was named for the character "Madame John" in George Washington Cable's "'Tite Poulette." Photograph courtesy of Gwen Nagel.

11. St. Roch Chapel. In Alice Dunbar-Nelson's "The Goodness of St. Rocque" Manuela comes here to offer her nouvena in hopes of marrying Theophilé. Dunbar-Nelson changed the spelling of the saint's name for her story. Photograph courtesy of Gwen Nagel.

12. 'Sieur George's House. Originally known as the Pedesclaux-Le Monnier House at 636-40 Royal Street, after the publication of George Washington Cable's "'Sieur George" it took the name of this fictional character's residence. Photograph courtesy of Gwen Nagel.

3
Alice Dunbar-Nelson and the New Orleans Story Cycle

Alice Dunbar-Nelson was twenty-four in 1899 when *The Goodness of St. Rocque and Other Stories* appeared from Dodd, Mead and Company in New York, a major publisher of the time.[1] African-American writers in the period enjoyed encouragement from such white writers as William Dean Howells and George Washington Cable and were able to find publication in the major periodicals, including the *Atlantic Monthly*, the leading magazine of the day. Indeed, Paul Laurence Dunbar gave Howells credit for introducing him to a national audience when he reviewed *Majors and Minors* for *Harper's* in June of 1896.[2] Charles Chesnutt placed his stories in the *Atlantic Monthly* and his books with Houghton, Mifflin and Company, the foremost publisher in the country. The fact that Dodd, Mead and Company was also Paul Laurence Dunbar's firm played some role in having *The Goodness of St. Rocque* appear with that company, and that connection was instrumental in generating public interest in Alice's volume of interconnected stories.

Gloria Hull gives Dunbar-Nelson credit for helping to institute a tradition of black stories, but she assumes that earlier writers had portrayed "only plantation and minstrel stereotypes," which was not the case. Frances Harper and Charles Chesnutt both preceded Dunbar-Nelson in the genre, and they were not at all restricted to clichéd representations. Nonetheless, Hull continues, arguing that Dunbar-Nelson's "strategy for escaping these odious expectations was to eschew black characters and culture and to write, instead, charming, aracial, Creole sketches that solidified her in the then-popular 'female-suitable' local color mode."[3] Hull is historically inaccurate in nearly every conceivable way. The Local-Color movement was not restricted to women in any sense. Indeed, the first two major practitioners of the mode were men, Bret Harte and Mark Twain. In *Crumbling Idols* Hamlin Garland maintained that the regional movement was the most important literary tradition in America, using the problems of common characters as the subject of important art, telling their stories in the vernacular, and establishing a truly indigenous literary movement distinct from the models of European literature.[4]

There was a widespread belief that this approach to literature would yield the highest form of art, not the lowest, a point made eloquently by Garland while Dunbar-Nelson was writing her stories. Nor did Dunbar-Nelson eschew anything; she wrote about the world she knew, the culture of creoles of color in New Orleans, depicting their fundamental humanity, social conflicts, and tragic dilemmas. For the most part, unlike her first husband, she did not write distinctly "dialect" literature but used the vernacular sparingly to reveal a character's participation in a subset of city life. When she did indulge in linguistic representations, she did it with great effect and thematic richness, as in "The Praline Woman," for example. Perhaps most significantly, she produced her most important book in the form of a story cycle, one in which all of the works share common settings, enlarge on a central core of themes, and draw from a shared cultural context.

To form the new collection, she drew on three selections from her earlier *Violets and Other Stories*: "A Carnival Jangle," "Titee," which she revised to give a more positive conclusion, and "Little Miss Sophie."[5] All three are set in New Orleans, feature localized characters and events, and depict the complex ethnic social structure of Louisiana culture. She also constructed a thematic pairing in the new book, works that draw on localized issues and deepen or contrast ideas introduced earlier.

Although it is notable for being set in New Orleans, and drawing on the cultural variations of that society, "Titee" (44–55) explores a different theme, social approbation based on a misunderstanding of a boy's character and motivation. Written during a time Dunbar-Nelson was teaching in the public schools, the background of the action involves Titee's violations of the codes of institutional behavior and commitment to his own affinity for the natural world and the impoverished section of New Orleans in the Third District, with its railroad section, levees, and swamps. The teacher, whose perspective provides a key judgment, regards him as an "idle, lazy, dirty, troublesome boy" who nonetheless knows a great deal about nature in the surrounding area and on the ocean, where he has sailed with fishermen. Although his situation is not race or caste specific, he would seem to be a Creole of color, for his friends are "little Creole and Spanish fellows, with dark skins," which would exclude the white Creoles of the French Quarter (212–13). He lives in a world of violence and deprivation; even his mother beats him for minor infractions, and he fights with the other boys at school. The crux of the action revolves around the fact that he undergoes a change, stops eating, and carries his food in his pockets, gradually growing thinner. What has happened, the conclusion reveals, is that on his ramblings along the railroad tracks, he has discovered a starving old man, and he has given his breakfast and dinner to him every day. When Titee does not return home on schedule, his family goes in search of him, and he is found, appropriately by his dog Tiger, having broken his leg. Titee insists that they carry him to the cave hiding the old man, where he gives "grandpa" his food. Titee dies soon after of "the cold and rain, and the broken leg" and is laid to rest in St. Rocque's cemetery, the appropriate place for him in that the historic saint was said to cure the disabled. Central to the Third District, this cemetery and chapel figure significantly in other stories.

"A Carnival Jangle" (76–82) is credited with being the first fiction in America to depict the riotous atmosphere of Mardi Gras, and it thus contributes something unique to the Local-Color tradition.[6] Perhaps the most notable dimension of the story is the impressionistic rendering of the scene that anticipates the polyphonic prose within the imagist movement nearly twenty years later. But Dunbar-Nelson's description fits perfectly into the prose experimentations of Amy Lowell, John Gould Fletcher, and D. H. Lawrence as well as the "Chicago Studies" Hamlin Garland wrote in 1902.

Dunbar-Nelson's narrative method captures the sounds, colors, and frenetic activity of the carnival: "There is a merry jangle of bells in the air, an all-pervading sense of jester's noise, and the flaunting vividness of royal colors; the streets swarm with humanity,—humanity in all shapes, manners, forms,—laughing, pushing, jostling, crowding, a mass of men and women and children" (76). Things seem to happen so rapidly that they defy comprehension: "A madding dream of color and melody and fantasy gone wild in an effervescent bubble of beauty that shifts and changes and passes kaleidoscope-like before the bewildered eye" (77). In the midst of this bustle, the protagonist, Flo, emerges, without description or explanation, and some friends take her to secure a costume from a wizened woman who is compared imagistically to an alligator, conveying a vague sense of threat. There is only one costume remaining, that of a young man, "*un petit garcon*," and Flo dons the outfit and rejoins the revelry. In Washington Square she watches an Indian dance, which historically would have been members of the black community in Native-American costumes, since they are referred to as "mimic Red-men." This practice was probably inspired by the appearance of Buffalo Bill's western show in New Orleans in 1884, for the very next year faux "Indians" appeared in the procession.[7] One of the chiefs spies Flo, thinks the figure is someone who has offended him, and seeks to revenge the affront by stabbing Flo in the back with a stiletto. The young woman falls dead. No one seems to care except her grieving mother, who sits at the bedside of the body of her daughter while the party goes on outside in the street.

The culture of New Orleans is thus portrayed as encompassing treachery, crime, murder, and violence as well as the celebrative chaos of Mardi Gras, and Flo dies as a result of mistaken identity. There would seem little justification for maintaining, as does Elizabeth Ammons, that the protagonist dies for "invading traditionally male territory, including and especially the white male territory of high Art."[8] Flo is hardly a practitioner of art of any kind, apart from wearing a costume, and her invasion of the male realm does not cause her death. Rather, she dies at the hand of someone who believes she has *not* crossed over, that she is indeed a man, the one who had offended him.

Perhaps the most culturally significant story borrowed from Dunbar-Nelson's earlier volume is "Little Miss Sophie" (140–54) in that it rests on top of the complex social matrix that underscores Cable's "'Tite Poulette" and "Madame Delphine." Although many of the works in *Goodness* are set in New Orleans either by direct reference or implication, the racial identity of the key characters is often uncertain, sometimes, as in "Titee," because it is not a central thematic issue. In "Sophie," however, it is a subtle but crucial element in the psychological orientation of the characters and suggests a back story that explains the conflict.

"Little Miss Sophie" is a story that falls into the "tragic quadroon" tradition that flourished in the first half of the nineteenth century in Europe.[9] Those works, as Werner Sollors has described, provided variations on the general plot of a wealthy white gentleman who takes a woman of color as a mistress, usually a mulatto or quadroon. The woman in these works is invariably sold into slavery, betrayed romantically, or abandoned unceremoniously, leaving her destitute and hopeless. Such stories and plays normally end in her suicide, sometimes her murder, despite the selfless devotion of the woman for her beloved. Dunbar-Nelson's story falls solidly into this tradition, with the addition of the localized *plaçage* arrangements as a backdrop.

Significantly, the first important work on the theme was by a black writer born in New Orleans, Victor Séjour, who was a free quadroon. Born in 1817 into a society that denied schooling for black children, he was sent to Paris to be educated in 1836, and his story "Le Mulâtre" appeared in *Revue des Colonies* in March of the next year. It portrays slave life in Santo Domingo and the deadly attempts of white master to force himself upon a beautiful slave woman.[10] A year later, Madame Charles Reybaud published "Les Épaves," a novella about the *Code Noir* narrated by a mixed-race woman, Zoe, and set in Martinique in 1720. The subject quickly became popular, so much so that Hans Christian Andersen wrote a romantic play produced in Copenhagen in 1840 titled *Mulatten* (The mulatto). It created a sensation and was revived in 1868 and 1873. Essentially a stage adaptation of Reybaud's "Les Épaves," it was adapted in a Swedish version that ran at the Royal Theater in Stockholm.[11]

Even more popular in America, the subject became the focus of scores of novels and stories set in the antebellum South, as Anna Shannon Elfenbein has established. Beginning with Richard Hildreth's *The Slave* in 1836, a steady stream of novels soon appeared, including Joseph Hold Ingraham's *The Quadronne* in 1841, Henry Wadsworth Longfellow's "The Quadroon Girl" in 1842, and Mayne Reid's *The Quadroon* in 1856.[12] In these and other works, the conflict derives from a racial and sexual basis. In many cases the beautiful young woman, being pursued by a white man, commits suicide rather than succumb to his advances. In some instances the woman's black lover kills the white man to avenge a sexual conquest. To be original, George Washington Cable needed to find an original approach to the social-caste plot. As the first important American writer after the Civil War to explore the racist basis of plaçage and related practices and to depict the tragic dimensions of such a tradition, he did so with a unique situation: those relationships in which there was genuine love and commitment on both sides despite racial disparities.

In "Sophie," Dunbar-Nelson deals with a more common pattern, the white gentleman who establishes a romance with a woman of color and then abandons her when he marries a white woman, an all too frequent occurrence within the history of plaçage relationships. Even though Dunbar-Nelson was herself of mixed ethnic heritage, she is much more delicate and indirect about racial matters in her stories than the reformist Cable, who not only wrote fiction directly on the issue but lectured across the country on behalf of civil rights for people of color. "Sophie" offers only hints about the protagonist's ethnicity, but it is not the case, as Kristina Brooks maintains, that she is of "unverifiable identity" and that the center of the story is the problem of "identification."[13] Sophie, rejected by her lover, by all indications a white Creole gentleman, is described as being a "little Creole old maid," which, in Dunbar-Nelson's fiction, would mean "Creole of color." The passengers on a street car (an electric one introduced into the city in 1892) make reference to Neale's "little Creole love-affair" with his "dusky-eyed fiancée," as direct an indication of racial identity as Dunbar-Nelson gets. In addition, she lives in the Third District, with people of mixed blood, and she sews at a factory, a job no white woman of the time would have accepted.

Traditional Louisiana laws and social ethics propel the direction of the plot. As a younger woman, Sophie fell in love with a white Creole gentleman,

Louis Neale, who cared enough about her to give her an important Roman ring, a family heirloom that is later crucial to his financial status. The *Code Noir* forbade their marriage, being of differing races, and they apparently had not yet established a formal plaçage arrangement, which would have required a legal procedure, a house or apartment for Sophie, and a small income sufficient to support her in comfort. These arrangements were standard for more than a century in New Orleans society, with many Creole men never marrying but committing themselves to their mixed-race family. Nor was it the case, as Jordan Stouck maintains, that the relationship between Neale and Sophie could not be "affirmed" in New Orleans society because of their different races.

Indeed, plaçage marriages were common in Louisiana, with quadroon balls twice each week to facilitate introductions and a special court system to codify the arrangements, and nearly half of Creole gentlemen established one.[14] Stouck also mistakenly assumes that black women involved with white men were "slaves," which was not the case. Under the *Code Noir*, all women in a formal plaçage relationship were declared legally free.[15] However, in some cases the white man abandoned his mistress when he courted a white woman, which seems to be what has happened in this instance. The special poignancy of the situation arises from the fact that Sophie is emotionally committed to Neale, so in love with him as to be willing to sacrifice her own life for his sake; he, on the other hand, remembers her not with affection but with guilt. When he needs the ring he gave Sophie to fulfill the requirements of his uncle's will, "he's ashamed to try to find her or the ring" (147). So he will forsake a fortune out of embarrassment, and she learns about it by overhearing the conversations in the street car.

The plot thickens over the fact that in her poverty, Sophie has pawned the ring, having "kissed and wept and fondled it," and she does not have the money to retrieve it. Rather than ask him for assistance, she is determined to sew more, eat less, buy back the ring, and present it to Neale as a token of her undying love. The rumors fly about the neighborhood about why she is working so diligently, none of them with genuine foundation, and at last she is able to secure the ring and write a note to Louis presenting it to him. Rather melodramatically, before she can deliver the present, she dies of starvation and her body is described on her deathbed, rather ironically, as "white" in death, with a "cold, happy face" (154). This rather simple plot is presented with a good deal of artistic sophistication. The narrative perspective shifts from a close identification with Sophie's mind in the beginning, to a generalized "neighborhood" point of view as the gossips speculate about her new dedication to work, to an omniscient stance at the end. There are temporal shifts as well from the opening "present" to a flashback (142–43) to the day

Sophie inadvertently came to church in the middle of a wedding and discovered that the groom was her beloved Neale. Sophie is so deeply stricken that she faints.

The focus returns to the present briefly (143) only to shift to the past once again to cover the arrival of Sophie in the Third District five years earlier when she had been rejected by Louis Neale. She was racked with sobbing that inspired speculation on the part of Michel, the grocer, and Madame Laurent, who keeps the rabbé shop, the gossip world of "In Our Neighborhood." In a resumption of present time, after the wedding scene, Sophie, riding in a street car, hears that Neale's firm has failed and he has lost his uncle's inheritance because of his inability to produce the Roman ring that Sophie pawned, and she resolves to earn the money to retrieve it. A stream-of-consciousness passage establishes her determination: "Still he must have it, it was his; it would save him from disgrace and suffering, and from trailing the proud head of the white-gowned bride into sorrow. He must have it,—but how?" (148). She seeks the guidance of the Virgin (people of color were required, under the *Code Noir*, to be Roman Catholic in Louisiana), and she leaves the church with a plan to return the ring to Neale. For weeks Sophie sews twice her normal volume, starves herself, and saves her money while the gossip mill around her spins fantasies of jailed relatives. Finally, on Christmas Eve, she has the money to buy back the ring, which she does, fondling it with extravagant love, a transference of what she still feels for her lover. On Christmas Day, she writes a note to Louis to accompany the ring, but she dies before it can be delivered, leaving some ambiguity as to whether it was ever brought to Neale.

As a relative novice in fiction, even in these three early stories Dunbar-Nelson nevertheless introduced into her fictional aesthetic the ability to write from multiple points of view within a single story, contrasting in parallax how Sophie's life is perceived from different angles. She also handled spatial and temporal shifts gracefully and with dramatic effect. She deserves to be credited with exploring new territory in Southern literature, the world of Creoles of color in New Orleans, with their complex history and role in the social spectrum, their unique cultural heritage, their pride and psychological conflicts. It was with some justification that Paul Laurence Dunbar, an ardent suitor at the time, wrote to her that "your 'Little Miss Sophie' is as graceful, poignant, and charming as anything Grace King ever wrote. Everything you have written shows remarkable thought behind that—talent."[16] It may be true, as Robert Whitlow contends, that coincidence plays too central a role in the plot,[17] a tendency that runs throughout Dunbar-Nelson's fiction, but the heart of the stories is on character, social values, and ethnic identity and rarely on event.

The first of the new stories is the titular "The Goodness of Saint Rocque" (3–16), which is built on romantic fulfillment based on local traditions and practices. Indeed, it demonstrates how rich the Local-Color tradition can be. Without a sense of the cultural traditions unique to the Crescent City, there is no way to understand the fundamental conflicts, the religious tension, and the final significance of the conclusion. In one sense the story presents a standard plot, a love triangle that is resolved in the course of the action. It is the local values, the multi-ethnic culture, the richness of the society that gives substance to the events. The narrative stance relates to the thematic development in that it presents the views of members of the immediate community, the people who know the characters, see them daily, and share their values. Dunbar-Nelson often used this technique, although almost never with consistency throughout an entire work. Thus, the perspective shifts to varying points of reference and information in various sections.

This narrative shift is mirrored by a changing temporal structure that highlights key conflicts and creates suspense by revealing consequences prior to the incipient events. For example, the story begins in media res at a moment after a picnic at which the protagonist, Manuela, was ignored by her beloved Theophilé, who turned his attentions to Claralie. That event, the middle of the plot, explains what is not evident at the beginning: why Manuela has had a "sleepless, tearful night" and why she now has swollen and discolored eyes (3). She has clearly been weeping over the betrayal by her lover, as becomes apparent later, and it is not at all as Thomas Strychacz argues, that her eyes are swollen because she has been beaten.[18] She has been crying, and she wears a veil to cover her dismay. She is hurrying along Marais Street, a meaningful fact in that it leads in the direction of St. Rocque's chapel, the partial purpose of her journey. But the meaning of her quest, the point of it all, is not evident in the opening section, which has a unique time scheme with simultaneity of action and telling, the narration coming at the instant of the events, not in retrospect.

That changes in the second part, a flashback to the picnic the day before at Milneburg-on-the-Lake, a brief train ride from the center of New Orleans and a popular nineteenth-century leisure destination. Here are gathered what is described as "Creole girls and boys," a term Dunbar-Nelson uses throughout her work to mean, almost invariably, "Creoles of color." It is a joyous event with music, dancing, fishing, swimming, boating, and a good deal of courtship around the edges. The pleasure of the event is undermined for Manuela, however, for Theophilé pays no attention to her but instead courts the "blonde and petite" Claralie. Within the social culture of New Orleans there was a good deal of discrimination based on color, and the lighter the shade the higher the social stature. Claralie, extremely light and flirtatious, has the advantage over the darker Manuela, who feels a "bitterness of spirit" as she watches her suitor dance and dine with her rival and escort her home from the picnic. Manuela goes home with Henri, for whom she feigns interest. The names at the picnic suggest something of the cultural mix of the society, "Claralie," "Theophilé" and "Henri" revealing a French background and "Manuela" a linkage to Spain or the Caribbean. Ethnically, there are reasons for Manuela's lover to prefer another woman.

That is what leads her to seek supernatural assistance in her attempt to lure Theophilé back to her, the subject of the third section, which resumes the "present" time of the opening. The motivation for Manuela's walk down Marais Street and across St. Rocque Avenue is now clear: her determination to win back her beloved. She goes to a little house in the poorer neighborhoods of the city to consult a voodoo woman, the "Wizened One," probably a quadroon from the Caribbean, given her dialect. She is described as being "yellow" and "turbaned," hallmarks of the mixed-race population, and she works her magic with Tarot cards (8). Her first question for Manuela is "an' fo' w'y' you come here? Assiez-là, ma'amzelle," her use of language defining her background, social level, and ethnic identity. A mistress of her trade, she tells Manuela that Claralie is making a nouvena in St. Rocque's to win Theophilé's love and advises Manuela to do the same and to wear a voodoo charm around her waist. These simple comments draw on a wealth of local tradition.

It is significant that the belief system among Creoles of color combines the voodoo traditions of the Caribbean with Roman Catholicism, which had been established as the official religion of Louisiana by the *Code Noir*. As Mary Anne O'Neal has pointed out, Cable portrayed this theological mixture in several of his stories and in *The Grandissimes*, but "Dunbar-Nelson was the first to treat the subject casually, as an integral part of daily life," as it is in that neighborhood.[19] O'Neal also comments on the relevance of the details of the Wizened One's house, the customary crushed brick on the front stoop as protection against evil spells, for example, supported by the "yellow-washed" sidewalk. The décor of the house suggests the Caribbean influence, especially that of the thousands of Africans who lived for a century in the French colonies and migrated to New Orleans in the early decades of the nineteenth century.[20] The room inside combines such artifacts of Catholicism as an altar, a portrait of St. Joseph, and a crucifix coexisting with Tarot cards and emblems of voodoo. Sitting in front of a magical woman who speaks French, wearing both an African charm and a proper Catholic veil, Manuela embodies the blended customs of the local culture. Her objective, however, is clearly to win back the affections of the young man she loves; it would seem unduly harsh to conclude, as Strychacz does, that "her primary motivations are jealousy, possessiveness, competitiveness, and pride."[21] But Manuela's response to Theophilé's indiscretion is not the reasoned calculation of revenge but the crushing weight of emotional betrayal, a matter she attempts to further rectify at the chapel of St. Rocque.

St. Roch (only Dunbar-Nelson spells the name "Rocque") is a famous figure in Europe and in New Orleans, and his religious significance has occasioned a good deal of folklore. Born in France in 1295, he was a legendary priest thought to be able to prevent, or cure, the plague, which he was said to have done as a mendicant pilgrim in Italy. A popular cult grew up around his miraculous powers, and churches were erected in his honor, from the Scuola Grande di San Rocco in Venice to the Bílá Hora in Prague, which features a statue of St. Roch. Since there were major yellow fever epidemics in Louisiana throughout the nineteenth century, his assistance was much invoked, and he was given credit for those who were not infected and those who recovered from the illness. In the American epidemic of 1866–67, Father Thevis prayed to St. Roch to protect his parishioners, vowing to erect a chapel in his honor if none of the people died. None did, and the chapel was constructed in 1871. But another legend in New Orleans is more pertinent to Dunbar-Nelson's story, the fact that St. Roch was the patron saint of bachelors. The variant of that idea in Louisiana pertained to women, not men. The dominant folklore held that if a maiden prayed to him on Good Friday, made the Way of the Cross, and lit a candle, she would be wed before the year was out.[22] That is the legend that the author was familiar with and the one that motivates Manuela to continue her walk down Marais Street to St. Roch Avenue, where she would turn left to reach St. Roch Cemetery and the adjacent chapel.

It is there that the fourth section continues the present action, with Manuela in the chapel. The narrative method has shifted in that no one in the neighborhood goes with her, as they were not at the conversation with the Wizened One, so it is a restrained omniscient point of view that describes the action in the scene. Still wearing her veil, thus continuing to grieve for the vagaries of Theophilé, she walks quickly through the white gates of the cemetery, buys a candle at the small lodge inside the grounds, and glides into the tiny chapel, where she sees a "wide table" before the altar filled with "wish candles" from other young ladies with similar objectives. She beseeches St. Rocque's assistance, lights her candle, and leaves the chapel, significantly caressing a young boy's head on the way out. She has already assumed a maternal role. Her spirits lifted, she becomes "cheerful," and her entire attitude has been improved (10–11).

The next scene, the following Sunday, demonstrates the power of the good St. Rocque. In previous weeks Theophilé had spent the Lord's Day with Claralie, but this time he calls on Manuela. Although their visit is brief, when he leaves she fondles the charm about her waist and prays to St. Rocque, covering her bets. Theophilé sends bonbons during the week, and the following Friday, Manuela lights her second candle in the chapel. On Sunday, he offers her his arm after Mass, crushing Claralie, who tosses her head to feign unconcern. The next Friday heightens the confrontation when both Manuela and Claralie arrive in the chapel at the same time, presumably there for the same reason. This meeting sends Manuela back to the Wizened One, who comforts her by saying "she ees 'fraid, she will work, mais you' charm, hit weel beat her" (12). On Sunday, Theophilé is nowhere to be found, but the two women exchange "murderous glances" in church. These encounters consistently stress Claralie's light color, her blonde hair, and her blue eyes in contrast to Manuela's darkness and black eyes. In subtle ways, the narrator heightens the ethnic dimension of the romantic struggle.

The penultimate section of the plot presents the key action, as all of the characters attend a party in honor of Theophilé's younger sister, Louise. Claralie is there in her "dainty white skirts," and she flirts with "mischievous" looks at her host. Manuela, on the other hand, confident of her supernatural support, is "proud-looking" in her yellow dress, and she pays no attention to Theophilé until he asks her to dance. As they stroll in the garden, they have "an engrossing tête-a-tête" that is explained only by implication as he leads her to the head of the family table where she sits next to his mother and, as the narrator suggests, "there is but one conclusion to be deduced therefrom" (16). The final section clarifies the meaning of these events.

The conclusion is brief but artistically complex. For one thing, the time of the telling is in the future, after the wedding of Manuela and Theophilé and subsequent to the "present" time of most of the action. It once again reveals the collective judgment of the community in an omniscient, speculative sense, formulating as "if you had asked" each of the characters a question about what brought about the union. Manuela would have looked "wise," knowing that she had the assistance of both St. Rocque and the Wizened One. Claralie would have rationalized sour grapes and insisted she preferred Leon. The groom would have suggested that he was only teasing Manuela. The Wizened One would have offered a charm, but St. Rocque is given a special place at the end, for "he is a good saint" and "if you believe in him and are true and good and make your nouvenas with a clean heart, he will grant your wish" (16). All of the projected speakers answer within the locus of values ascribed to them, but none proffer a humanistic assessment: that Manuela loved Theophilé truly, that he was sensitive to that fact, and that her newfound self-assurance, born of her voodoo charm and her prayers to

St. Rocque, gave her a confidence and presence that her lover found irresistible.[23]

"The Goodness of St. Rocque" is thus a complex story, one that introduces a setting and a locus of traditions and values that resonate throughout the story cycle, as is standard in the genre. New Orleans and its immediate environs are the setting for all of the stories, and the multifaceted historical background of the culture energizes the conflicts in each plot. The melding of Caribbean voodoo practices with European Catholicism lends a rich interpretive possibility to the motivations of the characters and the meaning of the final outcome. Subsequent works broaden the rich nationality mix of the setting, but the central issues throughout the volume spring from the social mixture that comprises New Orleans.

Another story on the theme of romantic fulfillment is "La Juanita" (195–208), which features dramatic action within a rather predictable plotline. As is characteristic of Dunbar-Nelson's stories, it is not the action that is of primary interest, although a conclusion that brings happy lovers together in marriage is a rare commodity in the fiction of the period. The point of view is fascinating in that it encompasses the generalized knowledge and perspective of the townspeople of Mandeville, a small town on the northeastern shore of Lake Pontchartrain, an estuary that flows into the Gulf of Mexico. A steamer came daily from New Orleans, forty miles away on the southern shore, and that was the principal connection to the outside world. Largely isolated, the local community has managed to perpetuate ideas and prejudices about ethnicity that had gradually receded decades ago in the rest of the state.

These stereotypical attitudes still dominate the action in that the protagonist, La Juanita Alvarez, a white Creole of Spanish and French blood, loves an American, the most objectionable ethnic group in the mind of her Grandpère Colomés, with whom she and her mother have lived since the death of her father. Closer to the hatreds fueled by the Louisiana Purchase, which brought about dramatic cultural transformations, he provides the conflict by objecting to any union of his granddaughter with this outsider, Mercer Grangeman, "big and blond and brawny" in contrast to the bright white skin and jet black hair of Juanita. The removal of this impediment comes through a sailing regatta in which Mercer captains his boat in a race on the lake. During the contest, a storm erupts, threatening the entire racing fleet, which disappears from the view of the community, but Mercer leads all of the boats into a safe inlet until the storm abated, at which point the race resumes. Mercer, of course, wins not only the contest but the hand of his beloved and the approval of her grandfather, who comments that "some time dose Americain can mos' be lak one Frenchman." As the narrator reports, in typical plurality, "we danced at the betrothal supper the next week" (208), a rather saccharine outcome for a conflict rife with ethnic prejudice.

One of the stories that most enriches the cultural mix of characters is "Tony's Wife" (19–33), a grim commentary on the fruition of romance: an unhappy, destructive marriage. In its depiction of an insensitive, physically abusive husband who cares little about the welfare of his wife, the situation is an unfortunate reflection of Dunbar-Nelson's own first marriage, although, of course, the ethnicity of the characters is quite different. In any event, the plot is not what is important: it depicts a brief period in the relationship between a domineering husband, Tony, and a long-suffering "wife," although, in fact, the two are not legally married. In due course, he becomes ill and dies, leaving his entire estate to his brother. Tony's wife (her first name is never revealed; she lives entirely in her relationship to her husband) is left with nothing. Within the courtship group, this story joins "Little Miss Sophie" in emphasizing the theme of betrayal and victimization of the woman involved.

But the most important dimensions are setting and characterization, for it is the first work to move out of the French Quarter and immediate neighborhoods and into the Garden District that housed the enormous numbers of immigrants that flooded into New Orleans after 1803. Encouraged by the opportunities of a rapidly expanding economy and the demand for labor, poor people from a wide spectrum of nations came to the city and settled in a new section of the expanding metropolis. It is an impressive mix: beyond the Italian Tony and his German wife, a Jewish girl buys candy at their family shop on Prytania Street. On the same corner is Mrs. Murphy, the Irish grocer; Tony's brother John has married an Irish woman, Betty. The local priest, Father Leblanc, is French. The key issue is the Italian nature of Tony who, portrayed as dark and brutish, is described in animal imagery as "growling" when he is first introduced standing "beetle-browed and huge in the small doorway" (19). At the time of the publication of *The Goodness of St. Rocque*, this portrait would have had meaning in the Crescent City since by then some thirty thousand Italians had moved into the city. In 1890, when a Sicilian gang killed the Irish Chief of Police, David C. Hennessy, a deep resentment toward Italians erupted within the neighborhood.[24] Nowhere to be seen are Creoles of either color, and the inherent themes do not involve the prerogatives of racial mixtures. Instead, male domination is a key issue, especially within nationality stereotypes.

Tony's dark and massive presence lends an undercurrent of impending violence to the action: "He was a great, black-bearded, hoarse-voiced, six-foot specimen of Italian humanity" who is compared to Hercules in his muscularity (22). His wife, in contrast, is "meek, pale, little, ugly, and German," and she is totally incapable of contesting for her place in the family. Given that Tony comes from northern Italy (his brother is blond), there is in the background a historic conflict in the homeland between the German speaking population, which had lived there for centuries, and the Italians, the fundamental issue undergirding the eruption of World War I two decades later. In any event, Tony hates his wife, beats her and her mother, and cares nothing for her feelings. In a standard Dunbar-Nelson narrative device, there is neighborhood gossip about the situation promulgated by Mrs. Murphy, who is described as the "Pauline Pry" of the block. The reference is interesting historically: in 1887, Pry had published a famous book titled *Random Glimpses of Society* that presented social sketches and especially perceptive analyses of various character types. Mrs. Murphy, who sees nearly everyone daily in her grocery, would have ample opportunity to analyze the local familial dramas.

It is Tony's gout that initially frees his wife from domination, and as his illness increases she becomes "light-hearted" and cheerful. The narrator calls the attending doctor Æsculapius, a classical frame of reference. In Greek mythology Æsculapius was the god of medicine and healing. Of greater significance, perhaps, he was said to have raised the dead in return for gold, for which Zeus killed him. The Louisiana avatar seems to lack these powers, however, for he reveals that Tony will surely die very soon, at which his wife "sat in her chair and laughed,—laughed with a hearty joyousness" that reveals her inherent sparkle (28). Even approaching death, however, Tony continues his cruelty to her, refusing a wedding to ensure her inheritance of the property, shunning the priest who comes to administer last rites, and revealing that he has left everything to his brother John. His wife is thus left penniless at the conclusion. It is a grim portrait of marriage, gender domination, injustice, nationality types, and the hopeless resignation of a woman caught in a patriarchal economic structure.

"Tony's Wife" deals with the pain of romantic disillusionment on the part of characters who are German and Italian; "By the Bayou St. John" (85–92) does so for a young Spanish woman. On one level, the plot deals with the anguish of unrequited love, a common subject Dunbar-Nelson enriched with subtle artistry. The story begins with a lyrical evocation of beautiful nature being invaded by the modern, industrial world. The focus is the bayou that flows through New Orleans into Lake Pontchartrain, with water blending from the surrounding swamps that, at the time of the action, still covered much of the city. The name "Bayou St. John" derives from a French fort established on the juncture of the bayou and the lake in 1701 and called "Fort St. Jean" at the time, but when Spain gained control of the area it was known as the Old Spanish Fort. The protection it accorded led to the establishment of the Crescent City along its banks, and the Carondelet Canal allowed for increased navigation into the deep waters that supported local commerce.

Of greater pertinence to the fictional events is the fact that the bayou was a beautiful, quiet area frequented by lovers seeking privacy. That background is related to the anthropomorphic imagery used to describe it as "dark, like the passionate women of Egypt; placid, like their broad brows; deep, silent, like their souls" (85). The narrator reflects that "within its bosom are hidden romances and stories," one of which will form the narrative that follows. The intrusion of the industrial world is changing things, however, destroying the ancients oak trees that line the banks with the "ruthless vandalism of the improving idea" of mechanization (86). The conflict between traditional, natural values and "progress" is a key motif, one at issue in New England literature beginning as early as the 1840s, but despite mechanical intrusions, the bayou sustains the peace and beauty of "a mockingbird in a fragrant orange grove." Indeed, the stream is compared to the "Priestess of Isis," the second Egyptian allusion in the introduction but one that is not developed beyond the comment that it is "calm-browed, even in indignity." Humiliation is involved in the love plot of the second section.

The two characters are a man who engenders "the essence of Spanish passion" from his heritage even though he is an American (87). The woman, Athanasia, is "a repressed Southern exotic," a woman whose ethnicity is an uncertain mixture but is later revealed to be Spanish as well, common in the complex society of Louisiana. They are described as "a fitting couple to seek the bayou banks"; in other words, they are lovers seeking the peace of nature, the "tideless waters" and the reeds swaying in the breeze. It is here that their affection expresses itself, as "dark eyes" look into "dark eyes," and "Iberian fire into Iberian fire, soul into soul" (88). They embrace and talk of the future until the gentleman reveals that he is going to Europe and she should forget about him. It is here that the name "Athanasia" gains significance because within Catholicism the Greek Saint Athanasia of Aegina was widowed at an early age and became a nun; the suggestion is that this young woman may have to do the same. The young woman's grief is expressed in nature, the pathetic fallacy of the "drizzling mist" that grows cold and "the sobbing wind more pronounced in its prophetic wail" (90). There is no further action in the scene, but none is required.

The conclusion reflects the lyrical impressionism of the opening even though it takes place years later, when the bayou continues to flow, concealing its "hidden passions," one of which would seem to be the lingering love Athanasia still feels for her lover. The consolation comes in the beauty of nature, the song of the mockingbird, the chirp of the cricket, the orange and magnolia blossoms that are beautiful in smell and appearance. Somehow, the bayou has taken into its waters her "broken-hearted romance," another love thwarted, and yet it flows "dispassionately," unconcerned with the human heart.

Another broken heart on the bayou is Louisette's in "When the Bayou Overflows" (95–107), a standard romance tragedy that ends with the death of her lover three hours before his train arrives home. The setting is on the Bayou Teche, which snakes its way south from Port Barre to Patterson, with specific action near Franklin in St. Mary Parish. The romance is once again interethnic: Louisette is a young woman of color; her lover, Sylvester, is described as Cajun, "tall and slim and agile," yet another ethnic population represented in the volume. He and his mother, Ma'am Mouton, a long-suffering matriarch, speak and write in French. But the conflict is not ethnic but financial. The young lovers wish to marry, but they have no economic future. Sylvester decides to go to Chicago and make money rolling cigars and to return with a diamond ring when the bayou overflows in the spring. Ordinarily, he works in the winter in the cigar industry in New Orleans, but, as he explains, "I don't lak' New Orleans; it too near here, dere no mo' money dere" (97). Bayou Teche is a hundred miles west of the Crescent City, so Sylvester would be gone much of the winter in any event, he reasons, and there is much more money to be made in the North. Ma'am Mouton thinks of the windy city only in negative terms, a "misty wicked city, a thousand miles away" (101). Accessible by water up the Mississippi and the Illinois, Chicago had become a common destination for adventurous young men from bayou country.

Sylvester leaves home in October and thrives in Chicago with the help of a local friend, Joseph Lascaud, whose name suggests he is a Creole of color. Winter and early spring pass without incident, although Sylvester's letter home reveals that he is ill, foreshadowing the conclusion, when the two women come to the station to welcome him home and he arrives, dead, with Lascaud's explanation that he died three hours earlier, wanting to give Louisette her diamond ring. There is more romantic loss than fulfillment in Dunbar-Nelson's stories, more pain than joy, more disillusionment than psychological growth.

"Mr. Baptiste" (111–24) also ends with the death of the protagonist in another story with a rich historical background. Characteristic of Dunbar-Nelson's fiction, plot is not the central element: Mr. Baptiste is a street person in New Orleans who lives by gathering partially spoiled fruit from the ships and bringing it to the housewives in the area, who feed him in return. Caught up in a longshoreman strike on the docks, he is killed by a thrown rock and buried in a pauper's grave. On this level, the theme would seem to deal with the indifference of society and the cruelty of the vicissitudes of life. But behind the action there are a host of elements that add depth and interest.

"Mr. Baptiste" is a curious name since "Mr." denotes an American and "Baptiste" someone of French extraction. It is possible that he is simply French but has been in the country long enough to have dropped "M'sieu" in favor of the English appellation.[25] However, he never refers to himself in this way; Mr. Baptiste is what others call him, and the point of view is allied with the community perspective. That narrative stance is complex since it is a plural entity that seems to constitute the generalized view of events, knowing some things and not others (the narrator is not aware of how Baptiste came to have his name, for example), yet providing the best speculation about a curious fellow in their midst. He is described as not only "Creole" but "Latinized," suggesting that he is simply an impoverished white man who haunts the wharfs. It is, of course, possible, but not definite, that he is a Creole of color, as several scholars have assumed, but that is not confirmed by the text.[26] The best evidence supporting that assumption is his dialect, a mixture of French and English vernacular, but the linguistic differences between poor whites and people of color in the wharf areas of New Orleans were not great. Indeed, the Irish dockworkers regard him as a white Frenchman, as McMahon's comments make clear, and no racial animus erupts between him and the strikers. Rather, they object to his support for the black "scabs" who have taken their jobs, a historical situation of considerable interest.

The early section of the story establishes the personality of Baptiste, his daily habits, his innocuous life, his impoverishment. He is concerned that the new emphasis on shipping cotton will drive out the fruit trade and his means of survival will be in jeopardy. Indeed, he reports to Madame Garcia, whose ancestry would seem to be Spanish, that "dose 'longsho'mans, dey go out on one strike. Dey t'row down dey tool an' say dey work no mo' wid niggers" (115). Baptiste's account suggests a racial conflict at the basis of the strike, one emanating from simple prejudice, and in the course of the action it escalates into a major confrontation.

Dunbar-Nelson's portrayal of this plot element is based on an actual event, one she would have known about, perhaps even witnessed, since it resulted in the death of a man on the docks.[27] As Jürgen Grant has outlined, the event at issue is the longshoreman strike in New Orleans in 1894, during the time the author was teaching in the city.[28] Both black and white workers had been unionized by this time, with the agreement that there were to be standard wages and no pay differential among the races, in return for which the unions established that there would be no more than one hundred black workers on the docks at any one time. This framework guided a reasonably harmonious ethnic relationship among the longshoremen for more than a decade, despite the increasing number of Irish and Italian immigrants streaming into the city. With the financial crisis of 1893, which sank the entire country into a period of depression, hard-pressed companies began hiring large numbers of black laborers below union rates, and one shipping firm declared it would hire only African-American laborers. The white unions went on strike; a violent confrontation ensued on the docks; and one black dockworker, J. Gordon Taylor, lost his life when he dove into the river to escape injury.[29] "Mr. Baptiste" reduces the causative history of the strike to simple racial animus, when actually it was socially and financially multifaceted and based on polarizing employment issues.

When Baptiste walks along the wharf, observing that the fruit is spoiling and not being unloaded, he is confronted by an "Irishman" who declares that his only concern is the cotton cargo (118). The rhythmic song of black workers at their labors echoes along the water, and Finnegan leads his men in an attack on the interlopers working on the White Star steamer. This line, which produced enormous ships, including the *Titanic* a decade later, was famous for the volume of goods and passengers that could be hauled at one time, a perfect cargo for which was cotton. The confrontation generates racial hatred, although the violence is limited to the throwing of bricks and wood, not to shooting. Baptiste is not directly involved, although he cheers on the black workers, having no particular love for the Irish. McMahon throws a rock at him, and he is struck just before the militia moves in to quell the confrontation. He is buried in an unmarked grave in a cemetery for the poor.

"The Fisherman of Pass Christian" (37–64) further expands the negative themes of romance and marriage as well as the setting for the action. Although the key opera scenes take place in New Orleans, the outdoor activity is at Pass Christian, a resort community for wealthy Creoles in Harrison County, Mississippi, on the Gulf of Mexico. The name derives from 1746 when the deepwater pass into the harbor was named for Nicholas Christian L'Adnier, and it quickly became a recreation destination for the rich. The first yacht club in the South was formed there in 1849, for example, and it was an easy sail from the Crescent City.

Although the characters are not designated by ethnic category, they would seem to be white Creoles of considerable means, given their capacity for leisure and travel. The protagonist, a young woman named Annette, speaks fluent French and has plans to visit Paris in the near future. Her cousin, Philip, who has a proprietary interest in her, seems cut from the same social cloth. They are familiar with the cuisine at Henderson's Point on the Bay of St. Louis, and they move as easily in resort society as they do at the opera in the city. When Annette meets Monsieur LeConte, a tenor she takes to be a fisherman, she is impressed by his strength and character. Quickly drawn to him, she is open to his advances, especially when he "began to dance attendance on Annette" (53). She sails with him, walks hand in hand on the beach, and is smitten with adolescent infatuation.

But the situation takes an abrupt shift when she returns to New Orleans with her family and they attend the opening of the opera season with Eugène Scribe's *La Juive*, a popular work brought in from Paris. It deals with the forbidden romance between a Jewish woman and a Christian gentleman, an interesting subject for postbellum New Orleans, since Jews had been excluded from the state under the *Code Noir*, a law changed only after the conclusion of the Civil War. Annette is astonished to discover that her simple fisherman from Pass Christian is playing the lead role of Eléazar. The theme of the opera deals with religious tolerance, as does another later in the season, Giacomo Meyerbeer's *Les Huguenots*, which also stars LeConte. Historically, that opera opened in Paris in 1836 before coming to New Orleans for its American debut in April of 1839, and its revival began the season in New Orleans in October of 1893, the year of the action.[30]

In both roles, LeConte is a sensation, and it deepens Annette's devotion to him. The theme of these works would seem to suggest that perhaps there is an ethnic divide between her and LeConte that presents an insurmountable obstacle to their marriage, but there is no confirmation in the text of any such issue. Other presentations of the season also deal with tragic romance, as does Gaetano Donizetti's *La Favorite*, which would have been appropriate since in the nineteenth century its libretto was in French. It ends with the heroine dying in the arms of her lover. But none of these issues seem to be the problem between Annette and LeConte. Rather, his romance with the leading soprano, Madame Dubeau, is of greater moment, for she "was beautiful and gifted and charming" (62). Annette is crushed when she learns that they were recently married, and another of Dunbar-Nelson's romance plots ends in disappointment.

"M'sieu Fortier's Violin" (67–82) is a typical story in which the plot is less important than the cultural environment and the values of the characters. Dunbar-Nelson, of course, had a personal interest in classical music: as she assessed her own artistic abilities in a letter to Paul Laurence Dunbar, "I don't draw, but a little, I don't paint; I only sing in choruses and in the school room with my children; I play the mandolin, I am studying the violoncello."[31] She is also said to have played the piano and to have attended the French Opera House in New Orleans on a regular basis. Since it was perhaps the major cultural location in the entire city, and her family attended regularly, she would have known about the historical background upon which she built Fortier's situation.

The plot is extremely simple in a logistical sense: Fortier is an elderly man who plays the violin in the orchestra at the opera house. In the wake of a change of management, he loses his position, suffers financially, and accepts an offer to sell his violin to a wealthy "American" collector. He finds he cannot live without his beloved music and appeals for the return of his violin, and the American, Courcey, gives it back to him, allowing him to keep the payment for it as well. Although the plot presents conflict and resolution, it is a simplistic narrative if separated from a local knowledge of New Orleans society. In context it is an important historical document that preserves a moment of transition in the musical life of the city.

The French Opera House was built in 1859 on the corner of Bourbon and Toulouse Streets in a French design reflecting its close connection to Parisian musical traditions. Seating three thousand, it was the largest theater in the United States and immensely popular among all social categories throughout New Orleans.[32] As Dunbar-Nelson remarked in "People of Color of Louisiana," "the French Opera House was the first place in the country where grand opera was heard, and tell [*sic*] of the tiers of beautiful women with their jewels and airs and graces. Above the orchestra circle were four tiers, the first filled with the beautiful dames of the city; the second filled with a second array of beautiful women, attired like those of the first, with no apparent difference; yet these were the octoroons and quadroons, whose beauty and wealth were all the passports needed."[33] The top tiers were less expensive, occupied by the working class, and reserved for people of color, with the gradation of blackness increasing with height. But people throughout the social stratification of the city enjoyed the music, which often featured musicians and compositions imported from Paris.

A brilliant young woman, Dunbar-Nelson would have been aware of all the major transformations in the cultural life of her home city, and she used a well-known situation with the opera company as the precipitating circumstance for the conflict. Into its fourth decade of operation, the opera house was experiencing financial difficulties, in part because of a general economic downturn. As a result, the company was sold to an American syndicate, the Opera Guarantee Association, which had been established in October of 1893. That organization, pledging to run the operation on a business basis, fired the manager of the French Opera, Frederick Maugé, and a new director was brought in along with a new assemblage of musicians.[34] That is the very moment at issue in the story, as Fortier, an older violinist, has been replaced by a younger player.

Fortier's situation may have been based on the career of Edmond Dédé, a celebrated violinist with the opera who made cigars in the off-season, as does the protagonist.[35] It was not unknown for musicians to take other jobs during the long hiatus between seasons, and Dunbar-Nelson would have been aware of him and the amazing dexterity of his hands. She may have taken the name "Fortier" from a prominent New Orleans citizen, Alcée Fortier, who founded the local Association of the American Folklore Society, which was very active in the 1890s.[36] But the depth of the narrative, Fortier's deep devotion to his music, his financial circumstances, his conflict in relinquishing his beloved instrument, his dialect, domestic situation, and character are all invented and handled with impressive subtlety.

The story opens with the opera house closing for the evening and the darkness in what had been a glittering hall of light and music displaying wealth and beauty, especially on the part of elite women of the city. Their carriages and footmen arrive at the Bourbon Street exit to collect the "cloaked society" and carry them home in comfort. But the audience also consisted of a more bourgeois entity, the pedestrians who come out the Toulouse Street door from the cheaper seats in the *troisièmes* and *quartièmes* and walk through the night humming phrases from the arias they have enjoyed (68). These are people of color assigned to the balconies but who nonetheless participate in urban cultural life.

The description of Fortier emphasizes his age, not his ethnicity, which would seem to be French but is not explicitly delineated. An "old man," he has grey hair and, more importantly, "aged, trembling, nervous fingers," a disadvantage in his profession. He is apparently of the lower economic echelon in that he walks home in his "faded brown overcoat," exchanging a "hearty salutation" with the bartender, whom he seems to know well (69). His path is precisely outlined as he walks down Bourbon Street to his home on Bayou Road near Claiborne. This street leads to the French settlements on Bayou St. John, further suggesting, as does his name, that he and his wife, Ma'am Jeanne, belong in that ethnic enclave.

The evening of his quiet walk home had featured a benefit concert at the opera house, a tradition, as Robert Clark explains, that survived many decades in New Orleans. On the concluding night of a running show, a special performance would be held with the proceeds going to the principal singer, in this case "the leading tenor." Here Dunbar-Nelson reaches back to the year before the time of her action, to 1892, when, for his concluding performance Monsieur Paulin sang the lead in *Roland à Ronceveaux* to a tumultuous reception, especially for the aria "Superbes Pyrenées," the very piece Fortier sings to himself on his walk (72). That opera would have special meaning for an audience of French extraction in that it is based upon *Chanson de Roland*, central to the perpetuation of the mythology surrounding Charlemagne. It recounts a tragic encounter in 778 AD when the campaign against the Saracens in Spain failed and the retreating French forces, defended by Roland, were slaughtered in the Pyrenees in the area of Roncesvalles.[37] Enlarged over the centuries into epic stature, and celebrated throughout the Western world, the tragic retreat through the mountains has been used as the subject of poems, operas, and works of fiction. Through the allusion to the opera, Dunbar-Nelson incorporates this reference to the classic myth into her simple story of Fortier and his violin, deepening his connection to French ancestry.

In the midst of his journey home, he encounters Courcey, an American who wishes to buy his violin, and his friend Martel, who thinks it an empty extravagance. When Courcey asks about it, Fortier replies "Me a lovere, and to sell mon violon! Ah, so ver' foolish!" (73), revealing his localized dialect as well as his values. The narrative then shifts to follow the two Americans rather than Fortier. Even the name of Courcey's friend has allusive significance, for "Martel" derives from Charlemagne's grandfather, Charles Martel, drawing the action even further into "The Song of Roland."[38] Courcey refers to Fortier as "that little Frenchman" he met on his walks through French-town. He describes the violin as "beautiful and mellow as a genuine Cremona," which music lovers in the nineteenth century would have understood. The town of Cremona, Italy, was the home of Antonio Stradivari and was famous for the creation of the world's best stringed instruments. In effect, Fortier owns an instrument he values as much as a Stradivarius, and Courcey wishes to buy it for fifty dollars. For his part, Martel, knowing his friend well, is certain that it means no more to him than a souvenir he can deface. What is at issue is the American world of wealth and commerce in conflict with the French realm of culture and tradition. Fortier treasures his instrument for its sound, for the artistic dimension of his life, for his connection to the opera. Courcey sees it as an artifact; he does not play the violin and only wishes to display it, "own" it as another of his possessions. This confrontation between commerce and culture persisted throughout the nineteenth century in New Orleans, testifying to the difficulties of reconciling the value of aesthetics with the acquisitive instinct of a moneyed society.

The central scene is domestic, Fortier at home on Bayou Road in his "quaint little house" with his wife, Jeanne, and a white cat named Minesse. To supplement his musical income in the off-season, he rolls cigars, using his natural dexterity and fine hands to do a delicate job. The thematic significance is the diminished circumstances of the family: Jeanne has grown deaf over the years, and there is no verbal communication with her, so Fortier talks to the cat. He confesses that he is getting on in years, able to make only half as many cigars as previously. Their impoverishment provides the impetus for the subsequent action, which intensifies when Maugé is fired as manager of the opera and an American syndicate takes control, promising to function on a "strictly financial basis" (76). As a result, the aging Fortier is also fired, as he explains to his cat: "Minesse, we mus' go hungry sometime. Ah, mon pauvre violon!" (77). Nonetheless, despite his limited means, he pays admission to attend the opera, and as his finances decline he sits in cheaper sections, beginning with the front row in the deuxièmes, then the fourth row, and then the rear. In due course he climbs the stairs to sit in the third balcony, the troisièmes, where he feels at home among the common people. But he refuses to sit on the fourth level, the quatrièmes, that was customarily the black section, so he waits outside the hall on Toulouse Street, listening as best he can and watching the crowd exit. It is there that Courcey offers him fifty dollars again and, reduced to extreme poverty, Fortier accepts.

This transaction, and its aftermath, form the conclusion of the plot, sorting out the values of the characters involved. Courcey is wealthy and collects interesting possessions. His friend Martel sees the violin in a broader context and grumbles "at the essentially sordid, mercenary spirit of the world," feeling that an important transgression has occurred in taking an instrument from a man who loves it so deeply (81). Fortier retains his dignity, seeing them out with an "old-time French courtliness" that hides his despair. But Fortier feels he has "done sol' my child," and six days later he seeks Courcey out, offering to return the money. The American gives him back the violin and allows him to keep the fifty dollars as well, indicating that he has come to realize how much "passion" the Frenchman has invested in it.

This simple plot raises several important issues in the life of New Orleans, however. Among those is the vestigial importance of the arts in society as manifest in the opera house, a tradition enriched by its European past. Fortier's placement in the audience during his impoverishment reveals the stratification of society based on race and wealth, as does the means of conveyance to the theater. The idea that a poor man could value music above all else is a statement in the Hellenism versus Hebraism debate that raged throughout the second half of the nineteenth century, primarily in Europe. Lost in these issues is the unfortunate fact that Fortier's circumstances have not changed: he is still not employed by the opera, and he can earn only the most meager of livings from making cigars. He can continue to play the violin, but only for himself (his wife is deaf) and his cat, and there is no suggestion that his circumstances will ever be improved.[39]

Another character caught in implacable circumstances is Camille in "Sister Josepha" (155–72), a young woman of light color who, at the age of three, was left at the Sacred Heart Academy to be raised in the convent. Although the school is portrayed in terms of confinement and restriction, a half-life for an attractive young girl, the New Orleans Sacré Coeur was a famous school. Founded in 1886, it would have been in its growing phase during the composition of the story, but it was still a formidable academy, with hundreds of students and an imposing edifice set back from St. Charles Street. It is a short walk to St. Louis Cathedral, a sojourn that would allow the students to observe the vibrant life of a secular Crescent City, a matter at issue for young Camille.

Her name would have seemed ironic in the 1890s in the French culture of Louisiana since the most famous novel of the time was Alexandre Dumas's *La Dame aux camellias* of 1848, which quickly became a play translated into English under the title *Camille*. In 1853 it also appeared as a famous opera, Giuseppe Verdi's *La Traviata*. In all of these forms it is essentially the story of a romantic courtesan who suffers and dies from tuberculosis, leaving to grieve an innocent young man who has fallen in love with her. Her willingness to dismiss him to save his family from the taint of her reputation is a transcending and redemptive conclusion to the ending. That Dunbar-Nelson gave her innocent protagonist the same name would have raised eyebrows and created false expectations for the resolution of her simple plot. The short story begins with the revelation that the protagonist is not devout since she nods during prayers and is clearly interested in the outside world rather than the spiritual isolation of the convent. The narrator describes her as a beautiful, French-speaking young woman of color, with "brown hands" and a "rosy mouth" beneath her "black eyes" (157). Her name, "Camille," means "altar server," a functional entity in obeisance to a larger, more powerful, clerical structure, and so she seems destined to be. A flashback reaches back fifteen years to record the moment in her infancy when she was left at the convent with no record of her background, and she grew to be a "tropical beauty" who dominates the other girls and even some of the nuns. The rest of the plot revolves around two crucial decisions that Camille must make, both of them drawing on her status as a foundling and involving a sexual threat from the outside world, a startling conflict for one so innocent of secular society.

A key scene occurs in a flashback to a moment when she was fifteen and a couple offered to adopt her, a common circumstance in an institution for abandoned children. Although she has been sheltered from the profane world, Camille's instincts shy away from the "leers" of the gentleman and his "admiration of her physical charms," and she chooses not to leave with them (159). She is clearly aware of the sexual interest his attitude implies, and it frightens her. Kristina Brooks describes the decision as her desire to "avoid the institutionalized sexual victimization of *plaçage*."[40] It would certainly seem reasonable to assume that Camille is a young woman of color, but Brooks seems to misunderstand the long tradition of taking mistresses in Louisiana: a plaçage arrangement, in such a case, would not have been sanctioned by a judge, which was required as part of this complex tradition. The leers of the gentleman in question may well be sexual in nature, especially given Camille's apparent beauty, but his intentions would not have involved a formal plaçage commitment.

Her decision to stay in the convent leads to her status as a novitiate at sixteen and to the major conflict she faces two years later at the time of the action. Camille is drawn to the holy orders of the sisters she admires, but she is tempted by what she observes during her walks to St. Louis Cathedral, during which she could observe the vibrant life in Jackson Square, earlier known as the Place d'Armes in the French Quarter. The young woman clearly desires the activity of a wider world, but she is frightened by the secularization of society and her status in it as a woman of color. This section emphasizes her fascination for the young man in the military uniform who gazes upon her, and she is tempted to "flee into the world" and live a more active life. However, the night before her final vows, she overhears a conversation between Sisters Dominica and Francesca, who is sensitive to how confining convent life can be, and she suggests that Camille needs a more expansive environment. Sister Dominica, however, observes that the young girl has no identity other than within the church, no nationality, no certainty about her ethnic background, and only her beauty to aid her (171). Camille reflects on what she has heard, and, with a sob, withdraws behind the "heavy door" of the convent for the rest of her life. This plot line may well have been based on the life of Henriette Delille, who faced the possibility of a life as the mistress of a white man and chose instead to become a nun. She went on to found the Sisters of the Holy Family, an order for women of color within the church. She became famous for her good work and, after her death, was elevated to sainthood in 2010 for her lifetime of dedication.[41]

"Odalie" (183–91) is a companion story dealing with similar themes and ending with a young woman's decision to become a nun. A plot that ends in religious devotion begins with the most secular of celebrations, Mardi Gras. The narrator presents a rich evocation of "a pot-pourri of every conceivable human ingredient" in New Orleans for the joyous carnival, and yet there lingers the memory of the sad account of Odalie, a beautiful young woman who fell in love with a young man who did not know her feelings for him.[42] She was the daughter of a judge and lived in a French house on Royal Street, directly in the center of the French Quarter. She was educated by the Ursulines, an ancient order founded in 1535 in Italy for the education of girls. Her school, the Ursuline Academy in New Orleans, was established in 1727, the oldest school for young women in the United States, and was thus a suitably prestigious institution for the beautiful daughter of a judge. After graduation she lived at home in "convent-like seclusion," a description that adumbrates her final decision. Her duenna, aunt Louise, keeps "faithful watch" over her lest she should meet young men, but she encounters Pierre regularly at Mass, and one day their fingers touch in the holy water font, generating an all-encompassing infatuation.

During Mardi Gras, she observes Pierre dancing with a merry throng of young people, and he has his arm around the waist of an attractive young "butterfly." Odalie is stricken, unable to deal with what she perceives as betrayal, and she retreated into her home and "nursed her dear dead love" (190). After a time, unable to deal with the outside world, she asks to be taken to the convent to become a nun, and the story ends. Had she had some experience with secular life, with the normative interactions with young men of her age, and the constant shifting of attention and flirtation, she could easily have taken this minor betrayal in stride and either attempted to win over the attentions of her beloved, as does Manuela in "The Goodness of Saint Rocque," or abandoned her fantasy of innocent love for a genuine relationship with someone else. The innocence of the protected world she lived in at the convent and then at her overly restricted home has left her vulnerable to the most ordinary of adolescent affections, and her life is ruined as a result.

Although Dunbar-Nelson has sometimes been criticized for her unwillingness to write in dialect, a strong feature of her first husband's verse, "The Praline Woman" (175–79) demonstrates that she was fully capable of handling the vernacular when she chose to do so. A brief tour de force of language, this story is essentially a dramatic monologue in the patter of a street peddler who reveals herself and her life as she attempts to entice the crowds who pass by on Royal Street, one of the oldest in New Orleans and the location of numerous antique shops and art galleries in the French Quarter. Although there is an expository paragraph by an abstract narrator establishing the scene, and another reporting the ringing of the chimes in the cathedral, the bulk of the story is the hawking prattle of the woman who sells pralines made by her adopted daughter, Didele. The woman, Tante Marie, reveals her values, past events, and family tragedies as she speaks to potential customers. She would seem to be a Creole of color given her dialect, a mixture of African, French, and English common in the black community, and she exhibits considerable persuasive skill as she charms or abuses the crowd depending on their interest in her pralines.

She attempts to persuade a white woman to buy by stressing that her "chile, ma bébé" made the candies with her hands, which are "brune." Her adopted daughter is apparently also a person of color. When the white woman simply passes by, Tante Marie throws a playful curse after her: "No husband fo' you den!" (175). But she is not only vindictive; she can also exhibit piety, compassion, and ethnic prejudice, which she feels for the "Indien squaw" and the Irish. She presents the priest with a free praline, perhaps a theological insurance policy, which causes her to remember her unanswered prayers in St. Rocque's Chapel for her dying son. She is uncomfortable about white people, especially those from the North. Her monologue reveals that the time of the action is post–Civil War since she refers to "dose Yankee dat come down 'fo' de war" (176). Although she has no husband, she has lost two children, a daughter to yellow fever and a son to unknown causes (178). Her surrogate child is Didele, whom she found homeless on the street. In a sense her monologue is a slice of life on Royal Street, a revelation of commonplace characters in emotionally complex circumstances, with the dramatic conflict primarily in the background.

As individual works of fiction, Dunbar-Nelson's stories vary in technique and theme but exhibit an impressive artistic capability, from the linguistic richness of "The Praline Woman" to the evocation of New Orleans culture in "The Goodness of Saint Rocque," the historical context of "Mr. Baptiste," the gender restrictions of "Tony's Wife" and "Little Miss Sophie," and the religious background of "Sister Josepha" and "Odalie." Within this variety, a spectrum of dialects and ethnic values emerge to energize the fabric of the local society, from the Italian and German characters in "Tony's Wife" to the French Creole protagonist in "M'sieu Fortier's Violin" to the conflict between the Spanish and French young women competing for the same beau in "The Goodness of Saint Rocque." Dunbar-Nelson is skillful in portraying the physical features of the city and the surrounding bayous and brilliant in capturing the localized ethic in each quarter of the Crescent City.

Gloria Hull certainly offers a questionable judgment in her contention that Dunbar-Nelson used "conventional concepts of form, genre, and propriety that (given her lack of creative genius) bound her to divisiveness and inarticulation."[43] In her detailed presentation of Louisiana culture, she may be seen as part of the Local-Color movement, but she was the first African-American writer to depict the rich interactions of ethnic groups within the matrix of differing languages, religions, traditions, and fundamental values that so enlivened New Orleans at the end of the nineteenth century. As Pamela Menke has said, Dunbar-Nelson presents "a riot of colors and customs and ethnic multiplicity: Creole, Spanish, French, Irish, Black, white. As an African-descent, Creole woman, Dunbar-Nelson stands alone in her contributions to Southern local color."[44] For those reasons alone, her work is a considerable contribution to the fiction of the United States.

But beyond the merits of the individual stories, as a group they constitute an impressive cycle of interrelated works of short fiction. The rich historical atmosphere of New Orleans informs all of the episodes, drawing them together into an evocation of a dynamic culture with a strong appreciation of the arts, family traditions, ethnic ties, and racial conflicts. Indeed, the action takes place against a crucial historical framework without which the conflicts cannot be fully understood: the racial nature of the accommodations the unions made for dockworkers behind "Mr. Baptiste," for example, or the change in management of the French Opera House in "M'sieu Fortier's Violin," or the lingering values of plaçage arrangements that explain the emotional drama in "Little Miss Sophie." These background issues are not directly explained in the volume, but they are central to the conflicts that play out in the stories.

Another aspect of unification is point of view, a communal perspective that presents what is understood or said in the neighborhood, a method used in all but "The Praline Woman." This voice is informed, kindly, but limited in knowledge, sometimes presenting erroneous gossip rather than omniscient observations. The narrative intelligence is wise in the customs and values of the various districts of the city and is permitted access to the mind of the protagonist, but what is presented is laden with speculation rather than fact, with probabilities rather than certainties, with what could be desired rather than achieved. This local, "humanized," perspective is another element that unites the stories in the volume, giving them the flavor of normative life in the community.

The volume is also unified thematically, drawing stories into patterns of ideas, creating resonance based on local traditions and prototypical conflicts in New Orleans social life. Beyond the more generalized background issues of ethnic mixture and Creole values, romance emerges as a prominent central plot device in many of these stories. Of these, only "The Goodness of Saint Rocque" and "La Juanita" end happily, with a loving couple together at the conclusion. More typical is the tragic ending, with the death of one of the young lovers or the brutal rejection of a faithful devotee, as in "Little Miss Sophie." "By the Bayou St. John," "When the Bayou Overflows," and "The Fisherman of Pass Christian" also end in heartache for the passionate young woman, whereas "Tony's Wife" portrays an even more devastating outcome, the unwise marriage to a man who is abusive, demeaning, and cruelly dismissive. There is little depth to courtship in Dunbar-Nelson's fiction and virtually no satisfaction or fulfillment in its fruition. Couples are not portrayed happily wed with healthy families, nor do they exhibit sustained affection or deepening alliances based on shared experiences. Romance is largely a matter of appearances, social stature, or limited alternatives, not mature choices or common values.

Related to romance, the motif of sexual threat looms in the lives of some of the young women characters, as it does in the potential adoptive father in "Sister Josepha" or in the vague innocence of Odalie, who dares not face the complex world of courtship she does not understand. Both young women retreat into the convent as an escape from secular life, not as a devotion to faith. Ethnic issues are partially behind Josepha's decision since she is of indeterminate ethnicity but slightly olive in complexion, suggesting a mixed-racial background, making her suitable to white Creole society as a concubine. The death of Mr. Baptiste is the result of ethnic confrontation, but it is ironic in his case because he seems not to be black even though he supports the cause of the African-American dock workers. In "A Carnival Jangle" the death of Flo is the result of misidentification during Mardi Gras, with the potential for fatal violence looming ironically amid joyous celebration. "M'sieu Fortier's Violin" concludes more positively with the return of the instrument, but the protagonist's diminished circumstances have not been substantially altered and an impoverished future awaits him. In one sense the speaker in "The Praline Woman" presents the most positive case, with a robust personality that has persevered through domestic tragedy. Through the indirection inherent in her street chatter, hawking her wares, she reveals a rich personal history within the complex ethnic community of the Crescent City, and she has survived with a new family based on love and mutual support. Among all of the characters in *The Goodness of Saint Rocque and Other Stories*, she emerges as the most stalwart and resourceful of all, a woman of great emotional depth and personal substance who is financially only on the periphery of Louisiana society.

4
Kate Chopin's *Bayou Folk*

Until the 1970s, when *The Awakening* emerged from relative obscurity to become a major American novel, Kate Chopin's reputation rested solidly on her first collection of stories, *Bayou Folk*, published in 1894 by Houghton Mifflin.[1] By then she had already developed a national following for her short fiction in the leading magazines, including the *Atlantic Monthly*, *Vogue*, and *Century*, so a well-designed, integrated collection of Louisiana tales was heralded as an important contribution, despite a certain amount of misinformation appearing in the notices. An anonymous reviewer for *Current Literature*, for example, reported that "Mrs. Chopin herself is a Creole and has lived much of her life in New Orleans and on her Natchitoches plantation."[2] In fact, before her wedding to Oscar Chopin, Kate O'Flaherty lived in St. Louis, the city of her birth in 1850, but upon her marriage to a Creole, Oscar Chopin, she moved to the Crescent City in 1870, living there for most of that decade before moving for five years to Cloutierville, in Natchitoches Parish, in the northwestern part of the state. Then, having set the family financial affairs in order after the death of her husband, Chopin returned to her native Missouri in 1884, having never published a word of fiction. It is remarkable that all of her impressive Louisiana fiction, complete with detailed descriptions, street addresses, and accurate historical references, were written when she was no longer living in the state.[3]

But the reviews also contained many insightful remarks, including the widespread observation that Chopin's emphasis on the folkways, dialects, and unique social customs of her settings placed her firmly in the Local-Color school of American fiction, which was being celebrated as an important new development. Hamlin Garland had described the movement as the first truly indigenous approach to literature, one that captured not only the regional locations but the character of the American people, their conflicts and triumphs, their approach to life, the meaning of their lives.[4] But some commentators went beyond remarking on regional aspects, as did Maibelle Justice, in saying that the book was "a collection of short stories distinguished by crispness of dialogue, teemed with charm and tenderness, and glowing with all the intensity and passion of the Creole race. There is not a dull page in the book, for the simple reason that the author knows how to tell a story and is able to gauge her speed by the nature of her events."[5] But Chopin was not much impressed by the depth of the reviews, writing to herself in her "Impressions" diary that "in looking over more than a hundred press notices of *Bayou Folk* which have already been sent to me, I am surprised at the very small number which show anything like a worthy critical faculty. They might be counted on the fingers of one hand. I had no idea the genuine book critic was so rare a bird."[6] Indeed, there was much about the volume that even the most insightful initial readings failed to realize, beginning with the fact that the twenty-three stories are tightly unified by setting, theme, characterization, and a host of subtle regional issues that provide an overarching form and significance to the volume, making it truly a story cycle.

For example, the first three stories in *Bayou Folk* all involve the Santien brothers, including background references to the historic circumstance that the Santien place on the Red River in Natchitoches Parish once belonged to the family. A proud Creole, Lucien Santien founded this plantation of over a thousand acres in the early nineteenth century and farmed it with some one hundred slaves, amassing considerable wealth in the process. When his son Jules assumed control of the property, the Civil War erupted and the value of the land was diminished. Southerners tended to transfer their wealth to Confederate currency, which became worthless during Reconstruction, and the loss of the slaves removed the Santiens' most valuable asset. Beset with inheritance taxes, a legacy of debt, and the division of the remaining assets among three brothers, the plantation fell behind on the payment of the mortgage and was taken over by their creditor, Harding & Offdean of New Orleans. That is the situation at the opening of "A No-Account Creole," in which Placide Santien, working as a painter and carpenter, when he can find employment, is engaged to the daughter of the current caretaker of the plantation.[7]

Placide is not the protagonist of the story, but the title makes specific reference to his decision to renounce his engagement to ensure the happiness of his beloved. He thus saves his pride, behaves honorably, and, knowing that she loves another, retains his sense of Creole manhood. When it was first written, however, the title referred to his love interest, and it was variously "Euphrasie's Lovers" or "A Maid and Her Lovers."[8] One of Chopin's early stories, and one of the few heavily changed, it was composed and revised between 1888 and 1891, rejected by both *Harper's* and *Cosmopolitan* before appearing in *Century Illustrated Magazine* in January of 1894, just prior to its republication in *Bayou Folk*.[9] The principal revisions made to the original draft involved the portrait of Euphrasie, the subject of the love of both Placide and a Creole from New Orleans, Wallace Offdean, who comes to Natchitoches Parish to evaluate the status of the plantation prior to selling it. Chopin apparently felt that in the first version Euphrasie had not been drawn distinctly, for in her letter to the editor of *Century*, Richard Watson Gilder, she explained that "I have tried to convey the impression of sweetness and strength, keen sense of right, and physical charm beside. . . . I have further changed and eliminated passages that seemed to me crude; but I made no attempt to condense the story. I knew that I could not without evolving something totally different in the effort."[10] Gilder seemed pleased with the alterations, and the story was published.

Chopin's emphasis on characterization points to some central issues in the volume, for many of the characters, and personality types, return repeatedly throughout the book, including the educated, relatively wealthy, young man from the city; the attractive, country ingénue who becomes the subject of a romantic conflict; and the scion of an old plantation family that has lost its wealth and social position and has only its implacable pride with which to confront the new Southern culture wrought by Reconstruction. The Santien family is represented throughout *Bayou Folk*: Placide is the titular character in "A No-Account Creole"; his brother Gregoire is in "In Sabine"; his other brother, Hector, is featured in "In and Out of Old Natchitoches." As is common in story cycles, repeated characters are often one element of unity, and it is only in the aggregate of appearances that the full circumstances of the family can be understood.[11]

The narrative perspective is congruent with the emphasis on character in complex ways. The point of view is essentially omniscient in that there is access to the minds of several characters in a shifting pattern of viewpoints that allow for the dramatic revelation of personality through thought, speech, and action rather than by expository comment. Given Chopin's statement that she wanted to reveal more of Euphrasie, it is noteworthy that very little is shown about her innermost musing, the most important emphasis being her immediate infatuation with Offdean and the growing love for him that continues to the end. The most important revelation to come from access to the thinking of the other characters is the stress on psychological and emotional growth, especially for Offdean and Placide Santien.

The story is divided into nine numbered sections, a device Chopin used often with subtle effects. Basically, each section reveals the mental state of one person and establishes a baseline from which to chart internal conflicts and transformations. All three principal characters experience dramatic change, and each is deepened and emotionally enriched. The story opens with Wallace Offdean in New Orleans, where he is presented as a Creole businessman with a college education who belongs to a men's club and has not, at age twenty-six, established a firm sense of self. He has just lost money gambling, a traditional vice for his social class, but he has recently inherited twenty-five thousand dollars that he wishes to invest wisely, knowing that this money will define his future. The firm of Harding and Offdean (he would seem to be part owner) sends him to Natchitoches Parish on the Red River to assess the status of the old Santien place, an assignment he perceives as an opportunity to get away from the city and "take counsel with his inner and better self" (4). In large measure, the plot that follows traces his success in doing so.

The second part is similar in method but quite different in subject and theme. The narrative perspective shifts to deal with Placide Santien, and the focus is the opposite of Offdean's, whose section looks to the future: what he will do with his inheritance, how he will define himself, and what life awaits him once he gets to Natchitoches. The information about Placide speaks to the past: the glories of the old Santien place; the legacy left by Lucien, the patriarch who founded the plantation; the fallen grandeur of wealth and stature wrought by the Civil War, ineptitude, and circumstance; and the resentment for a lost world. The decaying house on the property is an emblem of the collapse of the family: there is moss growing on the roof, the land is not properly cultivated, and the slave cabins, still occupied, loom as a reminder of a sordid past of racial stratification (5–6). The Santiens are Creole to be sure, but they represent the impoverished up-country population that persists in speaking French and in clinging to a pride that is no longer supported by reality: Placide works skillfully at odd jobs, painting and doing carpentry for other people. This section also introduces a colorful character, Pierre Manton, Euphrasie's father, who speaks in heavy dialect that provides background information about his daughter. Although there is no passage that provides expository information directly, Pierre's comments reveal that his wife died when his daughter was very young and that she was raised by Mrs. Joe Duplan, a warm and generous woman on the Les Chênier plantation: "You know it's hair raise' Euphrasie sence hair po' ma die" (8). Pierre manages the property for Harding and Offdean, although without adequate resources.

The third section brings together Placide and Euphrasie, revealing that although he has lost the plantation, he has a house in Orville, one he has gradually improved anticipating his marriage to her. College educated, a fact never supported by anything he says or does, he is handsome, charming, happy, and loves her truly (11). Only eighteen, Euphrasie has been educated at the Sacred Heart Convent, as was Kate Chopin, although in St. Louis, not Louisiana. She is beautiful, with "thick chesnut waves" in her hair, and everyone loves her. Implicit in her description, however, are some unspoken suggestions: reared by Mrs. Duplan, educated in a convent, she has known very few young gentlemen, and Placide has won her heart by default. Although she has traveled with her surrogate mother to New Orleans in previous years, there is no indication those visits resulted in any courtship or even friendships, for she stays within her group, protected, isolated, innocent.

That is what sets up the development in section four when she meets Offdean and is immediately smitten, her infatuation revealed in an intense narrative identification with her mind (20). For his part, Placide does not like the stranger and calls him a "Yankee," to which Euphrasie corrects him by saying that Offdean is a Southerner from New Orleans. The suggestion is that there is a family resentment of Reconstruction, when Northerners came to the region either as soldiers or as carpetbaggers seeking cheap land. Intruders came from the North, in Placide's mind, and he despises them: they brought about the collapse of his family. The point of view plays a key role in another dimension in this part in that Placide and Euphrasie converse in French, which is translated into standard English by the narrator. When the two speak in English, it is given in regional dialect. Euphrasie reassures her intended by saying "of co'se I love you, Placide. Ain't I going to marry you nex' spring?" (19). But behind this expression of loyalty there is a growing complication.

The situation is best revealed in the next part by a black woman, La Chatte (the cat), who plays the role of the wise commentator on the romance. As two weeks go by and the relationships deepen, she observes Offdean: "Dat young man, ef he want to listen to me, he gwine quit dat ar caperin' roun' Miss 'Phrasie" (21). Part of her concern is that, as his surrogate mother, she knows Placide well; she feels affection for him despite the fact that he once pointed a gun at her and insisted that she cook for him. Her comments introduce elements important later: that Placide can be violent, that he possesses a gun, that he is willing to take a human life. Those facts later resonate in the conclusion of the romantic triangle. This conflict is temporarily averted, however, when Offdean is called back to New Orleans on business, and Euphrasie and Placide both follow to be part of Mardi Gras.

The carnival section is replete with significant motifs but no major development of plot. For example, Offdean wants to show Euphrasie the rich culture of the city, the "day processions and night parades, balls and tableaux, operas, and plays," but he never has an opportunity. Indeed, he sees little of her (26). She stays with Mrs. Duplan's mother, Madame Carantelle, "who had not 'crossed Canal Street' for many years," a comment that marks her as a Creole conservative who still resents the Louisiana Purchase of 1803 and the establishment of an American quarter, the subject of much of Cable's fiction. Notably, the good lady speaks only French. This section involves rapid shifts of narrative identification, entering Offdean's mind to reveal his incipient love for Euphrasie and Placide's to show that he is so deeply obsessed with her that he does not even contact his brother Hector for a tour of the city. What is revealed is that when Placide kisses her, she feels that she has sinned because it is Offdean who she now loves (33).

That is the central issue of part seven, during which Placide paints his house, preparing for his wedding, which is hard upon. The narrative intelligence shifts to the perspective of the African Americans in town, who find this home improvement interesting. 'Tit-Edouard, "a strolling *maigre-échine* of indefinite occupation," comments on the development: "Look lack Placide goin' pent mo''an de fence. . . . I seen 'im, me, pesterin' wid all kine o' pent on a piece o' bo'd yistiday" (34). They are correct, but his painting is simply an externalization of deep love for Euphrasie, a point central to the ensuing conflict. Meanwhile, Offdean experiences an epiphany that clarifies matters for him considerably. He admits to himself that he is in love with her, and he forges a plan to buy the old Santien plantation with his inheritance, marry Euphrasie, and spend the rest of his life in the country: "He saw the whole delicious future which a kind fate had mapped out for him" (38). That future cannot be realized, however, without the inevitable confrontation that comes in the next section.

Offdean comes to the main house filled with his new plan and confesses his love for Euphrasie, who is to be married in only two days to Placide, who overhears this profession of affection and is enraged. When Euphrasie tells Offdean that her wedding is to be in two days, speaking in a "whisper" that sounds like a "wail," he is stunned and runs off. Placide follows him with a gun in his pocket, intending to dispatch him at the first opportunity. As he threatens to shoot him, Offdean conceives of a strategy for his defense, one that draws on a sense of Creole honor. Staring at a pistol aimed directly at him, Offdean says that "the way to love a woman is to think first of her happiness," suggesting that Euphrasie loves him and that her fulfillment can come only with her rejection of Placide. Offdean rides off, leaving the young man in a confusing internal conflict of rage, love, remorse, pride, and uncertainty: "His face was white and set with despair now. The rage had all left it as he rode deeper on into the wood" (47). It is clear that he faces one final decision.

That choice becomes obvious in a conclusion that is fraught with irony, as

Pierre totally misinterprets the series of events. Placide breaks his wedding plans on the excuse that he has to paint a house in Orville, and he leaves Euphrasie a message saying that "Placide know better 'an anybody livin' w'at goin' make her happy," thus setting her free to marry Offdean. But her father, Pierre, thinks him a scoundrel for leaving his daughter at the altar: "I yaired people say Placide was one no-'count creole. I nevair want to believe dat, me. Now I know dat's true" (48). Euphrasie understands: "Placide has saved me!" Offdean arrives to kiss her hand, and the future is clear, thanks to the "no account" Creole who has proven that even an impoverished, upcountry, common laborer possesses inherent pride and character, an idea that will surface again in the volume.

The first story in *Bayou Folk* thus introduces a spectrum of issues that resonate throughout the book, beginning with the two major locations for much of the action: New Orleans, with its rich cultural life and social stratification, and Natchitoches Parish, with its plantations, villages, and faded elegance. The people along the Cane River are not exclusively Cajuns, as is often assumed in criticism, but also Creoles who have lost their wealth in the aftermath of the Civil War. The Santiens are the embodiment of that condition: their historical position far outshines their current status. Their former slaves still live in the simple cabins they were born in, and their perspective on the lives of the principal white characters provides a narrative counterpoint to the underlying themes, as does La Chatte's commentary. The theme of faded elegance, lost legacy, and diminished lives is sadly ubiquitous in northwest Louisiana in contrast to the endless opportunities afforded in New Orleans. It is significant, when compared to Cable's stories, that by late century the Creoles of the Crescent City have adopted the mercantile values of the dreaded Yankees who arrived with the Louisiana Purchase in 1803 and again with postwar Reconstruction in 1865.

Chopin's approach to fiction is here essentially that of Local Color, with an emphasis on setting, regional dialects differentiated along ethnic lines, and localized values based on historical events. Beyond those qualities, however, is an important emphasis on psychological transformation and growth: there is a typical love triangle involving an indigenous woman and a handsome stranger from New Orleans; Euphrasie feels passion for the first time; Placide accepts personal rejection and disappointment in favor of allowing her to find fulfillment with the man she loves; Offdean discovers his inner self at the same time he realizes that his future will be with Euphrasie on the Santien plantation. An emphasis on internal character development and psychological conflict is characteristic of Chopin's best work, and it is here established in the opening story.

"In and Out of Old Natchitoches" (51–77), is less rich in psychological growth but parallels the first story in many other respects. Originally published in *Two Tales* in 1893, it once again shifts settings from Natchitoches Parish to New Orleans and back again.[12] The central plot deals with romance and an incipient triangle with two men, Hector Santien and Alphonse Laballière, competing for the attentions of the beautiful young Suzanne St. Denys Godolph. However, that plot, played out rather predictably when Suzanne discovers that Hector's reputation in the city has been compromised by his gambling, is not as complex as the historical details behind the action.

What is only vaguely suggested on the surface emerges as crucially important socially and psychologically, even though it has been little understood in most Chopin scholarship. The protagonist, Suzanne, descends from one of the antebellum aristocratic families, the Godolphs, who owned a plantation in the parish and enjoyed considerable local stature. They lost their fortune in the war and ensuing Reconstruction, retaining a small parcel of land along the bayou. Their relatives, the Santiens, suffered the same fate, the central issue of "A No-Account Creole." Eight years before the present action, Alphonse Laballière purchased a neglected plantation and moved into the area to reclaim it. It is not clear if he bought the former Godolph land, although he purchases some of their property later. Suzanne has descended socially and economically and finds employment as a teacher in the local public school, one reserved exclusively for white children. Alphonse follows her closely with his eyes as she walks to work each morning, already drawn to her delicate beauty (51–52).

For his part, after he purchased his plantation, Alphonse discovered the decaying house was occupied by the Giestins, a large mulatto family that has been working the land. Chopin here draws on her historical knowledge of the ethnic complexity of Cane River life to enrich a minor circumstance. The area was settled by a dominant population of free mulattoes, a proud segment of society that had never been slaves and who emulated the genteel agrarian life they had observed in southern Louisiana. Before the Civil War most of them lived on the Isle Brevelle, which became known as L'Isle des Mulatres because they and their slaves constituted virtually the entire population. Until the war, many of them were wealthy, owning considerable land. For example, Marie Thérèze Coincoin had an estate of twelve thousand acres and almost a hundred slaves. These Roman Catholic Creoles of color developed the same sense of stature, codes of honor, and deeply seated pride that aristocratic whites displayed in the rest of the state.[13] The irony is that emancipation brought a profound social and economic decline for this unique segment of the colored population, for Northerners did not distinguish among gradations of blackness and regarded the free mulattoes simply as generalized people of color. They thus lost the privileged positions and wealth that their families had enjoyed for generations, and one such family, the Giestins, has been reduced to living in the abandoned house that Laballière purchased.

Not unduly focused on social rank, Alphonse moves into a former slave cabin while a new house is being constructed, leaving the Giestins in the main house, where he takes his meals. Chopin does much with local rumor informing the narrative perspective, and the "people said he was entirely too much at home with the free mulattoes" and that he "had more use for a free mulattoe than he had for a white man," reflecting local views (53, 54). Interestingly, Madame Giestin is described in the imagery of royalty, being "queenly" despite her subordinate status and leaving the room "with a tread like the Empress Eugenie's in that elegant woman's palmist days," an allusion to the beautiful and stylish wife of Napoleon III. She set the standards for elegant fashion in France until the end of her husband's reign in 1870 (54, 55). Giestin does not share such elevated imagery, but his attitudes show selfless concern for Laballière's reputation, and he suggests that the family should leave the plantation: "I reckon I tell you; it's betta you git shed o' me en' my family. Jis like you want, yas" (54). But Alphonse wants no such thing, asserting his right of free association and insisting they all have breakfast at the same table. Later, he brings young André Giestin to the school on his property and insists that the teacher, Suzanne, enroll him as a regular student (57). Rather than preside over an integrated classroom, she resigns her position and moves to New Orleans. In response, the proud Giestin moves his family permanently to L'Isle des Mulatres, escaping the discrimination that has insulted his son.

The schoolhouse scene is thus a pivotal moment, prompting Suzanne's move to the city and a shift in setting to New Orleans.[14] That change introduces Hector Santien into the action. The brother of Placide, Hector is also landless after the loss of the Santien place and, unknown by Suzanne, has, for eight years, made a living under another name as a gambler, a classic Creole vice. She sees only the elegant and gracious side of her distant cousin, and he is unfailingly courteous and proper in her company. There is an imagistically erotic scene between the two of them as Hector, presenting her with a single rose, sweeps it slowly across her face "as a lover might have done with his lips" (74). Suzanne lives at the home of Madame Chavan in the French Quarter, where only French is spoken, and they discuss the recent insult shown her by Alphonse. Madame knows about Laballière and describes him as "an aristocrat" who has ingratiated himself to Suzanne's mother, who writes glowing accounts of him as a "man of attainment" and "a man of courage, a man of heart; and the best of company" (68). He arrives in New Orleans to shower his attentions upon her, attempting to mitigate the encounter at the school, and he learns that she has spent much time with Hector, whom he knows under the gambling name of "Deroustan." Alphonse forbids her to walk the street with her cousin, fearing a compromise of her reputation, and she is convinced that, having fallen in love with Laballière, it is best to return to Natchitoches. It is on the train with him back to the Cane River country that she learns of Hector's assumed name and reputation as a "notorious gambler," and it clarifies that her future is with Alphonse.

The romance plot seems contrived, but the background issues help inform the entire volume. The Creole penchant for gambling, for example, explains how many privileged families came to ruin. Suzanne conducts her school exclusively in French, the only language spoken in the New Orleans section of the story. The unsuccessful attempt at school integration is a dramatically liberal idea in a conservative society, but the emphasis on racial stratification is one of the dominant themes that unifies the book. Related to that issue is the more localized historical role of mulattoes in the region, their previous positions of wealth and stature and their recent decline wrought by emancipation, an idea embodied in the Giestin family. All of these motifs continue to resonate throughout the ensuing stories in *Bayou Folk*.

"In Sabine" (78–95) is the third story to feature the Santien family and the theme of romance, although with significant variations on the concept. There is also a slight alteration of the setting in that the protagonist, Gregoire Santien, has just left Natchitoches Parish on his way to Texas when he stops briefly in Sabine, a Louisiana parish on the border. Although his family has lost their plantation, he seems to have sustained his dignity and sense of honor. He stops for the evening, hoping to sleep on the veranda at the home of Bud Aiken, a Texan who has married 'Tite Reine, a beauty from Natchitoches whom Gregoire met before. Thus, as in the first two stories, there are two men competing for the attentions of one woman, but the circumstances here are less sanguine: Bud dominates his wife, beating her for small infractions and once nearly choking her to death, something he would have done save for the intervention of a former slave, Mortimer, who threatened his employer with an axe. The plot revolves around the means by which she can escape from her husband and return to the life she had known before.

As is often the case in Chopin's stories, characterization is as significant as plot. Bud is a large man, bereft of sensitivity, a gruff Texan with crude manners and few social graces. Gregoire is a much smaller man, a Creole with a gentleman's code toward women who immediately accepts the responsibility to assist the young wife in escaping a rude and threatening marriage. In this he is assisted, rather heroically, by Mortimer, a former slave, who now works on the Aiken property. His first introduction reveals his character, for he is chopping wood, but not because he is employed to do so. As he explains to Gregoire, "I say dit Mas' Bud Aiken don't hires me to chop 'ood. Ef I don't chop dis heah, his wife got it to do. Dat w'y I chops 'ood, suh" (79). There is no further emphasis on racial issues, but it is clear that Mortimer is, in nearly every sense, a better man than his employer. 'Tite Reine appears in images of royalty as a "little queen" despite her total lack of stature and authority: she feeds the pigs and picks cotton. An Acadian from Cane River, she has changed during the brief period of her marriage, and "her eyes shone with tears and ill-concealed excitement" at the arrival of Gregoire (83). He ingratiates himself to his host and plies him with whiskey, and when Bud falls asleep Gregoire and 'Tite Reine make their escape back to Natchitoches.

The first three stories in *Bayou Folk* are a clear demonstration of the principles of the cycle, the inclusion of individual works that stand alone but are enriched in the context of the works around them. These stories introduce a recurring family, the Santiens, and more of their background and current struggles are presented in each case. The dominant plot device is the romantic triangle, although there are variations on the kinds of love involved and the stages of courtship at the center of the conflict, from beginning infatuations to confining marriage, from the arousal of desire to a mature concern for the welfare of another person. "In Sabine" presents the first of a series of wives in unhappy marriages, women who wish to leave their husbands.[15] Virtually all of the conflicts and issues of these early stories resonate throughout the rest of the volume.

One of Chopin's earliest stories, "At the 'Cadian Ball" (261–79), first appeared in *Two Tales* in 1892.[16] It is set in Natichoches Parish near the Cane River, the same location as the Santien opening and dealing with many of the same issues, especially the delicate social and romantic relationships between Creoles and Acadians. As the title suggests, the central event is a community ball, and the background issue is whether the local Creoles will comprise their superior social position and attend it. The men are generally tempted, drawn by the vitality and beauty of Acadian women; Creole ladies do not attend; the black population is evident only in looking through the window at the robust activity or in serving food and drinks to the celebrants. The party plays an important role in local courtship and marriage, and two relationships surrounding the event are resolved in the basic plot.

As is often the case in Chopin's fiction, structure is of fundamental significance. The first section, for example, deals with Bobinôt, an Acadian farmer who works hard in his fields, something his forbears would have been accustomed to doing. As he plows the field of cane, the emphasis is on his romantic obsession with Calixta, a local maiden of Spanish descent whose mother was Cuban, possibly part of the island influx into Louisiana in the nineteenth century. Despite her allure, Bobinôt has resolved not to attend the dance, but then he thinks of the danger of Alcée Laballière, the dashing son of a wealthy Creole family who has a weakness for attractive women. There was a hint of scandal about her and Alcée a year earlier when she went to the coastal parish of Assumption, but, so far as he knows, it is only a rumor. However, in "The Storm" it is clear that she had a rendezvous there with Alcée, as he obliquely suggests later in this story. In local gossip, her beauty and voluptuous nature are attributed to her Spanish ethnicity, "bon chien tient de race," a good dog holds to its breed. Ethnicity and nationality are at the heart of the conflict, and Bobinôt, at last, feels compelled to attend the dance.

The second section is in thematic counterpoint to the first, concentrating on Alcée and his ultimate decision to go to the ball. The son of a prominent and influential Creole family, he nonetheless works dutifully in the fields, especially when he risks a great deal of money planting rice for the first time and loses the crop in a storm. The narrative perspective is with his mind for most of the section, although an omniscient narrator intrudes to clarify that the action took place some years ago, most likely somewhere in the period between 1881 and 1892 since John L. Sullivan is alluded to by Alcée's servant, Bruce, as an indomitable opponent (268). Sullivan, the first American sports hero, became heavyweight champion in boxing in 1882 by defeating Paddy Ryan in Gulfport, Mississippi. He lost the title to Gentleman Jim Corbett in New Orleans in 1892, so there are multiple reasons everyone in the state would have known about him. He is apparently still champion during the action of the story.

As the first section focuses on Bobinôt and his obsession with Calixta, this part portrays the beautiful and innocent Clarisse and Alcée's passionate desire for her. She is described in terms that make her one with nature. Imagistically a healthy and productive plant, she is depicted as being "dainty as a lily; hardy as a sunflower; slim, tall, graceful, like one of the reeds that grew in the marsh" (264). For his part he is motivated by jealousy, as is Bobinôt, and he resents the indolent dandies with fine manners and elegant clothes who visit the plantation while he is working. Overwhelmed with love for her, he kisses her and tells her of his burning desire, but she rejects him, shocked at his ungentlemanly behavior. That is when he decides to attend the Acadian ball, where he is certain to see Calixta, with whom he shares memories of a previous affair. A second reason is the mitigation of his grief at the loss of the rice crop, which has cost him dearly, despite his hard labor. Those two incentives compel him to go, along with the simple desire for a fling (268).

The first two parts thus offer juxtapositions of protagonists, romances, and motivations leading up to the scene at the ball itself. This episode begins with Alcée's late arrival at the dance hall, after the midnight serving of the chicken gumbo. The Acadian party is vibrant with joyous activity, violin music, and gambling, but it is a family affair, with *le parc aux petits* to take care of infants (270). Chopin's description is a model of Local Color, as Ewell has pointed out, and its immediacy and specificity, down to the smells and noise of the party, bring a vibrant realism to the scene.[17] Alcée's very appearance at the ball creates a stir because his recent financial disaster is well known in the community, and he is thought to have extraordinary panache to even appear in public (270). The narrator reports the generalized view as expressed in gossip, that the Laballières are rich and have sufficient resources in the family to ease over a crisis.

Alcée is suave and debonair, cutting a dashing figure at the party. Bobinôt, on the other hand, is "dull-looking and clumsy," unsuitable as a match for the radiant Calixta. As Per Seyersted has observed, this description suggests a significant ethnic point, that the Acadians "still give their daughters such old-fashioned Gallic names as Fronie and Ozéina, however, and basically they are still the French peasants their ancestors were when they left the old country."[18] For her part, Calixta is the belle of the evening: "All the men agreed she was at her best to-night. Such animation! And abandon! Such flashes of wit!" (271). She shows her drollness, and her preference for the Creole, in a taunt aimed at Bobinôt: "Hé, Bobinôt! *Mais* w'at's the matta? W'at you standin' *plantè là* like ole Ma'ame Tina's cow in the bog, you?" (272). It is clear that the younger generation is making a transition to English in social situations whereas older people speak French to one another and sustain the traditions of their ancestors, reading Parisian newspapers and clinging to the customs of their youth.

Calixta's jib at Bobinôt is in stark contrast to her behavior in the scene that follows, her flirtation with Alcée outside in the shadows. He plays with the ring on her finger, brushes his lips on her ear, and suggests that they both take a holiday in New Orleans. He alludes to the affair they had in Assumption the year before and implies that it can be resumed if only they can get away. She is responsive to his advances, her senses "reeling" at his touch, but their flirtation is interrupted by the arrival of Clarisse, obviously protecting her interest in the wealthy planter. At the plantation, she had condescended to the ball; now she arrives with the ruse of delivering an urgent message. Alcée immediately forgets Calixta and leaves without a thought until Clarisse reminds him of his manners and he bids the Cuban girl goodnight.

The next section deals with the consequences of her being ignominiously discarded, a sexual plaything for the wealthy Alcée. In the midst of her incipient passion for the Creole, she now feels the pangs of rejection and is hurt. When Bobinôt finds her outside sitting on a bench, her appearance reflects her emotions: "She looked ghastly in the faint, gray light struggling out of the east" as dawn approaches (276). He walks her home from the ball, and she surprises him with an unanticipated proposal: "You been sayin' all along you want to marry me, Bobinôt. Well, if you want, yet, I don' care, me" (277). She is clearly responding to Alcée's rejection of her, not to her affection for the Acadian, something made clear when she refuses to kiss him (278).

The story ends where it began, with the drama between Alcée and Clarisse, as they ride home together after the ball. She confesses that there was no tragedy at home, only her realization that he would see Calixta. She also reveals that she knows about Alcée and the Spanish girl in Assumption: "I thought, Alcée—maybe you were going to—assumption. I got wild. An' then I knew if you did n't come back, *now*, to-night, I could n't stan' it,—again" (279). The "again" clarifies that she knew about the earlier escapade and could tolerate it once but no more. She professes love for him, and his passion shifts focus: "Calixta was like a myth, now. The one, only, great reality in the world was Clarisse standing before him, telling him that she loved him" (279). The sound of pistol shots rings through the air, signaling that "*le bal est fini*," and the story ends with two courtship plots having been resolved.

Few of the stories in the book refer directly to the Civil War, although many suggest the devastating economic and psychological effects of Reconstruction among the class of Creoles who, in antebellum days, were living on the extensive plantations along the Cane River. "Beyond the Bayou," however, is unique in that the protagonist is a former slave named Jacqueline, and the focus is on the devastating psychological damage done to her by the violence of the fighting (99–110).[19] During the war one battle was fought at Bellissime, where Jacqueline lived in a cabin across the bayou from the plantation house, and it was there that the wounded owner of the property, P'tit Maître, staggered in covered with blood. He recovered; she did not. She suffers from a form of post-traumatic stress disorder from the incident, and although at least a decade has passed since the event, she has never crossed the bayou in all that time. She lives preoccupied with "the fear of the world beyond the bayou, the morbid and insane dread she had been under since childhood" (104). However, she has grown to love the white children of the master, especially the young boy she calls Chéri. In the present action, the boy sustains a wound in a hunting accident, and Jacqueline saves his life by carrying him across the bayou to treatment at his home. Her world is thus enlarged by her altruism, born of selfless love, and her reward is not only the gratitude of the boy's family but the expansion of her own experiences "as she watched for the first time the sun rise upon the new, the beautiful world beyond the bayou" (10). An epiphany in a female protagonist is a common climax in Chopin's stories, but there are elements in this case that are remarkable.

For one thing the key character is a black woman who has been psychologically damaged by war and is known locally as "La Folle," the crazy one. Her obsession with "place" was occasioned by fear not by fantasy nor depression. The transformative event involves love, but this affection is not profane nor it is self-fulfilling; it is a deep and meaningful devotion of an older woman of color for a white child, a conventional theme given an unusual application.[20] As Ewell points out, the bayou has served as a psychological as well as a physical barrier limiting Jacqueline's life, and crossing it allows her to rejoin the communal life of the plantation. Her long years of solitude are over, and the vehicle of her personal growth was love. There seems little evidence to support the contention by Bonnie James Shaker that her love for a white child serves as "justification for the continued white dominance."[21] Rather, Jacqueline experiences self-assertion both in her rescue of the child and in her determination to see him the next morning, when she sits on the top step of the veranda waiting for the boy to awaken (110). Brutality in the form of war drove her into psychotic retreat; personal love for a child brought her out of it and into a beautiful and more expansive life. Even the marginalizing Louisiana racial codes could not contain the power of her maternal affection.

"The Return of Alcibiade" (113–25) presents a variation on the theme: undying paternal love in the wake of the Civil War. It also involves another instance of psychological aberration in that a father who has lost a son in the conflict is unable to grasp that fact and clings to the expectation that Alcibiade will return for Christmas dinner with his family.[22] One of Chopin's earliest stories, it was published in a slightly different version in *St. Louis Life* in 1892 before inclusion in *Bayou Folk*.[23] As is typical of Chopin's fiction in this period, the plot is simple while the characterizations and themes are more complex. Fred Bartner is an outsider from New Orleans coming into Natchitoches Parish on business when a buggy accident causes him to stop for assistance at the home of the elderly Jean Baptiste Plochel, whose senility and grief has caused him to live in the past, in the Civil War years, awaiting the return of his son. He is lovingly cared for by his granddaughter, the young and beautiful Esmée, who beseeches Bartner to pretend to be the long-lost son to give the old man his day of happiness. He does so, touched by her emotional generosity and delicacy of feeling, and the story ends with the peaceful death of Jean Baptiste and an incipient romance between Bartner and Esmée, who are beginning yet another form of emotional alliance. Thus affection abounds: father for son, Esmée for Jean Baptiste, Bartner for her, and she for Bartner.

But there are other notable issues. Once again Chopin presents a double plot with love as the central emotion on both levels.[24] Retrospection also has two applications in this context: Jean Baptiste lives in the past, his mind arrested prior to the notification that his son had been killed; for him the war is still being fought and his plantation is worked by slaves (123). His mental illness is a benign aberration that allows him to sustain the belief that his boy will eventually return. That he mistakes Bartner for his son is a manifestation of time and the supremacy of hope over reality. The time of narration is twelve years after the events depicted, back before the completion of the New Orleans and Shreveport railroad. Thus, Bartner is compelled to travel by buggy. From such a perspective the narrator should know whether the beginning romance between Esmée and Bartner ripened into marriage, but that information is withheld.

Chopin's handling of language is also of interest: the characters speak French to one another, which is translated into standard English by the narrator. The African-American characters, however, speak English in dialect, as in the opening when the wheel on the buggy needs repair and the young boy suggests that "we kin stop yonda at ole M'sié Jean Ba's an' fix it; he got de bes' blacksmif shop in de pa'ish on his place" (113). The Baptiste plantation seems elegant despite the situation, and Christmas dinner features turkey dressed with pecans. As patriarch, Jean Baptiste presides over dinner, thus ending his life on a moment of elation. Esmée, whose French name means "esteemed" or "loved," is persistently associated with images of flowers, with violets or roses, with nature and the continuity of life. When she reveals at the end that she will move to New Orleans to live with her aunt, the implications for a future romance between the two of them seem clear. The fruition of love, which permeates the story, transcends the conclusion.

The plot of "A Wizard from Gettysburg" (230–44) involves essentially the same situation except the dementia is on the part of the returning Confederate soldier, Bertrand Delmandé, home from the Battle of Gettysburg at least two decades after that conflict in 1863.[25] His wife, Madame Delmandé, is now sixty-five, which must be roughly his own age (235). His son, St. Ange Delmandé, now controls the Bon-Accueil plantation, a name that appropriately means "good reception." Bertrand was wounded in the head, and his mind was altered in such a way as to deny the passage of time; he thus lives in the past. As the narrator recounts, "on that field of battle this man had received a new and tragic birth. For all his existence that went before was a blank to him. There, in the black desolation of war, he was born again, without friends or kindred; without even a name he could know was his own. Then he had gone forth a wanderer; living more than half the time in hospitals; toiling when he could, starving when he had to" (236). But now, at home, he begins to remember fragments of the past, although often in a confused way. He takes the grandson named after him, the young Betrand, for St. Ange, and he calls him by that name consistently. The teenage boy brings home a tattered man he takes to be a tramp; he could not recognize his grandfather because he has never seen him, having been born after the war. The boy, who aspires to be a physician, tends the old man kindly, much to the consternation of the black laborers, who object to his presence and find it inappropriate for such a distinguished family. One of them says, in wonderful regional speech, "Ma'ame Bertrand an' Marse St. Ange ain't gwine stan' dat, I knows dey ain't. Dah! Ef he ain't done sot 'im on de gall'ry, plumb down in his pa's rockin'-cheer!" (233). In due course the boy reveals that because of financial circumstances, he must drop out of school. The old man insists that "St. Ange must go to school," and other fragments of his memory come back, leading him to dig up a box filled with gold he had hidden before he left home. Even though the boy's education is thus insured, the conclusion has a tragic element in that the elder Bertrand does not recognize his aged wife, and he entreats her for hospitality for himself and his two children (244).

"A Wizard from Gettysburg" does much to unify the thematic elements of *Bayou Folk*. It is one of the stories to focus on the aftermath of the war, its psychological consequences for a family. That motif is tied to "a conventional postwar fantasy, the recovery of lost treasure."[26] The gold thus allows this family to escape a more common postbellum situation, the degradations of poverty for a once aristocratic plantation family, the irony being that it is the demented old soldier who is able to renew their wealth, playing the patriarch even in his confused state.[27] It was not so unusual for wealthy Southern families to be impoverished after the war. Many of them converted their entire wealth to Confederate currency, certain that the war would end in their favor. Their land, used almost exclusively for the production of labor-intensive crops such as cotton, hemp, or tobacco, was almost worthless after emancipation, when the cost of workers rose dramatically. Indeed, the black farmhands on the plantation are not at all deferential, insisting that the boy send the old man on his way. Chopin often uses mental disturbance to emphasize the enormous psychic cost of the conflict, the aberrant transformation of the individual mirroring the larger picture of what had happened to the entire South. Amnesia is thus a valuable narrative tool for presenting a lost narrative, and, supported by the other elements of Local-Color fiction, it underscores the compelling regional drama of the late nineteenth century.

Two other stories set at the time of the Civil War are "A Lady of Bayou St. John" and "La Belle Zoraïde," in some ways Chopin's finest and most complex work of short fiction. They share a common setting in New Orleans, some of the same basic set of characters, similar themes of lost love, and an artistic integrity that underscores the seriousness of the fundamental issues. "A Lady of Bayou St. John" (304–13) originally appeared in *Vogue* in September of 1893 prior to its inclusion in *Bayou Folk*.[28] Emily Toth has pointed out that the composition of the story followed Chopin's visit to the Columbia Exposition in Chicago earlier that year at which she observed the extensive exhibit of Impressionistic paintings, especially Mary Cassatt's mural *Modern Women*, which united innovative artistic techniques with the newly energized concern for the role of women in society, their psychology, and their rights. Toth suggests that the description of the protagonist, Madame Delisle, "resembles a painting, with 'the brilliancy of her golden hair, the sweet languor of her blue eyes, the graceful contours of her figure, and the peach-like bloom of her flesh.' The Frenchman who woos her is also out of an Impressionist painting, dressed for a boating party: 'clad always in cool, white duck, with a flower in his buttonhole.'"[29] Beyond surface appearances, however, the plot involves some equally modern issues that the society of the 1890s found singularly uncomfortable.

The basic situation is that the comely young Madame Delisle is left at home in New Orleans while her husband, Gustave, is in General P. G. T. Beauregard's Confederate regiment in the Civil War. In a sense the specificity of Gustave's commander is of no consequence in the ensuing action, but Chopin's extensive knowledge of history would have suggested him as the perfect leader to entice a Southern gentleman to serve in his unit. Born in New Orleans, Beauregard was the commandant of the United States Military Academy at West Point at the inception of the war. He immediately resigned and became the first Brigadier General in the Southern forces, in charge of the attack on Fort Sumter and, three months later, the First Battle of Bull Run at Manassas, Virginia. He was in command at the Battle of Shiloh and the Siege of Corinth in Mississippi. After the war he returned to his birthplace and became a railroad executive, expanding service throughout Louisiana, and he promoted the institution of the Louisiana Lottery, a favorite of the Creole gambling community. He died a few months before the composition of the story and was buried in Metairie Cemetery in New Orleans.[30] In 1893, as everyone in the city would have known, the mention of Beauregard in this context would suggest that Gustave is a proud and loyal Creole of the city who is following one of its great heroes.

The plot is simple, if with an interesting twist. Madame Delisle, as she is always called, is a beautiful and fetching young wife with narcissistic tendencies: she sits for hours looking into a mirror, "admiring the brilliancy of her golden hair, the sweet languor of her blue eyes, the graceful contours of her figure, and the peach-like bloom of her flesh. She was very young" (304). She is attended by a faithful woman of color, Manna-Loulou, a devoted servant and raconteur who seems to have no life apart from her mistress, who seems a child to her. Manna-Loulou, who may be a slave, tells her a story every night at bedtime to usher her into sleep. In the long absence of her husband, Madame Delisle has attracted a suitor, Sépincourt, a Frenchman rather than a Creole, a dandy instead of a gentleman. He stops by nearly every day, and the sympathy grows between them to the point that he feels free to suggest that they run away to Paris together, and she, the memory of her husband having grown dim, responds "Paris, or anywhere—with you—ah, *bon Dieu!*" (307). Sépincourt has inspired passion within her, and he kisses her repeatedly. However, that night she learns that her husband has been killed in the war, and she is transformed into a grieving widow, faithful to his memory. A romance of any kind with Sépincourt is now unthinkable for her. The conclusion reveals that all of this happened decades before the time of narration and that Madame Deslisle has remained devoted to her dead husband: "The memory of Gustave still fills and satisfies her days. She has never failed, once a year, to have a solemn high mass said for the repose of his soul" (313). What is ultimately of interest is "that psychological enigma, a woman's heart," and the frailty of marital fidelity (312).

Despite the twist of the conclusion, much of the story is thematically standard for Chopin's fiction. An ingénue serves as the focal point; she is awakened to passion by the attentions of a forbidden gentleman; she ultimately retreats from the world into a fantasy of lost love and never fulfills the romantic dreams that obsessed her. Her transformation allows her to remain a child in some respects, never having to commit to a genuine sexual relationship.[31] The point of view is omniscient, entering the minds of Madame Deslisle and Sépincourt and moving through time with total knowledge, telling events in retrospect. The narrator is objective, making no value judgment about the contemplated infidelity. The setting is the Bayou St. John, a marsh on the edge of the Creole section of New Orleans; the traditional values of that culture are very much at play even though invaded by a "Frenchman," meaning that Sépincourt was not born in Louisiana but emigrated from France. In the aesthetic tradition of the story cycle, all of these concepts relate in important ways to other works within the volume, especially "La Belle Zoraïde," written the same year and featuring many of the same characters in this very setting.

On the very day that "A Lady of Bayou St. John" was published, Chopin wrote a companion story dealing with essentially the same issues. "La Belle Zoraïde" followed the earlier story in *Vogue*, appearing on January 4 of 1894.[32] Readers of the magazine could easily have remembered the recent portrayal of Madame Delisle, her transient passion for Sépincourt, and her surprising loyalty to her dead husband throughout her widowhood, so they would have understood that she has experienced loneliness and has been clinging to faded memories. Lost love would mean everything to her, and she would be receptive to an account of another woman who had a similar but even more tragic experience.

However, in this case Chopin crafted a plot of extraordinary subtlety and aesthetic integrity, perhaps the most important artistry of her career. The beginning of "La Belle Zoraïde" is an omniscient opening that establishes the setting and the tone in preparation for an internal first-person tale told by Manna-Loulou. It is a hot summer evening, and the view across the Bayou St. John shows a few lights across the *marais*. Given the lack of strong winds, a "lugger" makes its slow way across the water. The specificity of this kind of sailboat, with its three square lugsails, suggests a narrator with an intimate knowledge of the region and its nautical traditions.[33] Someone on the boat sings a song in French, a lover's lament that his mistress has left Louisiana and he has no more happiness, thus foreshadowing the events of the internal narrative Manna-Loulou will tell. She obviously speaks French for she responds to the music with sympathy, and her emotion triggers her memory of the tale of Zoraïde. As in "A Lady of Bayou St. John," Manna-Loulou attends Madame Delisle and tells her a bedtime story each night, and it is this recitation that constitutes the rest of the narrative.

The opening frame thus moves from a distant view of the bayou to a boat moving across the marais, to the gallery outside the house, to the bedroom inside, where the important psychological action will take place.[34] It establishes that Manna-Loulou sees to the needs of Madame Delisle with loving tenderness, treating her as a vulnerable child. Indeed, some of her services establish Christian parallels: "The old negress had already bathed her mistress's pretty white feet and kissed them lovingly, one, then the other" (281). Manna-Loulou is as "black as the night," suggesting both purity of race and her station at the bottom of the social stratification of Louisiana. Her response to the setting and her account of Zoraïde indicate intelligence, sensitivity, and an extraordinary skill as raconteur. Indeed, save for her economic status, she would seem to be superior to her mistress: she is free of vanity and narcissism and responsive to the needs of others.

As a first-person narrator, she would have her own reasons for the choice of a tale to tell, and with her narration she can manipulate her mistress, presenting events in a quiet and respectful tone while simultaneously weaving a plot that is calculated to have an effect in the present. The opening description of Madame Delisle is also important. It establishes that she is wealthy, sleeping in a "sumptuous mahogany bed," attended by a faithful "old negress"

(281). Although it is not clear how many years have passed since the conclusion of "A Lady of Bayou St. John," she has apparently remained loyal to her husband, for she still wears a wedding ring. She is beautiful, with golden hair, although her role in the action is entirely passive. It is Manna-Loulou who compels the events, the tone, the direction of the action. Madame Delisle's almost total dependency upon her servant infantilizes her, compromising the depth of her character and diminishing her tragedy.

The opening presents the dramatic context of the telling, the circumstances of the internal narrator, and the meaning the tale would have for the listener. The introduction is related from an omniscient point of view, but the internal narrative is told by a different technique, by Manna-Loulou speaking in first person and relating a story of a woman of color who lost love in two dimensions and who was driven mad by the impact of it. The key figure is a slave, Zoraïde, a young woman of mixed blood, who found passion in her first love, which was denied to her by Madame Delarivière, a mistress who dictates nearly every aspect of her slave's life.

Manna-Loulou weaves a tale about characters very close to herself and Madame Delisle involved in romantic conflicts that would have special meaning for the mistress, since they result in lost love, loneliness, and a life without a husband and children. The internal story also features a faithful slave who adores her owner and is loved in return, at least so long as she obeys commands. The tale begins with the description of Zoraïde, a beautiful young woman who, although a slave, has been raised as a lady of privilege in the home of Madame Delariviève: "From a toddling thing she had been brought up at her mistress's side; her fingers had never done rougher work than sewing a fine muslin seam; and she even had her own little black servant to wait upon her" (282). Zoraïde is light skinned, the color of "*café-au-lait*," designations that conveyed stature among persons of color in New Orleans society. She is not destined to become a plaçage wife nor a tragic quadroon, a common figure in fiction in the nineteenth century, for Madame Delarivière is intimately concerned in the selection of a proper husband for such a protected and delicate young lady. Speaking directly to Zoraïde, she reminds her that "when you are ready to marry, it must be in a way to do honor to your bringing up" (282). To ensure that it is, Madame clearly intends to orchestrate the arrangements herself, albeit with extraordinary generosity: "Your wedding gown, your corbeille, all will be of the best; I shall see to that myself" (282). The offer conveys an assertion of wealth, status, and control. Although she is benevolent in many respects, it would also seem that the mistress, no longer married herself, has a complex scheme in mind that uses Zoraïde to strengthen Madame's relationship with an eligible white gentleman.

That man is Dr. Langlé, who owns a personal servant, M'sieur Ambroise, and Madame Delarivière has determined that it is he Zoraïde will marry. For her part, she hates him: she "detested the little mulatto, with his shining whiskers like a white man's, and his small eyes, that were cruel and false as a snake's" (282). It is a central conflict, and there is a good deal of cultural context that deepens the terms of the dispute. In this case M'sieur Ambroise is personally repugnant to Zoraïde because he is a mulatto and she a quadroon or octoroon, and he is beneath her in social station. She has never been a servant and is lighter than he. She also mistakenly seems to assume that she has total discretion in the matter. In one sense she does. Under the *Code Noir*, an owner could not force a slave to marry anyone. Furthermore, a strict reading of the law would indicate that a marriage between them would have been illegal, since unions were restricted to precise racial mixtures. On the emotional level, she does not love him and is not attracted to him. Zoraïde, however, does not wish to reject him openly, so for a time she declares, in diplomatic tones of respect and deference, that she is so happy with the current situation that she does not want to change anything for the near future.

The truth is that Zoraïde has another man in mind, Mézor, a tall and masculine slave she has seen dance the Bamboula in Congo Square, the setting of the dramatic scene in Cable's "Posson Jone'" where the parson gets drunk. This square was the one place in the Crescent City where the African dances could be performed without interference, and people of color would gather on Sunday for a musical celebration of black culture, often with sexual overtones. Mézor performs nearly naked, and his raw sexuality stirs Zoraïde to passion: He "was as straight as a cypress-tree and as proud looking as a king. His body, bare to the waist, was like a column of ebony and it glistened like oil" (283). The royal image used to describe an African suggests that a slave society perverts the natural order for he is, outside of imposed social codes, clearly a person of stature worthy of the beautiful and refined Zoraïde, and their mutual love is instantaneous. He is also owned by Dr. Langlé, so a union between them should have been easy to arrange.

Instead, Madame responds with outrage, finding betrayal in Zoraïde's independent attitude and feeling that her loving treatment over the years has earned her both trust and absolute authority: "You deserve to have the lash laid upon you like any other slave; you have proven yourself no better than the worst" (284). She forbids Zoraïde to have any further contact with Mézor, but the lovers find ways to consummate their attraction, which results in pregnancy. When it begins to become obvious, Zoraïde confesses: "Nénaine, you would not let me have Mézor for my husband; but I have disobeyed you, I have sinned" (285). It is a carefully calculated confession, beginning with the respectable term "godmother" for Madame Delarivière and delivered with tones of submission and helplessness, pleading for understanding and mercy. None is forthcoming.

Madame uses her influence on Dr. Langlé to sell Mézor to a plantation in a distant state, and Zoraïde never sees him again. Then, when the baby is born, a "griffe" daughter, the child of a fully black father and a quadroon, Zoraïde is told that it was born dead, and the child is spirited away to a plantation along the coast. Zoraïde is psychologically transformed by these events, and she takes a small bundle of rags as her infant, treating it with insane dedication, so that even when her real child is brought to her, she rejects it and prefers her surrogate infant. She becomes known as a "folle" and ends her days lonely and demented, clinging to her bundle of rags (290).

At this juncture the internal narrative spoken by Manna-Loulou ends and the omniscient point of view resumes, presenting the ironic conclusion. In the context of this riveting narrative, filled with romantic drama built within the context of the racial codes of Louisiana, the slave asks her mistress if she is asleep, as though she is sufficiently obtuse and insensitive to have been bored by the story of Zoraïde. Madame Delisle responds poorly, ignoring the major issues of slavery, control, psychological cruelty, and the power of lost love, and comments vapidly on a tangential point: "Ah, the poor little one, Man Loulou, the poor little one! Better had she died!" (290). That may be true, but she ignores the treatment of Zoraïde by her owner, the instinctive natural love between Zoraïde and Mézor, and the mental destruction wrought by the insensitive mistress.

Of course, it is Manna-Loulou who controlled the internal narrative, and she might well have hoped that Madame Delisle would see parallels in her ownership of a slave and that of Madame Delarivière's domination of Zoraïde, which resulted in unhappiness for all involved. As Lynn Cothern has pointed out, the internal narrator thus "functions as an intermediary between the privileged world of her mistress and the plight of the slaves who had been stripped of all rights."[35] In that sense, it is a manipulative tale, didactic in intention, reformative in objective. The tale of Zoraïde is told in respectful tones, deferential throughout to the sensitivity of Madame Delisle, who could hardly find fault with any of the implications. The fundamental point is how slavery allows for the ruthless exercise of power of one person over another, and the construction of that authority in altruistic rhetoric does not assuage the ultimate tragedy of what happened to a beautiful and sensitive young slave. Manna-Loulou, having told such a narrative to her mistress, might well be hoping for more benevolent treatment in the future, especially from a woman who had suffered the death of her husband

and knew something about lost love. She might well assume that Zoraïde's passion for Mézor would be something Madame Delisle would understand, given her flirtation with Sépincourt.

Another character whose mind has been arrested in the past is Uncle Oswald in "The Bênitous' Slave" (143–46), an unusual work for Chopin in that it resembles the antebellum idyllic South portrayed by Thomas Nelson Page and other romantic plantation writers. Originally published in *Harper's Young People* in 1892, it seems an odd choice for a magazine for children in that it deals with pathological psychology in an elderly former slave.[36] Narrated in first person by a character who hears the story in the town of Natchitoches just after meeting Uncle Oswald, the plot concerns the man's insistent desire to return to his "owners" despite having been free for several decades. Diagnosed as mentally ill, Oswald is being taken to an institution when he meets a descendant of his former master, a little girl named Susanne, and he follows her home, content that he has returned to his rightful place in the world. He has internalized a social status that was forced upon him, and it is only within the constraints of that paradigm that he can be at peace. It is an insightful variation on the mental illness motif that runs throughout the book, and it certainly exceeds Barbara C. Ewell's conclusion that the story is "little more than a stock, sentimental portrait of the loyal ex-slave and his kindly ex-masters."[37] It also extends the historical impact of slavery far beyond abolition, suggesting that as an aberrant institution it had manifestations that were psychological as well as social and economic.

The psychological aspects of "Ma'me Pélagie" (245–60) are also central themes, although the issue is an obsession with lost grandeur, wealth, and social stature.[38] The Valmêt family lived in the mansion they built on their plantation in 1840 that was destroyed in the Civil War. The oldest of three children, Ma'me Pélagie has lived for thirty years with a single purpose at the center of her life, the restoration of the mansion, the manifestation of familial standing in the Old South. She lives with a younger sister, Pauline, brother Leander having fled to the city many years before the "present" action in the 1890s. The two women, uncompromising in their dedication to a single idea, save every penny against the dream of restoration. All of that changes when Leander, a widower, sends his young daughter, La Petite, to live on the plantation and, disenchanted with the lack of culture and social activity, she threatens to leave for the city. Both sisters have grown to love the child, and they sacrifice their savings to build a new home and fill it with the kind of entertainment the girl enjoys. Ma'me Pélagie, however, has lost her sustaining purpose, and she ages quickly in her empty life: "While the outward pressure of a young and joyous existence had forced her footsteps into the light, her soul had stayed in the shadow of the ruin" (260). So the story ends with her lost dreams, with her farewell to the mythological image of the aristocratic plantation South of gentlemen and ladies leading a genteel agrarian life.

The plot of the story is thus simple, a metaphor for the postwar situation throughout the region, where dreams were forced to give way to unpleasant new realities. As Per Seyersted has pointed out, this is one of Chopin's few works of serious fiction on a popular Southern theme, although Grace King focused much of her work on the subject.[39] It was easy for the reading public of the day to accept the idea that former aristocrats would invest much of their attention on a glorified construct of the golden past, and the domestic consequences of the war fell largely on women, the loss of youth and home and family. As Ewell has stated, "with her grand dreams of rebuilding, Pélagie is, in some ways, one of Chopin's strongest characters, ably managing a large plantation, once defying an enemy army, and loving faithfully not only her lost sweetheart Felix but also her sister."[40] That the emotional devotion of the family comes to include a niece serves to intensify the internal conflict Pélagie must resolve, for much is invested in the dream of the past, including her love of ancestors. That this drama is played out next to the charred remains of an old mansion is pertinent to the original title of the story, "In the Shadow of the Ruin."[41]

This story reflects Chopin's standard Southern themes of the 1890s, including the costly legacy of a lost war that has broken families and fractured lives. Here, as in other works, the love of surrogate motherhood is instrumental in restoring a healthy future for a child, who finds normalcy where there had been only an obsession. Since Edgar Allen Poe's "The Fall of the House of Usher," American fiction has often used the ancestral dwelling as an embodiment of the multigenerational soul of a family, its welfare tied directly to the psychic well-being of the protagonist. Chopin not only used this idea, she did so with impressive artistic grace.

"Ma'me Pélagie" uses all of the standard aesthetic devices of the Local-Color movement, from the deft handling of dialect to the representation of regional values and localized circumstances. Her characters could exist in this situation only in the South; there was little devastation in the North, and expansion was creating a vibrant and burgeoning new culture on the West Coast of the United States. But the subtle handling of point of view, which shifts between the two sisters, reveals the psychologically transformative nature of the conflict for both of them.

These matters are best explained in terms of structure. The first of the numbered sections dwells on the dream of the restoration of the mansion, although Pélagie has taken over the management of the plantation and runs it well. Now fifty, she has devoted over half her life to that idea, living in a small log cabin while saving her money for the restored house. Her emotional life is restricted entirely to her sister, Pauline, a deferential younger sibling who returns undivided affection. Into this family unit, at the end of part one, comes La Petite, disrupting the psychic structure they have established, "and they made room between them for this young life" (249). The second section covers the adjustments needed to incorporate the child into the household, and the central alteration is in the emotional life of Pauline, who is reborn with love for the young girl. Thus it is the younger sister who is devastated by La Petite's decision to leave the plantation: "I must live another life; the life I lived before. I want to know things that are happening from day to day over the world, and hear them talked about. I want my music, my books, my companions" (251). Pauline faints and cannot be comforted, and Pélagie, demonstrating her love, holds her in her arms. The child has been a "savior" for Pauline, and the loss of the child would leave her without purpose in life, without hope of happiness.

Section three is the most dramatic in its internal action, for it is here that Pélagie must say goodbye to the glories of the past and embrace life in the present. In the night she steals to the ruin, "but she never before had been there with a heart so nearly broken. She was going there for the last time to dream her dreams" (254). There, at the ruined mansion, she revisits scenes from decades before, and her visions reveal the meaning of the house to her. She sees a "robust old white-haired man," a father or grandfather, chiding her for returning home so late. She remembers a former lover, Felix, who took her in his arms with a promise of marriage before he left, only to be killed in the fighting. She sees important visitors to the grand house, Lucien Santien, for example, the patriarch of another clan, and Monsieur Lafirme, among a host of others. But all was lost, even in her fantasy, with the cannon at Fort Sumter and the devastation that followed, including the invasion of the mansion by marauding Union troops "drinking the wines, shattering the crystal and glass, slashing the portraits" (257). She recalls having slapped a soldier who ordered her to leave the house, her strength emerging even in her youth. A fire consumed much of the building, and all that is left is the image of Pauline as a small child clinging to the knees of her older sister, terrified by the violence and destruction. These memories have sustained her entire adult life, and now, she says farewell to this dream, to this vision that has given direction to her every day.

Section four is devoted to the transformation, to the new house and vibrant young life within it. Leander moves back to the plantation to join his sisters; La Petite is enthralled in the new world, playing the piano and enjoying the activity of a bustling household; Pauline has everyone she loves about her, and she blossoms with restorative youth. It is only Pélagie who suffers: "In her deep, dark eyes smouldered the light of fires that would never flame" (260). She grows old very quickly, for despite the resplendent life about her, "her soul had stayed in the shadow of the ruin" (260). It is a brilliant conclusion to an insightful story, one rendered with remarkable sensitivity and artistic grace.

Yet another story on the theme of familial love is "A Rude Awakening" (126–42), first published in *Youth's Companion* in 1893, suggesting that it was suitable for young people.[42] It deals with the Bordon family of Acadians living in Natchitoches Parish, where the father, Sylvester, is a lazy and negligent parent to his motherless children: Lolotte, Nonomme, Jacques, and Veveste. He works, reluctantly, for Joe Duplan, a wise and generous man who often intervenes to assist families in the area. In this case he has hired Sylveste, as he is called, to haul three bales of cotton to the railroad station, but in the morning he goes fishing rather than tending to his duties. Distraught at their poverty and lack of food for a sick child, Lolotte, a girl of seventeen, drives the wagon to deliver the cotton. The horses run out of control, and she is injured and taken to a hospital. Her father assumes she has drowned in the river when he searches for her, and his grief inspires a benevolent transformation. When he finds her alive in the Duplan household, "he only sobbed, kneeling upon the floor beside her, kissing her knees and her hands, that sought his" (139). Duplan shames him with a speech about how he should be a man and assume parental responsibilities, and Sylveste vows to try his best.

The story is quintessentially Local Color in most respects, with a regional setting, variations on the local dialects, and a sentimental ending. However, the narrative method is omniscient and the language of the narrator is standard English. The people of good conscience are Aunt Minty, an old black woman who kills one of her own chickens to feed the sick girl, and the Duplans, at the other end of the economic spectrum, who take Lolotte in and guide her father in establishing a new work ethic. Sylveste's pledge to work harder in the future is certainly laudable, but Per Seyersted would seem to be a bit generous in concluding that he "has something of the true gentleman in his dignity and lack of affectation."[43] His transformation is thrust upon him by circumstance, not manifest from internal nobility, but it could be said of him that he exhibits genuine love for his daughter, although it takes a serious accident to reveal it. Bonnie James Shaker is also overzealous in claiming that "the Bordons, a poor Cajun family living in rural postbellum Louisiana, triumphantly and harmoniously integrate themselves into hegemonic white American culture."[44] Sylveste's reluctant assumption of his parental duties is a positive step, to be sure, but there is nothing "triumphant" about it nor have they achieved the status to exercise "hegemonic" power in society. They are still an impoverished clan, scratching out a living on poor soil and running odd jobs for other people, and there is no indication of significant economic status. The rise is in moral terms, not social or financial, and such values are not dependant on caste position. Aunt Minty is the most decent and generous person, and she is without social stature. Joe Duplan is a wealthy Creole gentleman, and he brings a similar decency to bear on family problems that are not his own. The crux of the issue is not social status but the depth of familial love, which joins "A Rude Awakening" to a host of other stories in the volume.

Another short work involving a husband's pledge to do better is "Madame Célestin's Divorce" (163–69), which provides a variation on the marriage theme and the introduction of divorce, an issue central to Chopin's first novel, *At Fault*.[45] Artistically, the story is a model of simplicity and control, with only two active characters (the husband, Célestin, is important but never appears) and a single location, the picket fence in front of Madame's home. Lawyer Paxton, who lives nearby, passes the house every day on his way to the office, and he has obviously been taken by her beauty and openness. Almost every morning she speaks to him, sharing her marital problems, especially her periodic abandonment by her husband, whom she has not seen for six months. Inspired by his desire to marry her himself, he urges her to consider leaving her husband, and she agrees. Each meeting at the fence between them becomes an increment of the plot, and each moves her resolve closer to a marital termination and drives his fantasies about marriage to such a comely Creole woman. Finally, she proceeds to court, but the judge instructs her to discuss the matter with Père Duchéron, who urges her, she reports, to consider the scandal and discuss the matter with the bishop, which she does. Her resolves holds firm, and Paxton refines his wedding plans, even considering a move out of Natchitoches Parish. The final paragraph, however, reverses the course of action. Madame reports to Paxton that her husband returned the night before and "promise[d] me on his word an' honor he's going to turn ova a new leaf" (109).

Chopin is somewhat given to surprise endings that reverse the course of things, a device common in the 1890s in Local-Color fiction. The restricted Louisiana setting, the localized values, and the persistent Creole dialect establish the regional nature of the story. Indeed, the relationship between Paxton and Madame Célestin is revealed entirely in dialogue, his educated lexicon and her more relaxed parlance. In style and structure, character development and theme, the artistic coherence is impressive and deftly controlled. Per Seyersted has observed that here "Kate Chopin reached a new peak in her artistry. Everything is infallibly right in this story about a contemplated divorce caused by M. Célestin's desertion of his wife."[46] Even the evolving plot proceeds with plausible increments: It quickly becomes clear that their relationship is sympathetic and warm, with mutual respect, admiration, and sexual attraction. His desire to marry her is well developed, involving incipient love as well as regard for her beauty. Her motivation to divorce is largely driven by her husband's almost total neglect of his responsibilities. A union with a professional man, a lawyer, who goes to the office every day, would bring stability into her life. On the other hand, by staying with her husband, Madame Célestin can remain within her comfortable domestic sphere, escaping the censure of the church and society, avoiding the outside world with its complex evaluations and choices.

In many ways "Love on the Bon-Dieu" (170–92) presents the simplest level of love and familial issues, courtship, even though there is no traditional romance involved.[47] Rather, the plot is set within the context of religion, opening on Père Antoine's veranda on the eve of Easter Sunday, where Lalie has come to get a letter from the priest allowing her to purchase new shoes for the holiday, paying for them out of her meager income from selling eggs. Several important matters are presented in this opening, her beauty and poverty among them, and the humane compassion of the priest underscores what evolves into an ethical and emotional drama. The ethnic identity of the central characters is not specified, although Nina Baym's suggestion that they are impoverished Acadians seems the most reasonable assessment, especially given their dialect.[48] Chopin rarely depicts poverty within Creole society, and the young man does manual labor, something generally restricted to lower-class employment, so he is not likely Creole (172). Acadian poverty is one of the distinguishing traits that differentiates them from their French neighbors. In contrast, Linda Wagner-Martin assumes that Lalie is African American,[49] which seems unlikely because people of color are most often described as such, as is Tranquiline, "an amiable old black woman" (182). In any event the characters are clearly Roman Catholic and the views of the priest are important in their lives.

The next scene features the priest welcoming, in French, handsome young Azenor, setting the stage for the ensuing romance. The conversation is a means of establishing the fundamental impediment to any serious courtship between the young man and Lalie: she is decidedly lower class, poor, and tainted by having a grandmother who has grown senile. Further, in their destitute state they have been forced to move into a wretched dwelling on Le Blôt farm, a cabin the black laborers refused to occupy (175). Driven almost exclusively by sexual attraction, Azenor quickly becomes interested in her, in her beauty and "figure," one "as slim and delicate as a flower-stalk" (178). Chopin often uses nature imagery in this way, suggesting that a relationship between them would be healthy and reproductive. Despite the approbation of the local people, who caution Azenor that Lalie is "real canaille, her," his affection for her grows, increased by her sensitive and compassionate comments about her grandmother. But the young woman is nearly starving to death and becomes seriously ill with fever, which inspires him to bring her home for convalescence. In this context their mutual love is revealed as he tenderly sees to her needs, and the final paragraph indicates his intention to marry her. The plot thus moves progressively from attraction to sexual allure to deeply committed love, a transformative affection so deep that Azenor is willing to risk his own health to care for her. His feelings for her transcend the community reproach that surrounds their romance as well as her poverty and lack of social standing.[50] He has found maturity and sensitivity in his relationship with a destitute but beautiful young woman, revealing Chopin's capacity to instill even the most basic of courtship plots with psychological depth.

Chopin's most famous story, "Désirée's Baby," is thematically congruous with the rest of the volume, exploring variations on romantic and familial love, social stratification, race, and death.[51] First published in *Vogue* in 1893 under the title "The Father of Désirée's Baby," it is one of the few stories in the book set prior to the Civil War, and it is her only work to focus directly on miscegenation.[52] Often praised for the power of its racial theme as well as the artistry of its style and construction, Fred Lewis Pattee observed in his *A History of American Literature Since 1870* that it was "well-nigh perfect" and concluded that Chopin was the great genius of short fiction.[53] Even earlier, in 1911, Robert Cecil Beale pronounced that this work alone established the author in a "lofty" position in the history of literature.[54] In 1932 Daniel Rankin suggested that it was one of the greatest stories ever written, an evaluation echoed in 1937 by Reilly.[55] "Désirée's Baby" has been widely admired and anthologized ever since, especially after the Chopin revival of the 1960s. There is, indeed, much to admire, not the least of which is the power of the racial theme in the historical context of the time, when the *Code Noir* was still in force, forbidding, with the power of severe punishment, sexual contact between the races. At the same time, the plaçage tradition contravened those restrictions but required formal ratification of financial arrangements. On the level of social custom, racial matters were taken very seriously in Louisiana, especially for a wealthy aristocrat living on a well-established plantation, and the story must be read in that context.

"Désirée's Baby" (147–58) derives much of its depth not only from its subject matter but from the deft manipulation of its artistry, within which small touches and subtle suggestions create a wave of meaning that culminates in the tragic irony of the conclusion. The setting is in farm country on the Cane River in Natchitoches Parish where two plantations, Valmondé and

L'Abri, are located a good distance apart. The narrative technique is omniscient with a shifting identification with the minds of various characters, showing, in parallax, the contrasting evaluations each person makes of the developing situation. The method is also essentially minimalistic, with subtle suggestions of meaning inherent in offhand remarks by the characters or in the movements they make about a room.

The action begins with Madame Valmondé who, the day being so pleasant, decides to drive over to L'Abri to see Désirée and the baby. The name of the plantation is ironic in that it means "the shelter," a benevolent refuge it does not afford the young mother. Indeed, the Aubigny residence is dark and foreboding, a place of violence and cruelty, as is slowly revealed. The brief trip gives Madame opportunity to daydream a bit, and she remembers the day her husband found the infant Désirée by the pillars at the entrance to Valmondé plantation nearly two decades before. They decided to keep the foundling and raise her as their own daughter despite the racial uncertainties of her birth, a matter that generated local speculation. The emphasis in this opening is on parental love for the beautiful young girl, and the adoptive mother and father conclude that a "beneficient Providence" sent them a perfect child on whom to bestow their affection. The mystery of her birth looms over the subsequent events, however, bending the meaning of them in accord with regional values. But the tone of the opening is one of deep and abiding love, the unconditional affection of adoring parents for a child.

The second section shifts to the time Armand Aubigny first saw Désirée when she was eighteen and fell in love with her. This event is also driven by affection, but the incident carries with it ominous additional information, that he had been born in Paris and lived there until age eight. His mother died in France and apparently was never seen by anyone in America, hence her race remained a lingering question from that point onward. France, of course, enjoyed liberal racial policies even in the early nineteenth century, and an interracial marriage would not have been unusual there. One of the ironies in the situation is that when the French drafted the *Code Noir* in 1685 to govern slave matters in the colonies, they did not apply the same codes to the home country, and interracial relationships were common. An educated New Orleans audience at the end of the century would be aware of the disparity, and many more readers at the time of initial publication would have suspected a biracial parentage for Armand than would even consider the suggestion a century later. At the time of the action, however, Armand wishes to marry Désirée, and there seems to be no obstacle from his point of view. Monsieur Valmondé, however, acutely aware of the uncertain origins of his daughter, "wanted things well considered," but the passion of the moment propelled an almost immediate wedding.

The first two sections thus provide a fragmentary background for the two main characters and suggest uncertain aspects of their parentage. The third part resumes the "present" action of the opening, Madame Valmondé's visit to her daughter after not seeing her for four weeks. The imagery associated with L'Abri as she arrives is ominous, the roof "black like a cowl" surrounded by "big, solemn oaks" with branches that shade the house "like a pall" (149). Two references to the past are also negative: the reminder that Armand's mother had died in France without ever coming to America, and the comment about his cruel treatment of slaves, unlike his father's "easy-going and indulgent lifetime." Unknown to the son, the father had married a woman of African descent.

This part presents Désirée for the first time as a mother, with a son at her breast and a "yellow nurse woman" by the window. Racial mixing is apparently common on this plantation, and the servant is a quadroon. Madame Valmondé also appears as a loving mother, embracing Désirée tenderly, but as she looks at the infant she exclaims "this is not the baby!" (150). Significantly, she speaks in French, as do all the characters, and the narrator translates into English. It is clear that she sees African features in the child. Désirée totally misunderstands her mother's remark, thinking that it refers to how much he has grown. She seeks confirmation from the "yellow" woman, Zandrine. Désirée then mentions the volume of the child's crying, saying that "Armand heard him the other day as far away as La Blanche's cabin" (150). That Armand was in the mulatto's cabin suggests that he may have been seeking sexual gratification with one of his slaves; her children are referred to as quadroons, meaning that they have a white father, and he is certainly a candidate, which would compromise his later outrage regarding ethnicity. Chopin then handles Madame's response with great delicacy: "Madame Valmondé had never removed her eyes from the child. She lifted it and walked with it over to the window that was lightest. She scanned the baby narrowly, then looked as searchingly at Zandrine, whose face was turned to gaze across the fields" (150). Madame Valmondé is preoccupied with the racial implications of what she sees in the baby. She looks at Zandrine to examine similarities of color and confirmation, and the suggestion is that the servant "knows" and looks out the window to avoid having to confirm, in her demeanor, what the mother suspects. She asks "what does Armand say?" out of fear that the father is aware. Armand's behavior has changed since the birth of the baby, especially in his treatment of the slaves, with whom he is now less harsh. There are hints in the description of his "dark, handsome face" that he may be the one of mixed blood, but this point is not further developed at this juncture.

The fourth section moves ahead four months and deals directly with Désirée and Armand. Apparently, Madame Valmondé is not the only person to have noticed the race of the child, for there is an "air of mystery" among the slaves on L'Abri, and Armand's attitude has undergone an "awful change" (152). Désirée's intense maternal love has prevented her from seeing anything unusual about her child, but now it is her turn to look at the baby and back at one of La Blanche's "quadroon boys," which inspires a startling epiphany as she sees the resemblance: "The blood turned like ice in her veins, and a clammy moisture gathered upon her face" (153). As in Greek tragedy, it is a moment of insight that impels the catastrophic conclusion. When she asks her husband to explain, he responds, bluntly, that it means "the child is not white; it means that you are not white" (154). She writes to her mother, seeking refutation of the accusation, but her mother only asks her to return home with her baby. The Valmondés entertain liberal views of racial issues, and their love for their daughter far transcends ethnic prejudices. Désirée does not find the invitation comforting. When she asks if he wants her to leave the house, he says "Yes, I want you to go," and the stage is set for two avenues of concluding action (155).

The first is Armand's self-righteous vindication: "He thought Almighty God had dealt cruelly and unjustly with him; and felt, somehow, that he was paying Him back in kind when he stabbed thus into his wife's soul" (155). The narrative perspective is here identified with his mind, his justifications, and it reveals that he does not love his wife any longer. When she says goodbye, "he did not answer her. That was his last blow at fate" (156). In response, she walks with her baby into the bayou and presumably drowns, committing suicide rather than facing the racial complexity of the situation. She never questions his assumptions of her racial identity nor his certainty about his own.

That leads to the denouement, the scene at L'Abri in which Armand is burning everything that reminds him of Désirée and the baby, her clothing, the cradle, letters from her. In examining these he finds one from his mother to his father revealing that she had African blood and that Armand is thus multiracial (158). It is a stunning conclusion, one that has garnered almost obsessive attention for more than a century. This revelation casts a different light on the action in several dimensions. The parents of Armand and Désirée are all revealed to be morally and racially enlightened, perfectly capable of thinking beyond ethnicity to the character of the people around them. Armand's father knowingly married a black woman, which would have been perfectly legal in nineteenth-century France. His mother was willing to marry outside her own race, and she was aware of the opprobrium that her son's background would bring in America, so she kept it hidden from him.

On the Valmondé side, they deliberately adopted a child not knowing her racial identity. Later, when it appears she has black blood, they are lovingly eager to take her back into the household.

It is thus the younger generation that harbors rigid racial attitudes. Désirée would seem to be somewhat benign on ethnic matters, celebrating when her husband shows kindness to the slaves, although she does not question the practice of involuntary servitude at any point. She dies, in part, because she cannot live with the rejection of the man she so desperately loves. Further, she apparently does not want her child, whom she assumes to be biracial, to live in a racist society. Neither parent considers the possibility of a return to France, where Armand lived the first eight years of his life, and where ethnic identity would play no role in their relationship. Armand entertains the most negative view of race, so the ironic sentiments of his mother hits hardest on him: "I thank the good God for having so arranged our lives that our dear Armand will never know that his mother, who adores him, belongs to the race that is cursed with the brand of slavery" (158). The destructive potential of racial attitudes is brought home with searing irony, a sting that can be felt more than a century after first publication of the story. A tragic figure in the classical sense, he realizes the truth too late, and that recognition makes all the difference.[56]

What ultimately emerges, however, is a generational gulf in ethnic attitudes. Armand's parents, one white, one black, were obviously able to transcend race and embrace their love for one another, and they entered freely into a legal marriage in France. Even in Natchitoches Parish, free persons of color were widely accepted into society, and many of them attained wealth and prestige, as did the mulattoes on the L'Isle des Mulatres.[57] Désirée's adoptive parents were eager to take a child of unknown racial identity into their family and raise her, lovingly, as their own.[58] When she writes home to her mother suggesting that she may be of mixed race, her mother is willing to take her and her baby into the fold of the Valmondé plantation.[59] The children of these parents, however, demonstrate retrograde ethnic attitudes: Armand is cruel to his slaves and drives Désirée out of the house when he suspects she is of mixed blood. For her part, Désirée is unwilling to live as a black person in the South, and she dies, killing her baby, rather than endure such a life. That she is totally wrong about the facts in the case does nothing to mitigate the searing indictment of racism at the heart of Chopin's most famous story.

"A Visit to Avoyelles" (223–29) is a Local-Color tale and a grim inversion of the heroic legend of the outsider who arrives just in time to save the beautiful maiden in distress. It originally appeared in *Vogue* in 1893 under the title "The Lover of Mentine," which added additional irony to the conclusion.[60] Presented as the community perspective of the events, the background is that as a younger man Doudouce had a romance with Mentine, who is now, seven years later, married to Jules Trodon, who farms the thin soil of Avoyelles Parish. The rumors, always with an element of uncertainty, suggest that Mentine is terribly unhappy in the marriage, saddled with at least four children, living in poverty with a man she does not love. In his fantasies Doudouce sees her reaching out to him for rescue, and he is determined to go to her and bring her away from a life of hardship and toil. That motivation sets up the twist in the stereotypical romance plot.

Doudouce journeys to the Trodon farm and finds Mentine as he had suspected, carrying an infant with two young children underfoot. Her dialect places her among the unlettered poor: "*Mais* Doudouce, that ent you, *comment!* Well, if any one would tole me this mornin'! Git a chair, 'Tit Jules. That's Mista Doudouce, f'om 'way yonda Natchitoches w're yo' maman use' to live. *Mais*, you ent change'; you' lookin' well, Doudouce" (225). He is uncomfortable wearing his Sunday best, suggesting that he, too, works the soil, and neither of them fit traditional romantic characterizations. She has grown older, with lines in her face and a distorted shape. Jules arrives from the fields, and they dine together, Doudouce realizing that he loves Mentine still: "But he loved her now as he never had. Because she was no longer beautiful, he loved her" (229). The shock of the ending comes when Jules walks away, returning to the fields, and Mentine gazes lovingly after him, obviously a devoted wife despite the poverty of her situation.

It is thus Doudouce who is left bewildered at the realization that although her physical circumstances are what he had expected, her emotional life is rich and fulfilling, and she still loves her husband. It is thus one of Chopin's rare stories of female fidelity within marriage, of the permanence of romantic devotion. As Allen F. Stein formulates it, "Chopin thus does offer something both new and disturbing: . . . a woman whose continuing happiness with her husband marks and perpetuates an imprisonment of which she is blithely unaware."[61] Far from longing for rescue, Mentine seems happy in her squalor, and the romantic expectations of the familiar chivalric plot are thus deflated and made grimly inappropriate.[62]

Another drama about love with a racial subtheme is "Loka" (193–206), which fits into a series of works involving parental or surrogate affection for children.[63] Once again the plot is less important that the inherent attitudes and values displayed by the characters. A Choctaw girl, Loka is one of Chopin's few Native American protagonists and one here portrayed in stereotypical terms as lazy, violent, unattractive, and "big-boned and clumsy" (194). As Ewell has suggested, "the Choctaw life Loka has escaped is virtually synonymous with dishonest and brutish behavior," a singularly negative portrait of an ethnic minority group.[64] Loka is briefly employed at an "oyster saloon" in Natchitoches, but she is discharged when she breaks glasses over the heads of the customers. The community is at odds of what to do with her when Madame Laballière suggests placing her with a large Acadian family who could use some assistance around the home. Thus, Loka comes to live with Baptiste and Tontine Padue and their children on a small farm in the southern part of the parish.

The remainder of the plot deals with that family and Loka's place as an outsider attempting to fit into a new society. She does not speak French, the standard language of the area, and her English is substandard, despite her protestations to the contrary: "I kin talk English good's anybody; an' lit' bit Choctaw, too" (195). She is deliberate in her tasks about the house and indifferent to responsibility, but her redeeming quality is her love for Bibine, an infant boy. Her internal crisis comes on a day she is left alone with the baby, and she contemplates escaping from her duties. Gazing intently into the woods she experiences a vision of "Marot, the squaw who drank whisky and plaited baskets and beat her" (199). Marot had wanted Loka to "steal and cheat, to beg and lie" when they went out to sell baskets, but there was something within the girl that resisted such behavior, and she ran away, coming to Natchitoches. Her vision broadens to include the sounds of the bayou and the creatures living in it, a verdant wilderness she misses deeply, and she takes the baby and disappears into nature.

When the Padues return home, the house is empty with no sign of Loka or the baby, and they are not to be found in the surrounding homes and fields. A short time later, however, she is spotted climbing over the fence on her way to the house, and Baptiste gallops out and brings back the infant. Later, Loka explains what has happened, saying that "Bibine an' me, . . . we was lonesome—we been take lit' 'broad in de wood" (204). Madame Padue is outraged at the despair she felt when the baby was missing, and she wants the girl dismissed, but Loka explains that it was her love for Bibine that caused her to take him with her. Baptiste argues Loka's case, saying that she is not inherently bad, that the strictures placed on her have been too severe, and that, fundamentally, "we got to rememba she ent like you an' me, po' thing; she's one Injun, her" (206).

Thus the conclusion brings the focus back to the racial issue dealing with the behavior and fundamental nature of the indigenous population. Loka has had difficulty merging into Acadian culture, but she has learned to love a baby and returned from her flight because of him. Now, transformed by affection, she wants to continue to have him in her life. It is not, as Shaker has argued, that "the narrative treats Loka less as a sympathetic subject than as an object through which to teach white southerners a kinder, gentler management style for governing people of color."[65] Chopin's fiction is not didactic in such practical terms; rather, she has shown another instance in which a young woman rebels against the restrictions imposed upon her, undergoes a transformative awareness of herself, and emerges a person of her own making. The important conflict, the internal one, is inside Loka, not outside in the world of social acceptance. For that reason, it is strange that the narrative perspective in the concluding scene stays with the point of view of Baptiste Padue, not with Loka, thus conveying this important psychological change only from the outside.[66] It is Loka's feelings of love for Bibine and responsibility to the Padue family that bring her back, not issues of law or race or fear.[67]

Other stories in the volume deal with singular issues but always with some relevance to the central themes of the book. "Old Aunt Peggy," for example, recalls a negotiation at the moment of emancipation in 1865 when a former slave, Peggy, presented her former masters with her request that she be allowed to stay on the plantation: "Massa, I ain't never gwine to quit yer. I'm gettin' ole an' feeble, an' my days is few in dis heah lan' o' sorrow an' sin. All I axes is a li'le co'ner whar I kin set down an' wait peaceful fu de en'" (111). Touched by the extraordinary fidelity of this newly freed woman, the plantation owners set aside a cabin for her, complete with a favorite rocking chair. But the entreaty turns out to have been a sinecure rather than a deferential gesture, for Aunt Peggy has lived comfortably in her idleness for decades, supported by the largess of her former masters, and she now claims to be 125 years old, although the narrator interjects "possibly she is older" (112). This is the kind of relationship Grace King might write about, one in which the slave proved more clever than the master, and one in which bargains are honorably kept.

A story with a similar theme of fidelity and love between a white man and a former slave is "For Marse Chouchoute" (210–22), Chopin's first contribution to *Youth's Companion*,[68] suggesting that she considered it to be a tale for children, and the first, as Shaker has said, "to address the change in Louisiana's post–Civil War social order from an antebellum slave society to postbellum emancipation."[69] A model of Local-Color tendencies, it captures Creole and black regional dialect, the complex relationships between the races after the war, and the sacrificial loyalty some "negro" boys felt for the white men they admired. The plot is characteristically simple. Armand Verchette, called "Chouchoute" by all around him, is a handsome and charming fatherless gadabout with no sense of responsibility or discipline. Somehow he secures a job bringing the Cloutierville mailbag from the village to the railway station three miles away. His constant companion is a young black man, Wash, who venerates his every move. What emerges is that Wash is the deserving character, selfless and generous, while Chouchoute is thoughtless and destructive. One spring evening, when he should have been carrying the mail, he stops by a dance, eagerly joins in, and totally forgets his duties. Wash, on the other hand, takes the horse at the last minute and races to the railroad, arrives late, and, galloping alongside, throws the mail bag onto the moving train, only to be mortally injured. Attending to the dying boy, Chouchoutte hears Wash explain what happened: "Dar warn't a minute, so I gits top o' Spunky—I neva seed nuttin' cl'ar de road like dat. I come 'long side—de train—an' fling de sack. I seed 'im kotch it, and I don' know nuttin mo''cep' mise'ry. . . . I boun' to git well, 'ca'se who—gwine—watch Marse—Chouchoutte" (222). Even his last words express his concern for his friend, a somewhat idealized portrait of vestigial love and loyalty of former slaves, and their descendants, to the white "gentlemen" they admire.

If the story is a didactic tale aimed at children, as Nancy A. Walker assumes, it would seem to emphasize loyalty and self-sacrifice for others.[70] Shaker, however, puts the emphasis on Chouchoutte and the meaning of the events for him. She argues that the story "teaches America's first generation of young white males to reach adolescence since Reconstruction their proper relationship and responsibility to others in society through the inculcation of white, Anglo-Saxon, Protestant middle-class values."[71] Of course Chouchoutte is a French Roman Catholic, and he demonstrates the weakness for frivolity and the life of gaiety that characterized Creole life in Louisiana for two centuries. It was the "American" ethic that invaded local society in 1803 and created the conflict between two approaches to work and responsibility that invest the stories of George Washington Cable.

"A Turkey Hunt" (159–62) is more of a sketch than a story, but it presents black characters on a plantation in a humorous and yet meaningful way.[72] Although some scholars have commented that it offers but a "superficial view of human behavior" and a central character who is but a "figure of humor,"[73] other readers have been more sensitive to the psychology behind the simplistic mask. Peggy Skaggs, for example, is insightful in remarking that Artemise, a young black girl, "has one outstanding characteristic, a placid self-containment that suggests she feels quite complete within herself."[74] Told in first person, the plot involves three missing turkeys who turn out to have been locked in the chicken coop. What is of the moment is character revelation, as the simple Artemise, who appears incapable of the most simple tasks, emerges as correct in her assessment of the location of the missing fowl. A flashback reveals her limitations, as she is unable to light a fire, for example, and the narrator condescends to her as does Aunt Florindy, the cook. Yet despite the fact that the entire household was sent to search for the missing turkeys, it is Artimise who finds them. She has intellectual resources hidden by her circumstances, a common situation for freed slaves in postbellum Louisiana.

Another charming sketch is "Boulôt and Boulotte" (207–09), which deals with impoverished twins in Natchitoches Parish who finally receive money to buy shoes, a luxury among their peers.[75] They walk into town on a Saturday afternoon, but the narrative perspective remains with the children back home, who eagerly await the return of their friends and the display of the new footwear. When the twins come into view, it is clear that they are carrying their shoes, not wearing them, and they are met with derision: "You go buy shoes, an' come home barefeet like you was go" (206). The shoes are then described, a pair of brogans for Boulôt and high heels with buttons for his sister. She defends their actions: "You 'spec Boulôt an' me we got money fur was'e—us? . . . You think we go buy shoes fur ruin it in de dus'?" (209). The twins walk into their house, and the sketch ends.

The most important aspect of this brief account relates to gender differentiation and the Local-Color representation of dialect and social customs. As Ewell has commented, insightfully, "this extremely brief and very straightforward work exemplifies many of the most successful aspects of Chopin's craft, including her ability to pique our interest, her manipulation of perspective, her sharp and vivid focus, her ability to avoid a maudlin tone even when writing about the very young and the very poor, and especially her deft use of local color and regional speech."[76] Certainly the dialect of the Acadian poor is fascinating in itself, but the representation of a moment of confrontation in which the female twin proves to be the more assertive and resourceful is significant. Throughout *Bayou Folk* it is often the case that women, even young girls, discover strength within themselves in a moment of conflict, and normally that realization is transformative. This sketch is so brief that any subsequent demonstrations of stolidity are not covered, but it is clear that Chopin's theme of the assertive New Woman begins early in the lives of her characters.

"A Very Fine Fiddle" presents a brief plot in which a daughter sells her father's vintage violin, making a huge profit.[77] She replaces it with a new one that he plays once and sets aside, vowing never to touch it again (96–98). The situation recapitulates the plot of Dunbar-Nelson's "M'Sieu Fortier's Violin" in its emphasis on the value of music in French culture, in the capturing of the local dialect, and in the contrast between the wealthy outsiders who purchase the instrument and the impoverished protagonist who values it highly for noncommercial reasons.

"A Gentleman of Bayou Têche" (291–303) first appeared in *Bayou Folk*, and it focuses on the sensitivity of an Acadian, Evariste, who is asked by a visiting artist to pose for a painting. He first assumes that he should dress in his Sunday best for the sitting, but he is asked to look as though he just came out of the swamp. When he is told by a black woman, Aunt Dicey, that the caption of his image will probably read "dis heah is one dem low-down 'Cajuns o' Bayou Têche," he is embarrassed and resolves to return the two dollars he was given for posing. Later, the son of the painter, Archie Sublet, overturns his pirogue in the swamp and is saved by Evariste, who dives into the water to rescue him. In return Sublet agrees to allow Evariste to chose any title he wishes for the painting, and the Acadian responds that the caption should read "Dis is one picture of Mista Evariste Anatole Bonamour, a gent'man of de Bayou Têche" (303).

There is cultural significance beneath the surface plot, beginning with the basic point that "the resolution of the story both establishes Evariste's humanity and allows him to resist being categorized as an exotic specimen."[78] Beyond his poverty, Evariste is Acadian, illiterate, trusting, and poor, but he is capable of embarrassment; he has his own feelings of dignity and does not wish to be humiliated in a magazine.[79] Cable wrote about the Bayou Têche as well, of course, but Chopin gives the region a complex dynamic, beginning with the fact that the local black population condescends to the Acadians, thinking them without guile and unaware of insidious cunning. Aunt Dicey says to Evariste's daughter, Martinette, "I jis studyin' how simple you an' yo' pa is. You is bof de simplest somebody I eva come 'crost" (294). Later, when Evariste has rescued the Sublet boy and is invited to dine with the artist, the black waiter expresses superiority to the Acadian: "It was with visible reluctance and ill-disguised contempt that Wilkins served them" (301). Many Cane River black people had once been the slaves of the aristocratic plantation owners and identified with the names and stature of those families, looking down on uncultured and impoverished Acadians, who occupied the lowest level of society. What the conclusion emphasizes, however, is that wealth is not a necessary component of a sense of self-worth, despite the inculcated stratification of society. Evariste, notwithstanding his simplicity, has performed a heroic act worthy of admiration, but he remains the same character. It is the artist, Sublet, who has been forced to adjust his values, to regard the rustic farmer as a man worthy of respect rather than as an example of regional charm and peculiarity.

It is intriguing that an artist seeking local color for a painting should be featured in another art form within the same tradition. Chopin was quite aware of the regional tradition, of course, and the same year she published *Bayou Folk* she reviewed Hamlin Garland's *Crumbling Idols*, which advocated Local Colorism as the highest and most original American literary form. Chopin endorsed that idea, arguing that "the youthful artist should free himself from the hold of conventionalism; that he should go direct to those puissant sources, Life and Nature, for inspiration and turn his back upon models furnished by man; in a word, that he should be creative and not imitative."[80] Writing in St. Louis, Chopin focused almost exclusively on Louisiana settings and characters, finding within the complex social dynamic of a multi-ethnic culture the psychological, social, and personal conflicts that enriched her decade of writing. Unlike King, Chopin's work does not celebrate the fallen aristocracy of Louisiana nor lament its passing. She most often deals with individuals in the present; King's characters live in the past, time having passed them by.

Beyond portraying characters throughout the social strata, however, Chopin uniquely focuses on feminine gender issues that were new to American literature. As Davis has indicated, her work is "distinguished for the frankness with which she approached sexuality, the amorality with which she described such problems as divorce and adultery, and for the serious consideration she gave to the restrictions of marriage and childbearing and the uses of freedom."[81] In a similar vein, Taylor contends that Chopin's ultimate significance "lies in her particular use of Local-Color techniques, and of regional and historical themes and allusions, that challenged European male and English and American female fictional definitions of femininity and female sexuality. She made an important contribution to debates about gender of relevance to the South of the 1890s."[82] The individual stories in the volume represent a significant advance in the art of storytelling in both subject and technique, something that Fred Lewis Pattee was quick to acknowledge. He observed that "without models, without study or short-story art, without revision, and usually at a sitting, she produced what often are masterpieces before which one can only wonder and conjecture."[83] Among the number of outstanding stories in *Bayou Folk*, "Désirée's Baby," "A No-Account Creole," and "La Belle Zoraïde" are certainly among the finest works of fiction of the 1890s, and their standing in the literary hierarchy grew with each decade of the twentieth century. Although somewhat obscured by the monumental achievement of *The Awakening*, the stories in *Bayou Folk*, and the volume itself, deserve a prominent position in the literary history of American Realism.

Conclusion

The Literary Legacy

As a subject of serious literature, Louisiana emerged in the second half of the nineteenth century as the most complex and vibrant geographic area in the country. Unique among the states for its founding as an extension of the French empire, its four decades of rule by the Spanish, its incorporation into the United States by the Louisiana Purchase in 1803, and its complex mixture of cultures, languages, religions, and traditions, New Orleans and its surrounding plantations and bayous provided a virtually inexhaustible wealth of issues for literary exploration. The French Creole obsession with culture and refinement gave elegance to the city, but the predilection for gambling, drinking, and dueling weakened the foundations of society, and the stratifications of race, caste, and wealth further separated the elite from the mass of the population.

Despite the national interest in the New South and the enormous popularity of Local Colorism, the area had not been a major setting for fiction until the work of George Washington Cable, Grace King, Alice Dunbar-Nelson, and Kate Chopin, all of whom established themselves as important national figures in the world of letters. Although as a group these writers portrayed essentially the entire spectrum of life in the Crescent City, they all focused on a subset of characters and themes for a short-fiction cycle, often revisiting locations, issues, and even characters in a series of stories. As a result, their volumes fulfilled the highest demands of the cycle tradition, the norms of Local Colorism, and the rigorous ethical explorations that had become standard in American Realism.

Although Cable lived in the Lower Garden District of New Orleans at 1313 Eighth Street, his fiction is set primarily in the French Quarter in actual buildings on historically accurate streets. The protagonist of "'Sieur George," for example, is said to live on the fourth floor of his apartment building, as indeed he did, on the corner of 640 Royal Street at the intersection with St. Peter Avenue, later a tourist attraction as the first structure of that height in the city and one of several landmarks derived from the author's fiction. "Madame Delphine" takes place in a area known for the residences of *plaçage* quadroons, as does "'Tite Poulette," which involves a dwelling now commemorated generically as "Madame John's Legacy," a two-story structure at 632 Dumaine Street. Cable knew the city well, as he demonstrated in his historical studies, especially *The Creoles of Louisiana* (1884) and *The Negro Question* (1888), the subjects of which reveal the major issues of his fiction.

As Per Seyersted has indicated, Cable "used his short stories . . . to dramatize the conflict between the French and the Yankee civilizations, showing the Creoles' resistance to change and their inevitable retreat in front of the growing pressure from *les Américains*."[1] His knowledge reached back to the founding of Louisiana and the complex social and political adjustments required by its transformations from French rule to Spanish, back to French, and finally to incorporation into the rapidly growing United States. His understanding of the people and their region was rich and analytical, representing prejudices, weaknesses, impressive achievements, and cultural strengths, but always with an emphasis on the Crescent City, including the subtleties of ethnic streets, taverns, and neighborhoods. Grace King, however, resented Cable's portrayal of society, arguing that "Cable proclaimed his preference for colored people over white and assumed the inevitable superiority—according to his theories—of the quadroons over the Creoles. He was a native of New Orleans and had been well treated by its people, and yet he stabbed the city in the back, as we felt, in a dastardly way to please the Northern press."[2] Despite her criticism, the city eventually honored Cable for his career and went on to name a number of historic buildings after places in his stories that derived from genuine locations. The Café des Exilés was on Royal Street, for example, and Ursin Lemaitre's smuggling negotiations would probably have been conducted out of Jean Lafitte's blacksmith shop at 941 Bourbon Street, which was well known for such activities. The topographical details mentioned throughout the eight stories of *Old Creole Days* comport to cartographical verification. All of this is especially remarkable in that Cable set much of his work decades before the Civil War and prior to his birth in the city. Thus, he had to reconstruct the streets and buildings and conditions of a much earlier era, something he did with impressive accuracy.

Grace King also knew the city extremely well and, as did Cable, wrote historical books about it in addition to fiction. Her *A History of Louisiana* in 1893 was followed by *New Orleans: The Place and the People* in 1895, suggesting that the period of composition of *Balcony Stories* was during the same years that she was deeply engrossed in the study of the life of her region, a concern that finally concluded with *Creole Families of New Orleans* in 1921. When she went on an extended trip throughout Europe, she recorded that when she returned home "New Orleans was never more attractive as a heroine of literature. The early winter was dazzlingly beautiful and the heart could not but feel inspired by a subject that offered so many wonderful sides, not only to history, but to the imagination that enhances it. My mother was born here and, splendid *raconteuse* that she was, she turned every episode of her life into a good and colorful story."[3] If Cable's fiction primarily depicts the antebellum South, King chose to write about a period she had personally witnessed, Reconstruction and its aftermath in New Orleans and the surrounding area.

The people she knew and understood the best were the privileged elite of the city, and she presented them with impressive insight, handling the subtleties of feeling in "The Old Lady's Restoration" and "A Delicate Affair" with startling awareness, for example. The crushing realities depicted in "La Grande Demoiselle," based on two of her former teachers, would have been especially close to her family in their home at 1749 Coliseum Street, just across from Coliseum Square. Her perceptions into the dominant religion of New Orleans gave rise to the pathos of "The Little Convent Girl" and "The Miracle Chapel," just as rationality and empirical science inform the background of the key character in "A Drama of Three." King's portrayal of one of the few important African-American characters in her fiction in "A Crippled Hope" suggests the limitations of her personal experience with slavery: the relationship between white owners and black slaves is discussed in only the most benevolent and idyllic terms. With the exception of her portrayal of black life in Louisiana, however, King worked close to her personal knowledge, showing the areas of the city she knew best, dealing with the dramas and conflicts that had unfolded all around her throughout her childhood and adolescence.

Alice Dunbar-Nelson, whose mother had been a slave in Louisiana, grew up in New Orleans as Alice Moore, took a teaching degree in 1892 from Straight University, and taught in the public school system for six years before marrying and moving north for the rest of her life. As Mary Anne O'Neal has pointed out, Dunbar-Nelson came from a background very different from the other three writers: "She was the only one of these writers who obtained a college degree and the only one who had a career other than writing. Because of her race, she regarded history much differently than did King or Chopin. She referred to Reconstruction, for example, as 'a halcyon period' and praised the accomplishments of Benjamin Butler, a man vilified by white New Orleanians."[4] Part African American, she used the term

"Creole" throughout her fiction to mean people of mixed race, unlike Cable and King, who retained the original sense of the term. However, racial designation did not in any way limit the range of her characters or the conflicts in their lives, and her themes focus primarily on the restricted lives of women of any color.[5]

Indeed, often the ethnic identity of her characters is uncertain, as it is in "The Goodness of Saint Rocque," although Manuela's name and complexion suggest either Spanish or, perhaps, African origin, unlike her rival, Claralie, whose blond hair and name indicate a French background, although they are both part of a "Creole" group of young people. They worship at St. Rocque's Chapel on Marais Street in the mixed-race section of the city. The German wife of the Italian Tony is clearly white, as are M'sieu Fortier, who goes home in the French section near Bayou St. John, and Annette in "The Fisherman of Pass Christian." Tante Marie of "The Praline Woman" is clearly of African descent, although there are hints of Caribbean influence on many of Dunbar-Nelson's black characters, as with the Wizened One in the opening story. Mr. Baptiste seems to be French, which heightens the irony of his death in the racial conflict on the docks. Two characters are of uncertain ethnicity but seem likely to have some African blood: Sophie, who was the mistress of a white man, a remnant of the plaçage marriages of the antebellum period, and Camille, who becomes Sister Josepha because of the hint of color in her skin.

"Sister Josepha" is the easiest story to locate geographically within the city because it takes place in the Convent of the Sacred Heart at 4521 St. Charles Avenue, a short walk from Jackson Square and St. Louis Cathedral, where she goes to pray. "Titee" takes place in the Third District just east of the French Quarter where he goes to school on Marigny Street. He catches crawfish in the Claiborne and Marigny canals. Odalie, of Spanish and French blood, lives on Royal Street, where a key character sells pralines, and celebrates Mardi Gras on Toulouse Street. Disappointed in love, she retreats to the Ursuline Convent on Chartres Street. The action in "A Carnival Jangle" is even more specifically located since the celebration proceeds down Bourbon Street, turns on to Toulouse and St. Peter Streets, and proceeds onto Rampart Street at the edge of the French Quarter.

It is clear that Dunbar-Nelson had a detailed knowledge of her home city, as did Cable and King, and the locations of their settings is significant in suggesting ethnic identity and social rank. The best educated of the New Orleans writers, Dunbar-Nelson also moved in the most cultured circles, with season tickets to the opera, good seats at the symphony, and a vibrant social life among the educated classes. Grace King was the best "connected" in social terms, and she often dined with traveling dignitaries and lecturers.

Cable, who fought for the Confederacy and was wounded in the Civil War, seems to have felt himself an outsider throughout his life in New Orleans, even more so than Kate Chopin, who had been born in St. Louis and lived only a decade in the city.

Kate Chopin and her family lived in several different houses in the 1870s, including one still standing at 1413 Louisiana Avenue in New Orleans, between Coliseum and Prytania Streets. Her husband, Oscar, had a short commute to his office at 65 Carondelet, just off Canal Street. In addition, they owned property in Natchitoches Parish, the center of which was Cloutierville, where she lived with her children for two years after Oscar died. It is notable that, despite the historical transformations in the rest of Louisiana, Natchitoches was a "homogeneous cultural entity which is still nearly untouched by Yankee influence. The problem of a dying civilization is therefore not to be found here."[6] Chopin wrote about the young living in the present; as Seyersted maintains, "she was not interested in a dying civilization, and she had no wish to rescue the past."[7] What is remarkable is that all of her fiction about Louisiana was written in Missouri after she had returned to St. Louis to live with her mother. Nonetheless, her memory of the Crescent City was precise, with streets and intersections clearly identified and the feel of life in the various districts accurately described.

In "A No-Account Creole," for example, the opening scene has Wallace Offdean and Fitch walking along Canal Street, which marked the perimeter of the business district where the Americans established financial institutions following the Louisiana Purchase in 1803. Fitch lives in the fashionable area of Prytania Street, as did the Chopins, although most proper Creoles had residences in the French Quarter. The action then moves to Natchitoches Parish for a time but returns for crucial scenes in the city that clarify issues of social rank and financial status. Offdean's love interest, Euphrasie, comes to visit friends in New Orleans, and they live on Esplanade Street, one of the most fashionable addresses in a stratified society based on wealth and position. The young lady, the address suggests, would be an acceptable wife for a businessman who had just inherited a small fortune. Her host, the mother of Mrs. Duplan, prides herself on not having crossed Canal Street for many years. Doing so would involve passing into the American district, where business is transacted and English is spoken, matters quite anathema to the Creole elite. When Euphrasie's Natchitoches suitor, Placide Santien, comes to the city, he stays with his brother Hector, a gambler who lives "in some obscure corner of the town" (28). Chopin's "A Lady of Bayou St. John" takes place in the west side of central New Orleans bounded by Esplanade Avenue on one side and the marsh itself on the west. A central character in both "A Lady of Bayou St. John" and "La Belle Zoraïde," Madame Delisle also lives in the immediate area, where she can watch boats on the bayou in the evening and still be part of the vibrant life of the city.

All four of these writers placed their stories in the French Quarter using the same major thoroughfares, historic buildings, and memorable locations. All of them also reached out to place action in the surroundings bayous and on the northern plantations, especially those along the Mississippi, although Chopin favored the region she knew best, the Cane River section of Natchitoches Parish. Cable gave his fiction the greatest temporal range, reaching back as far as 1803 and emphasizing the 1830s, a decade of swift cultural transformation for Louisiana. Setting his action in this period allowed him to address issues anachronistic at the time he was writing: slavery, the plaçage tradition, the insidious rigidity of the caste system, and the destructiveness of racial classification. His primary characters are Creole aristocrats, fallen gentry clinging to pretensions of status. He also focuses on quadroon women caught in a social structure that offered them few alternatives to concubinage, however benign some aspects of it might have been. Of the four writers, Cable most emphasized ethnic discrimination and racism as insidious forces within New Orleans society, more than even Alice Dunbar-Nelson, who stressed gender issues over those of racial identity. In fact, as Violet Harrington Bryan has pointed out, unlike Cable, "King, Chopin, and Dunbar-Nelson used the city to confront women's social issues, the restrictions of gender roles, especially as these influenced marriage and divorce, career, social networking, and motherhood."[8] In short, Dunbar-Nelson's work was not limited to the racial themes that many readers expected of her.

In fact, her stories present the lives of the broadest range of ethnic characters: French, German, Irish, Italian, African, Acadian, various degrees of Creole mixture, and characters of indeterminate ethnicity. The conflicts in her work explore a variety of issues, although the vagaries of romantic courtship prove central to her plots. The cruelty of an abusive marriage, an unfortunate theme in her own life, invests "Tony's Wife" with unique pathos, although the heartache central to "Little Miss Sophie" and "When the Bayou Overflows" gives her volume emotional depth. Grace King deals with psychology in very different terms, exploring pathological states in formerly wealthy women wrought by an inability to cope with diminished social stature and financial resources, as in "La Grande Demoiselle," although the war itself brought on sufficient human tragedy to initiate aberrant psychic conditions. Interestingly, Dunbar-Nelson does not touch that theme at all in her fiction, probably because few New Orleans men of color served in the Civil War, thus not many suffered the devastating effects of exposure to mutilation and death.

Kate Chopin, whose brother died serving the Confederacy, wrote most richly about the psychological consequences of battle for both soldiers and civilians, as she did in "The Return of Alcibiade" and "A Wizard from Gettysburg." She also produced the single most powerful work on the racial theme, "Désirée's Baby," one of the great works of short fiction in English. "La Belle Zoraïde," which combines the racial theme with emotional pathology, is a remarkably sensitive portrait of the mind of a slave, one who is a pampered surrogate daughter of an aristocratic woman. Indeed, Chopin's volume demonstrates an astonishing spectrum of themes and issues unique to Louisiana, especially for someone who lived there only slightly more than a decade.

The individual stories in these four volumes represent not only an impressive utilization of the life and culture of New Orleans as a subject for serious literature, some of them are also among the most respected works of short fiction in the nineteenth century. Kate Chopin's "Désirée's Baby" is perhaps the most powerful fictional indictment of racism in American literature. Quite beyond what strikes some people as a surprise ending, it is drawn with great psychological subtlety and artistic restraint, and the scene in which Madame Valmondé first realizes that the child is of mixed race, glancing at Zandrine for confirmation of the color, is taut with tension even though not a word of conflict is uttered. That Zandrine looks out the window at that moment suggests that she also knows the truth and does not want to betray that fact through expression or reaction, so she evades scrutiny by looking away. She sees the baby every day, of course, and she would be well aware of suggestions of African features or skin tones.

Largely neglected in comparison to "Désirée's Baby" is "La Belle Zoraïde," a deeply important story also set in the antebellum plantation country outside of New Orleans. The title alone signifies the most poignant irony as the beautiful and gentle protagonist, still a slave, is driven mad by the insensitive manipulations of her mistress, Madame Delarivière. The frank treatment of feminine sexual desire is even more powerfully presented than that portrayed in *The Awakening*, for example, and much is established through suggestion and implication. The stirring representation of the etiology of aberrant psychological states is remarkable for the nineteenth century, when relatively little had been written about such matters, and Chopin's handling of dramatized narration, the motivation for the telling, the systematic unwinding of the plot, and the power of the conclusion are nothing short of brilliant. These two stories alone fully justified her long and distinguished reputation as a fictional artist of the first rank, as Pattee declared in the early years of the new century.

Grace King also wrote individual stories of artistic integrity that present psychological themes with impressive dexterity, in particular "La Grande Demoiselle" and "A Delicate Affair." The first is of broad significance for the Deep South in that it deals with the fall of a young woman from a life of privilege and grandeur to one of humiliation and poverty, an issue unique to King's work but poignant and compassionate nonetheless. The opulent adolescence of Idalie Sainte Foy Mortemart des Islets is perhaps a bit overdrawn, but it is clear that the wealth she enjoys derives from the labor of the "slaves, slaves, slaves everywhere, whole villages of negro cabins" (22). Told from a communal perspective, from a narrator who has access not to the truth, as in omniscience, but to what is believed to be true by the local community, many of the details of her decline during the war and in the years that followed are not known and can only be supplied through social conjecture, a device later used with masterful skill by William Faulkner. Thus, the collapse of Idalie's social stature, as well as the burning of her mansion, can be portrayed only on the basis of "hearsay. When one has not been present, one knows nothing of one's own knowledge" (30). Unreliable narration is often thought to be a Modernist technique, but King used it with skill and sophistication, tracking the emotional and psychological adjustments Idalie must make in her decline, in her marriage to the undesirable Champigny, and in her employment teaching African-American children.

"A Delicate Affair" is also important for its subtle narrative mode. It is told in retrospective first person by a niece who, at the time of the action, was living with her widowed aunt in New Orleans. Reticent to a fault, the niece saw everything, heard everything, and did virtually nothing, since her actions are entirely absent from the narrative, although the aunt makes direct reference to her when Mr. Horace comes to call, saying that "she (nodding toward me) goes out, but she never learns anything. She is as stupid to-night as an empty bottle" (195). But the niece, as narrator, is not stupid but supremely perceptive, insightful, and aware of the delicate drama unfolding before her. The plot is intricate but not as important as the psychological transformations brought by the subtle manipulations of Mr. Horace, who fell in love with the aunt as a youth and adores her still, many decades after she married another man, and he attends her every Wednesday, supplying her with news and gossip. The aunt is persistently oblivious to the depth of his devotion, but the narrator sees it, understands it, and records his restraint. As a man who has lived with unrequited love throughout his life, he would be aware of how precious deep emotions can be, even on the level of friendships, and he manipulates a reconciliation of the aunt with an estranged former friend, a woman the aunt realized, too late, her husband had also grown to adore. From the moment of that epiphany to the climax of the story, the aunt had shut the friend out of her life. Now, after she was widowed, and her old friend is dying, Mr. Horace brings about a reconciliation and silently slips away, allowing the two friends to express their renewed affection. At the time of the telling, all three of the characters have died and are buried in St. Louis cemetery, leaving only the niece to narrate from memory her account of this delicate affair. It is fiction rendered with a sublimely soft touch worthy of Henry James or Edith Wharton, despite the fact that it has been almost totally ignored for more than a century.

Chopin's stories are impressive for their thematic power on the issue of race, King's for their delicate emotional restraint and consummate artistry. The works of Alice Dunbar-Nelson are important in literary history for the range of their subjects and characters. "Tony's Wife" is one of the earliest portrayals in American literature of an abusive marriage, a matter exacerbated by nationality conflicts in an immigrant neighborhood. "The Goodness of St. Rocque" presents ethnic difference at an earlier stage, in the courtship ritual of adolescents of Spanish and French descent. To ensure success, the young Latina girl enlists the aid of the Wizened One from the Caribbean who practices voodoo. She also beseeches the assistance of Saint Rocque, who, the local folklore insists, ensures the marriage of a young woman who prays to him. "Sister Josepha" is less benevolent in several senses. Catholicism offers a young woman of uncertain racial identity only a life of cloistered worship and worldly denial, a future she accepts because of caste. Perhaps the author's richest portrait is that of Tante Marie of "The Praline Woman," who reveals herself, her life story, her values, and her sensitivity entirely through her patter to customers as they pass by on the streets.

It is remarkable that Dunbar-Nelson had such a light touch on racial themes and George Washington Cable such an emphatic stress on the inhumanity and cruelty of the caste system. The paired importance of "Madame Delphine" and "'Tite Poulette" is that they are the two most important stories on the theme of the *Code Noir* and the plaçage tradition, the first forbidding interracial marriages and the second condoning a system of concubinage, both regulations functioning within the constraints of Napoleonic law. "Belles Demoiselles Plantation" benefits from a dramatic subject, thematic depth, and consummate artistry, all of which explain why it has become the most popular of Cable's short fiction. In one sense it demonstrates the long-term effects of the issues of the first two stories, the descendents of mixed-race relationships, as is the case with Injin Charlie, who owns considerable property in the French Quarter of the city, as was often the case with the children of plaçage arrangements. What Cable adds to this complex situation is this character's inherent nobility and humane generosity, traits that are expressed when he cares tenderly for the dying colonel and attempts to negate the agreement to trade property. Similarly humane, if outcast, is Jean-ah Poquelin, who suffers the contempt and abuse of the community with great dignity while he cares for his leprous brother, unbeknown to local society. It is not until he dies that the truth is revealed, upsetting the moral hierarchy the townspeople had embraced. These are socially and morally important accounts of American life, and no one wrote more powerfully about this spectrum of issues than did Cable in these remarkable stories.

Whatever the power of these individual works, the fact remains that *Old Creole Days, Balcony Stories, Bayou Folk*, and *The Goodness of Saint Rocque and Other Stories* are not simply collections of short fiction but story cycles, volumes that exhibit not only shape but artistic integrity and thematic congruence as unified aesthetic constructs. Each of the parts of *Old Creole Days*, for example, constitutes a complete work of short fiction, but the eight stories as a unit tell a narrative larger than the sum of the parts. The comprehensive tale of the book is one of complex and painful transformation for a society from the French Creole world of Louisiana to a new culture in 1803 dominated by American ideas, language, currency, customs, and values, all brought by the unwanted and deeply resented Louisiana Purchase. The effects of this event cut across all eight short works to give the unified whole a larger theme, the multidimensional transition the entire civilization underwent in the decades that followed. As part of that process, one component was the difficulty the entrenched elite had in accepting any changes at all, and, as is clear with General Villivicencio and his followers in "Madame Délicieuse," his intention is to reverse the entire process, to restore French language, newspapers, and government to New Orleans: "The staff of General Villivicencio were a faithful few who had not bowed the knee to any abomination of the Américains, nor sworn deceitfully to any species of compromise; their beloved city was presently to pass into the throes of an election, and this band, heroically unconscious of their feebleness, putting their trust in 're-actions' and the like delusions, resolved to make one more stand for the traditions of their fathers" (277). That attitude, or a more benign form of it, is in the life of the city throughout the rest of the book, and resentment for change persists for decades, gradually giving way, in a new generation, to English as the language of society and commerce, the American government as a controlling force, and business, rather than inherited income, as a legitimate means to wealth.

But much of the old way of life persisted in the social values of these people, particularly the Creole gentry. They still looked to Paris as the source of culture; they read French newspapers, educated their children in the language and history of France, and sustained European attitudes about courtship, marriage, mistresses, and the children of informal relationships. They are guided in such endeavors by the Napoleonic Code, which did not give way to American principles based on English Common Law. Thus the *Code*

Noir, formulated in Paris in 1685 and brought to Louisiana in 1724, became codified in the Louisiana Civil Codes of 1825, sustaining a set of standards for social conduct unique within the United States. These regulations are what prevent interracial marriage in "Madame Delphine" and "'Tite Poulette" and that resulted in the wealth of Injin Charlie in "Belles Demoiselles Plantation." The Creole traditions of the good life are what lead his relative, Colonel De Charleu, to an impoverished state in which he must, ignominiously, borrow money from his mixed-race relative: "He had gambled in Royal Street, drunk hard in Orleans Street, run his adversary through in dueling-ground at Slaughter-house Point, and danced and quarreled at the St. Philippe-street-theatre quadroon balls" (123–24). In short, he lived the way his father and grandfather had lived, in accord with European standards, sustaining the language and customs of an inherited social fabric. Jean-ah Poquelin attempts to do the same, although for more benevolent purposes, and his meeting with the governor is a classic example of resistance to change.

On the other end of the social spectrum is an isolated caste, quadroon women, destined to become either servants or plaçage mistresses, and no one in the United States had told this powerful story before Cable. Under the *Code Noir*, these women could not marry outside their narrow racial classification, and the prospects of having a normal family were limited. The sons of white fathers in a mixed-race relationship were also free persons of color, and they were often sent to be educated in France, from which they never returned. What the volume reveals is the series of common events: the grooming of the quadroon girl; her debut at the quadroon balls; the negotiation of the terms of her concubinage; the birth of her children; her sustained widowhood with the death of her older "husband." This domestic narrative was unknown in any other state in the country, and Cable first brought it to light in his remarkable story cycle.

Beyond the plight of the quadroons, the volume presents a broader drama of considerable historical significance. Political intrigue stirs in the back rooms of the city taverns, driven largely by Caribbean wars, and refugees stream into the narrow streets of the French Quarter. People from outside Louisiana come to New Orleans, fail to understand its complex cultural history, and encounter situations for which they are patently unprepared, a matter treated humorously in "Posson Jone'" and with dark seriousness in "'Sieur George." But in total, *Old Creole Days* introduced New Orleans to America in 1879, its French and Spanish history, its unique customs, its intransigent social problems, the glory of its cultural heritage. Cable was recognized immediately as one of the masters of regional fiction, and the course of American literary history was permanently enriched.

All of these four story cycles are set in New Orleans and surrounding regions, and all of them feature the multifaceted vernacular of the various classes within the city. All of them present characters descended from the French cultural elite and from the four decades of Spanish rule, which established a permanent legacy in the architecture of the French Quarter. All of these writers dealt with the racial issues embedded in the local culture, although in varying ways. However, the strata of society represented, the conflicts within that populace, and the temporal parameters of their dramas are all very different.

Cable's *Old Creole Days* is set before the Civil War in the heyday of French dominance of the cultural norms of the city. Grace King's *Balcony Stories* take place, with one exception, during Restoration and its aftermath, a period also filled with transformation but a series of changes of a very different sort. The narrative of her book is dominated by the psychic drama of economic decline and its psychological consequences. That is the overarching plot of the volume: the collapse of the Southern privileged class wrought by the Civil War, exacerbated by Reconstruction, and resulting in a social inversion in which former employees and servants now owned the mansions built by the leading families of Louisiana. Indeed, at the time of the telling, that is the situation as the women in "The Balcony" sit out of an evening and share tales. No one else in American literature has so dramatically presented a psychological glimpse of a dynasty in decline, and not again until William Faulkner did a writer attempt to deal with the complex issues involved. In a sense *Balcony Stories* gives the history of New Orleans in the nineteenth century, with the Creole aristocrat clinging to the past in "A Drama of Three" to the pampered and extravagant ingénue struggling with her sense of self in the destructive aftermath of the war. "The Old Lady's Restoration" is yet another permutation on the theme, with the uncertain resumption of wealth for a woman ignored and neglected after the loss of her fortune whose friends return amid the local gossip that it has been recovered. "A Delicate Affair" involved yet another form of loss for the same genteel set, the loss of a husband's fidelity and a friend's devotion recovered in old age through the intervention of another loving friend, whose romantic affection is unrecognized, unrequited, and never articulated. The overarching narrative of the book is this cultural adjustment to change, but it is less a eulogy than a probing study of resilience and vulnerability, of resentment and bitter acceptance by characters who would cling to the past if only it had substance to grasp.

Kate Chopin's *Bayou Folk*, her most celebrated book until the resurgence of interest in *The Awakening* in the 1970s, broadens the settings, ethnic issues, and thematic concerns of Louisiana fiction in the 1890s. Her twenty-three stories take place in essentially two locations: New Orleans and the bayou country of Natchitoches Parish along the Cane River. Many of these issues focus on a unique cultural class, that between the wealthy Creole establishment and the poor-white Acadians who work as tenant farmers and shopkeepers. Both groups are Roman Catholic and speak French as a first language, but Chopin's Cajuns are generally uneducated and resolve conflicts in the crudest of terms. The women are often beautiful and attract the attention of gentleman from New Orleans, thus introducing a conflict of backgrounds within white society that parallels the more standard racial tension in Cable's stories. The themes of the volume reflect this wider range of locations, ethnic divisions, and historic issues, reaching back to antebellum matters of race and caste, the postwar readjustments of life in the Deep South, and the psychological and physical damage wrought by the war. Of the New Orleans writers of the period, Chopin thus presents the broadest range of subjects and themes, perhaps because she was removed from the area at the time of composition and looked back on her life in Louisiana with a comprehensive perspective.

Despite its length and number of stories, *Bayou Folk* is nonetheless a unified cycle of short fiction, one that includes reappearing characters, continuing locations, and themes that resonate throughout the book, enlarging their impact in the aggregate beyond the importance of any one story. As a total artistic entity, the volume presents a broad range of characters who live within the unique social structure of Louisiana, the only state in which, by the time of the war, free persons of color outnumbered slaves, free mulattoes owned enormous plantations and had slaves of their own, and Acadians and French Creoles competed for the attentions of beautiful young women in the bayou country. Indeed, the quest of the Cajuns for respect and social standing is an important subtheme that helps unify disparate stories.

Only two of Chopin's stories reach back to more familiar themes of the South, to the days of slavery and the supremacy of caste, the subjects that so preoccupied Cable. "Désirée's Baby" and "La Belle Zoraïde" deepen the ethnic issues of many of the plots, and these works are among the most powerful condemnations of involuntary servitude in American literature. "Zoraïde" also deals with another motif that persists throughout the book, aberrant psychological states, an issue presented with impressive sensitivity and insight. Variations on the courtship ritual appear in half of the stories, and that matter relates to instances of dysfunctional or precarious marriages, a theme at the center of "In Sabine," "Madame Célestin's Divorce," and "A Lady of Bayou St. John." In total, this is a culture with a long history and a proud tradition, and it clings to a way of life that is rapidly fading. Unlike Grace King, Chopin largely ignores the Civil War and Reconstruction as prime issues and focuses on issues inherent within the local society itself, not those imposed from the outside, and that realization is crucial to understanding the lives in *Bayou Folk.*

That situation also pertains to Alice Dunbar-Nelson's *The Goodness of St. Rocque and Other Stories.* The conflicts of these fourteen works of short fiction all focus on disputes unique to New Orleans, issues of the deepest moment in the Crescent City that would be nearly impossible anywhere else. For example, Mr. Baptiste is killed in a historically genuine riot among Irish and African-American dock workers on the wharfs, a conflict with a vibrant legacy in Louisiana that would not have happened in another region. "A Carnival Jangle" involves a murder during Mardi Gras, also a unique event, and "M'sieu Fortier's Violin" draws on the history of the French Opera House to depict a salient moment when the largest musical theater in America was sold and came under new management. When the Spanish Manuela and French Claralie compete for the attentions of a young man, they do so in the context of an ethnic chronicle unmatched in any other region of the United States. The easy melding of Catholicism and voodoo, paralleled by similarly rapid shifts in language and dialect, are also indicative of late nineteenth-century culture in Louisiana. That a young girl of indeterminate ethnic identity is brought to a convent to be reared in "Sister Josepha" is also a local issue. That she remains not out of religious devotion but because she is uncertain of what secular life she could have in a rigidly stratified society relates to the complex role women of mixed race have played in Louisiana domestic interactions. Dunbar-Nelson's volume, in other words, tells a rich and dramatically varied ethnic story about living in the city, one filled with history, intrigue, violence, and little genuine opportunity for taking even one step on the path to the American Dream.

As a group, these four volumes of stories constitute an enormous contribution to the history of American fiction, establishing a rich cultural history of one of the great cities of the world, recording the complex interactions of people of different races and nationalities functioning within a social system based on a rigid stratification of caste and status, and giving literary expression to the inner lives of characters across the entire spectrum of the populace. For wealthy French Creoles, the history of the city is one of tremendous success in the first century of settlement followed by betrayal, political change, cultural adjustment, and economic and social decline. The tale of the Acadians takes place largely in the surrounding bayous, and it involves their poverty, their pride, and their difficult struggle to build a future for their families. The most complex element in this comprehensive saga is the African-American population, which had its own stratifications ranging from the free mulattoes who owned plantations and slaves on L'Isle des Mulatres, to the free persons of color who flourished in the culture of

New Orleans, to the slaves, who faced an often cruel and restricted future as an oppressed population. George Washington Cable, Grace King, Kate Chopin, and Alice Dunbar-Nelson did not ignore the deep social problems of their home city; rather, they used these circumstances as the subject of volumes of integrated and interwoven short stories in the rich legacy of the cycle tradition, and in doing so they produced some of the finest short stories ever written in English. *Old Creole Days, Bayou Folk, Balcony Stories*, and *The Goodness of St. Rocque and Other Stories* are central to the history of the nineteenth century as both art and cultural records, and they deserve renewed attention for their contributions to American literary history.

Notes

Introduction

1. See Claude M. Simpson, ed., "Introduction," *The Local Colorists: American Short Stories, 1837–1900* (New York: Harper and Brothers, 1960), 6. Simpson provides an excellent discussion of the growth of the Local-Color movement in the magazines.

2. Elizabeth Ammons and Valerie Rohy discuss the multiple languages for magazines serving various nationality groups in the introduction to *American Local Color Writing, 1880–1920* (New York: Penguin, 1998), x.

3. See Louis D. Rubin Jr., *George W. Cable: The Life and Times of a Southern Heretic* (New York: Pegasus, 1969), 41.

4. Rubin, *George W. Cable*, 60.

5. Arlin Turner, *George W. Cable: A Biography* (Baton Rouge: Louisiana State University Press, 1966), 6.

6. The two newspapers were *L'Abeille* and *Deutsche Zeitung*, still publishing in 1878 when Lafcadio Hearn arrived in the city. See Delia LaBarre, ed., *The New Orleans of Lafcadio Hearn* (Baton Rouge: Louisiana State University Press, 2007), xiv.

7. See Hans W. Baade, "The Law of Slavery in Spanish Luisiana, 1769–1803," in *The Spanish Presence in Louisiana, 1769–1803*, ed. Gilbert C. Din (Baton Rouge: Louisiana State University Press, 1983), 366–90.

8. I am indebted here to Gary B. Mills, *The Forgotten People: Cane River's Creoles of Color* (Baton Rouge: Louisiana State University Press, 1977), 195.

9. I am indebted for this observation to Lawrence N. Powell, *The Accidental City: Improvising New Orleans* (Cambridge: Harvard University Press, 2012), 115.

10. For a valuable discussion of the Spanish period, please see Ned Sublette, *The World That Made New Orleans: From Spanish Silver to Congo Square* (Chicago: Lawrence Hill Books, 2008), 96–97, 113.

11. Kjell Ekstrom, *George Washington Cable: A Study of His Early Life and Work* (Uppsala: A. B. Lundequistska Bokhandeln, 1950), 112.

12. In recent criticism, Shannon Lee Dawdy ignores any racial dimension to the term "creole" and defines it as simply "native born." See *Building the Devil's Empire: French Colonial New Orleans* (Chicago: University of Chicago Press, 2008), 5.

13. George Washington Cable, *The Creoles of Louisiana* (New York: Scribners, 1884).

14. Grace King, *A History of Louisiana*, with John R. Ficklen (New Orleans: Graham, 1893); *New Orleans: The Place and the People* (New York: Macmillan, 1895); *Creole Families of New Orleans* (New York: Macmillan, 1921).

15. Indeed, Alice Dunbar-Nelson offers an extensive history of slavery, manumission, and racial mixing in "People of Color in Louisiana, Part I," *Journal of Negro History* 1 (1916): 361–76. The second half of the article ran the next year as "People of Color in Louisiana, Part II," *Journal of Negro History* 2 (1917): 51–78.

16. For a more detailed discussion of the land rights of Creoles, see Kristina Brooks, "Alice Dunbar-Nelson's Local Colors of Ethnicity, Class, and Place," *MELUS* 23, no. 2 (1998): 5.

17. For an informative discussion of alternative meanings of the term "Creole," please see Richard Campanella, *Bienville's Dilemma: A Historical Geography of New Orleans* (Lafayette: Center for Louisiana Studies, 2008), 161.

18. See Kenneth M. Stampp, *The Era of Reconstruction, 1865–1877* (New York: Alfred A. Knopf, 1975), 80.

19. Dawdy gives an excellent account of the *Code Noir* in Saint Domingue and the revision of it when it was imported into Louisiana in 1724. She highlights, in particular, regulations regarding interracial marriage (Dawdy, *Building the Devil's Empire*, 198–200).

20. There are hundreds of books and articles dealing with the *Code Noir*. Among the ones that have been especially helpful are B. F. French, *Historical Collections of Louisiana: Embracing Translations of Many Rare and Valuable Documents Relating to the Natural, Civil, and Political History of that State* (New York: D. Appleton, 1851); Ira Berlin, *Many Thousands Gone: The First Two Centuries of Slavery in North America* (Cambridge: Harvard University Press, 1998); Walter Johnson, *Soul by Soul: Life Inside the Antebellum Slave Market* (Cambridge: Harvard University Press, 1999); and Theodore B. Wilson, *The Black Codes of the South* (Tuscaloosa: University of Alabama Press, 1965).

21. For an extensive discussion of the revisions of the *Code Noir* and the evolution of Louisiana law, see Richard Holcombe Kilbourne Jr., *A History of the Louisiana Civil Code: The Formative Years, 1803–1839* (Baton Rouge: Paul Herbert Law Centre Publications Institute, 1987).

22. Dawdy, *Building the Devil's Empire*, 203.

23. Quoted in Dunbar-Nelson, "People of Color in Louisiana, Part II," 59.

24. For a discussion of this military role for freed slaves, see Dunbar-Nelson, "People of Color in Louisiana, Part II," 67.

25. Anna Shannon Elfenbein, *Women on the Color Line: Evolving Stereotypes and the Writings of George Washington Cable, Grace King, Kate Chopin* (Charlottesville: University Press of Virginia, 1989), 15.

26. Powell discusses this tradition at some length (*Accidental City*, 286–93), although he seems not to realize that the children of *plaçage* arrangements were legally free at birth and carried the name of their fathers.

27. For a valuable discussion of this tradition, please see Sublette, *World That Made New Orleans*, 111, 244.

28. See Christopher Benfey, *Degas in New Orleans: Encounters in the Creole World of Kate Chopin and George Washington Cable* (New York: Alfred A. Knopf, 1997), 5.

29. For more information about Edgar Degas and New Orleans, including his relatives of mixed race, please see Benfey, *Degas in New Orleans*, 5, 124–26.

30. For an excellent discussion of these issues, including a chart outlining the progeny of the plaçage union, see Mills, *Forgotten People*, 72–76.

31. For a biography of Sister Henriette Delille, see Sister Audrey Marie Detiege, *Henriette Delille, Free Woman of Color: Foundress of the Sisters of the Holy Family* (New Orleans: Sisters of the Holy Family, 1976).

32. See Herbert Asbury, *The French Quarter: An Informal History of the New Orleans Underworld* (New York: Alfred A. Knopf, 1936), 135.

33. George Washington Cable, manuscript draft of "Foreword to 'Tite Poulette," file 62, folder 1, Williams Research Center, New Orleans.

34. *Civil Code of the State of Louisiana* (New Orleans: J. C. de St. Romes, 1825), 30.

35. See Dunbar-Nelson, "People of Color in Louisiana, Part II," 56.

36. Alice Dunbar-Nelson points out, however, that a school for orphaned children of color, the Ecole des Orphelins Indigents, was opened in New Orleans in 1840. In 1859 John F. Cook established a school for free people of color in the city. See Dunbar-Nelson, "People of Color in Louisiana, Part II," 67.

37. See Mills, *Forgotten People*, 96–97.

38. For an excellent summary of these arrangements, see Mills, 94–98.

39. Violet Harrington Bryan, *The Myth of New Orleans in Literature* (Knoxville: University of Tennessee Press, 1993), 6.

40. For a more detailed discussion of this point, see Virginia R. Domínguez, *White by Definition: Social Classification in Creole Louisiana* (New Brunswick: Rutgers University Press, 1986), 127.

41. See Turner, *George W. Cable*, 14.

42. Powell seems to be unaware of the long tradition of plaçage and its impli-

cations since in *The Accidental City* he marvels at the number of women of color who owned property in the city and enjoyed an income from rentals (305). Since plaçage mistresses tended to be a good deal younger than their gentlemen, the end result was a population of mixed-race widows who owned dwellings in the city. Such women often supported themselves by renting out rooms or apartments.

43. For more detailed information, please see Gwendolyn Midlo Hall, *Africans in Colonial Louisiana: The Development of Afro-Creole Culture in the Eighteenth Century* (Baton Rouge: Louisiana State University Press, 1994).

44. See Werner Sollors, *Neither Black nor White Yet Both: Thematic Explorations of Interracial Literature* (Oxford: Oxford University Press, 1997), 164–67. Sollor's book is an excellent exploration of the issue of mixed racial identity, exploring scores of works that utilize the theme, and much of my understanding of the matter derives from his research.

45. Victor Séjour's "La Mulâtre," *Revue des colonies* 3 (March 1837): 376–92.

46. Madame Charles Reybaud, "Les Epaves," *Revue de Paris* 50 (February 1838): 37–101.

47. Sollors goes on to discuss the play at considerable length (*Neither Black nor White Yet Both*, 174–78).

48. Sollors, *Neither Black nor White Yet Both*, 178.

49. For a discussion of this comic opera, see Sollors, 182.

50. I am indebted here to Elfenbein, *Women on the Color Line*, 14.

51. For an extended discussion of the "tragic octoroon" figure, see Elfenbein, 13–15.

52. Judith Fetterley and Marjorie Pryse maintain that white men held up their characters to ridicule whereas women writers preferred to present a narrator who was a local person herself. My research does not reveal this distinction. First of all, most Local-Color writers were from the region and familiar with the circumstances of the characters they portrayed, and they would have little reason to want to ridicule them. But the paradigm Fetterley and Pryse describe does not work either. For example, in *The Country of the Pointed Firs*, Jewett uses a sophisticated narrator from an Eastern city as a narrator, the very device Fetterley claims to be exclusively male. On the other hand, Hamlin Garland's *Main-Travelled Roads* is hardly a collection of stories that make fun of Midwestern farmers. In fact he argued in numerous essays that the lives of simple farmers were as important as those of European nobles or anyone else on earth. I find no significant differences in the gender of writers and the handling of the relationship between narrators and characters. See Judith Fetterley and Marjorie Pryse, *American Women Regionalists, 1850–1910* (New York: W. W. Norton, 1992), xi–xii, xvii.

53. Hamlin Garland, *Roadside Meetings* (New York: Macmillan, 1930), 256.

54. Hamlin Garland, *Crumbling Idols: Twelve Essays on Art Dealing Chiefly with Literature, Painting, and the Drama* (Chicago: Stone and Kimball, 1894), 58, 60.

55. Simpson offers an impressive list of Local-Color works in various genres (*Local Colorists*, 2). I am indebted to his guidance on this point.

56. For a detailed definition of the short-story cycle, please see the introduction to James Nagel, *The Contemporary American Short-Story Cycle: The Ethnic Resonance of Genre* (Baton Rouge: Louisiana State University Press, 2001). Among other valuable books on the subject, see Maggie Dunn and Ann Morris, *The Composite Novel: The Short Story Cycle in Transition* (New York: Twayne, 1995); Forrest L. Ingram, *Representative Short Story Cycles of the Twentieth Century* (The Hague: Mouton, 1971); J. Gerald Kennedy, ed., *Modern American Short Story Sequences: Composite Fictions and Fictive Communities* (Cambridge: Cambridge University Press, 1995); Rolf Lundén, *The United Stories of America: Studies in the Short Story Composite* (Amsterdam: Rodopi, 1999); and Susan Garland Mann, *The Short Story Cycle: A Genre Companion and Reference Guide* (Westport: Greenwood Press, 1989).

57. See, for example, Edmund Wilson, "Mr. Hemingway's Dry-Points," *Dial* 77 (October 1924): 340–41.

58. See Philip Butcher, *George Washington Cable* (New Haven: College and University Press, 1962), 42.

59. For a brief biographical overview of Cable's life, see Michael Kreyling, "George Washington Cable," in *American Realists and Naturalists*, ed. Donald Pizer and Earl N. Harbert, *Dictionary of Literary Biography*, vol. 12 (Detroit: Gale Research Company, 1982), 42–50.

60. For more of these kinds of intimate insights into Cable's life, see Lucy Leffingwell Cable Bikle, *George W. Cable: His Life and Letters* (New York: Charles Scribner's Sons, 1928). Also see Arlin Turner, *Critical Essays on George W. Cable* (Boston: G. K. Hall, 1980), xi.

61. See John Cleman, *George Washington Cable Revisited* (New York: Twayne Publishers, 1996), 102.

62. Rubin, *George W. Cable*, 46.

63. A good brief introduction to Grace King's life and work is David Kirby, "Grace King," in *American Realists and Naturalists*, ed. Donald Pizer and Earl N. Harbert, *Dictionary of Literary Biography*, vol. 12 (Detroit: Gale Research Company, 1982), 342–46. For more extended treatment, see David Kirby, *Grace King* (Boston: Twayne, 1980); and Robert Bush, *Grace King: A Southern Destiny* (Baton Rouge: Louisiana State University Press, 1983). I am also indebted to Mary Anne O'Neal, "New Orleans Realists: Grace King, Kate Chopin, and Alice Dunbar-Nelson" (dissertation, University of Georgia, 1999), 25.

64. For a brief biographical overview, see Sara deSaussure Davis, "Kate Chopin,"

in *American Realists and Naturalists*, ed. Donald Pizer and Earl N. Harbert, *Dictionary of Literary Biography*, vol. 12 (Detroit: Gale, 1982), 59–71. Also of value is Bernard Koloski, *Kate Chopin: A Study of the Short Fiction* (New York: Twayne Publishers, 1996). The two major biographies are Per Seyersted, *Kate Chopin: A Critical Biography* (Oslo: Universitetsforlaget, 1969); and Emily Toth, *Kate Chopin* (Austin: University of Texas Press, 1990). Toth establishes that Kate Chopin was born in 1850, not 1851, as has generally been reported (24).

65. Seyersted presents an extended discussion of Chopin's childhood in St. Louis (*Kate Chopin*, 13).

66. Helen Taylor, *Gender, Race, and Region in the Writings of Grace King, Ruth McEnery Stuart, and Kate Chopin* (Baton Rouge: Louisiana State University Press, 1989), 142.

67. Taylor offers a detailed discussion of Kate's relationship with Dr. Kolbenheyer (*Gender, Race, and Region*, 142).

68. Bryan (*Myth of New Orleans*, 64) questions whether Joseph Moore was actually her father, but the answer is unknown. I am indebted to Bryan for Dunbar-Nelson's address in New Orleans.

69. For an excellent biographical essay on Alice Dunbar-Nelson, see Ora Williams, "Alice Moore Dunbar Nelson," in *Afro-American Writers before the Harlem Renaissance*, ed. Trudier Harris and Thadious M. Davis, *Dictionary of Literary Biography*, vol. 50 (Detroit: Gale Research Company, 1986), 225–33.

70. Eugene Wesley Metcalf Jr., *The Letters of Paul and Alice Dunbar: A Private History* (dissertation, University of California, Irvine, 1973), 24.

Chapter 1

1. George Washington Cable, "'Tite Poulette," *Scribner's Monthly*, 8, No. 6 (1874): 674–84. All quotations, however, are from *Old Creole Days* (New York: Scribner's, 1883), 213–43. The volume first appeared in 1879 without "Madame Delphine," which was added to the 1883 edition, making it the preferred text. All subsequent references from *Old Creole Days* will appear parenthetically within the text.

2. Lawrence N. Powell in *The Accidental City: Improvising New Orleans* (Cambridge: Harvard University Press, 2012) goes further and calls the house "the best surviving example of a French-colonial dwelling" (204).

3. See Alice Hall Petry, *A Genius in His Way: The Art of Cable's* Old Creole Days (Rutherford: Fairleigh Dickinson University Press, 1988), 113.

4. For a more detailed account of her observations on the matter, please see Alice Dunbar-Nelson, "People of Color in Louisiana, Part I," *Journal of Negro History* 1 (1916): 361–76; and "People of Color in Louisiana, Part II," *Journal of Negro History* 2 (1917): 51–78.

5. Petry, *Genius*, 101.

6. Cable's letter is quoted in Lucy Leffingwell Cable Bikle, *George W. Cable: His Life and Letters* (New York: Charles Scribner's Sons, 1928), 58.

7. John Cleman is especially harsh in his criticism of Cable's handling of characterization. He says that "'Tite Poulette barely exists except as an object of desire and pity, and while Zalli is given some complexity, Kristian Koppig is wooden and conventional, and both are primarily interesting as typifying strands in a social and historical fabric." Please see *George Washington Cable Revisited* (New York: Twayne Publishers, 1996), 34.

8. Quoted in Petry, *Genius*, 24.

9. "Madame Delphine" has a complex publication history. It first appeared as a story in *Scribner's Monthly* in the May, June, and July issues of 1881 (volume 22, numbers 1, 2, 3). It then appeared from Charles Scribner's Sons as an independent volume later in 1881 before being incorporated as the lead story in the revised edition of *Old Creole Days* in 1883.

10. Anna Shannon Elfenbein, *Women on the Color Line: Evolving Stereotypes and the Writings of George Washington Cable, Grace King, Kate Chopin* (Charlottesville: University Press of Virginia, 1989), 65.

11. Edmond Gosse, "Madame Delphine," *Saturday Review* (London), 52 (August 20, 1881): 237–38.

12. There are only minor revisions in the movement from the magazine to the volume, with Cable replacing "Captain Lemaitre" with "He" in one instance and with a footnote inviting readers to consult the newspapers of the period in another. The other changes deal with punctuation and accidentals.

13. Elfenbein discusses this point at some length (65).

14. Cleman discusses this theme (*George Washington Cable Revisited*, 88). Petry attributes the responsibility for the *Code Noir* to the North, which does not make sense. These regulations were formulated before the establishment of the United States, but even as early as 1775 there was an active abolitionist movement in the North, which abhorred such regulations based on race and caste. See Petry, *Genius*, 25.

15. See George Washington Cable, "Belles Demoiselles Plantation," *Scribner's Monthly* 7, no. 6 (1874): 739–47.

16. Please see Bikle, *George W. Cable*, 58.

17. Petry offers a valuable discussion of the limited setting for the portrayal of the seven sisters (*Genius*, 60).

18. Petry gives the collapse of the house a much more Christian reading, as "the just punishment of ungodliness, and as a means of Christian conversion" (*Genius*, 60). Other scholars have also pursued this line of thought: Howard W. Fulweiler, in "Of Time and the River: 'Ancestral Nonsense' vs. Inherited Guilt in

Cable's 'Belles Demoiselles Plantation'," *Midcontinent American Studies Journal* 7 (Fall 1966): 53–59, maintains that the collapse of the house is the punishment for both his individual failings and the inherited guilt of the family. Donald A. Ringe puts more emphasis on the need for brotherhood, closer to my own position, which emphasizes the bond of familial loyalty established at the end. See Donald A. Ringe, "The Moral World of Cable's 'Belles Demoiselles Plantation,'" *Mississippi Quarterly* 29 (Winter 1975–76): 83–90.

19. Petry, *Genius*, 68.

20. Cleman, *George Washington Cable Revisited*, 28.

21. Arlin Turner, *George W. Cable: A Biography* (Baton Rouge: Louisiana State University Press, 1966), 59.

22. Arlin Turner, "A Novelist Discovers a Novelist: The Correspondence of H. H. Boyesen and George W. Cable," *Western Humanities Review* 5 (1951): 345.

23. For first publication, see George Washington Cable, "Posson Jone'," *Appleton's Journal* 25 (April 1, 1876): 422–26.

24. Turner, *Biography*, 63.

25. Petry gives a detailed account of the publication history of the story (*Genius*, 75).

26. See Kjell Ekstrom, *George Washington Cable: A Study of His Early Life and Work* (Uppsala: A. B. Lundequistska Bokhandeln, 1950), 99.

27. See Petry, *Genius*, 89.

28. Bikle records her father's statement about the time of the action in her biography (*George W. Cable*, 58).

29. See Lafcadio Hearn, "The Scenes of Cable's Romances," *Century Magazine*, 27 (November 1883), 40–47.

30. For a further discussion of Congo Square and the circus, see Turner, *Biography*, 13.

31. Petry, *Genius*, 76.

32. Petry argues that the growing Christian love is the major theme of the story (*Genius*, 84).

33. Louis D. Rubin Jr., *George W. Cable: The Life and Times of a Southern Heretic* (New York: Pegasus, 1969), 54.

34. I am indebted for the phrase "linguistic smorgasbord" to Petry, *Genius*, 89.

35. For first publication, see George Washington Cable, "Café des Exilés," *Scribner's Monthly* 11, no. 5 (1876): 727–36.

36. Cable's text has it as "Barbadoes" (87).

37. I am indebted for this point to Cleman, *George Washington Cable Revisited*, 44.

38. See Hearn, "Scenes of Cable's Romances," 40–47.

39. Dunbar-Nelson, "People of Color in Louisiana, Part II," 52.

40. I am indebted to Petry for her insightful observation on this point (*Genius*, 53).

41. See Bikle, *George W. Cable*, 58.

42. For more information on Ole Bull and his American concerts, see Sara Chapman Thorp Bull, *Ole Bull: A Memoir* (Boston: Houghton Mifflin, 1882).

43. George Washington Cable, "'Sieur George," *Scribner's Monthly* 6 (October 1873): 739–45.

44. Petry, *Genius*, 118.

45. It follows the title on page 739 of the magazine. The story was revised much more heavily than the others in the transition from periodical to book publication, with many substantive clarifications added along with the concluding paragraph.

46. Turner, *Biography*, 56–57.

47. Petry, *Genius*, 119.

48. George Washington Cable, "'Sieur George," *Scribner's Monthly* 6 (October 1873): 745.

49. Turner, *Biography*, 57.

50. For further comment on Cable's editorials, see Turner, *Biography*, 48.

51. George Washington Cable, "Jean-Ah Poquelin," *Scribner's Monthly* 10 (May 1875): 91–100.

52. See Turner, *Biography*, 61.

53. Turner, *Biography*, 61.

54. Petry, *Genius*, 93.

55. See Cleman, *George Washington Cable Revisited*, 38.

56. Rubin, *George W. Cable*, 57.

57. For the first publication of the story, see George Washington Cable, "Madame Délicieuse," *Scribner's Monthly* 10, no. 4 (1875): 498–508.

58. See Bikle, *George W. Cable*, 58.

59. Petry, *Genius*, 137.

60. Turner, *Biography*, 62.

61. Cleman gives an insightful analysis of the general (*George Washington Cable Revisited*, 42).

62. See Petry, *Genius*, 132.

63. Hearn, "Scenes of Cable's Romances," 40–47.

64. See Grace King, "The Glorious Eighth of January," *New Orleans: The Place and the People* (New York: Macmillan, 1928), 211–51.

65. King, *New Orleans*, 211–51.

66. Philip Butcher, *George Washington Cable* (New Haven: College and University Press, 1962), 40.

67. See Petry, *Genius*, 131.

68. Petry, 131.

69. See Pattee, *The Development of the American Short Story*, 256–57, for further discussion of Cable's use of New Orleans as a subject.

70. See Turner, *George W. Cable*, 84. He also comments on Cable's plan to precede each story with a Creole song, an idea similarly rejected.

Chapter 2

1. All references are to Grace King, "Monsieur Motte," *New Princeton Review* 1, no. 1 (1886): 91–133, and will be given parenthetically within the main text.

2. King's letter is quoted in Helen Taylor, *Gender, Race, and Region in the Writings of Grace King, Ruth McEnery Stuart, and Kate Chopin* (Baton Rouge: Louisiana State University Press, 1989), 51.

3. I am indebted here to Robert Bush, *Grace King: A Southern Destiny* (Baton Rouge: Louisiana State University Press, 1983), 58.

4. Grace King, *Memories of a Southern Woman of Letters* (New York: Macmillan, 1932), 61.

5. Bush, *Southern Destiny*, 61.

6. See Taylor, *Gender, Race, and Region*, 51, for example.

7. Taylor, 54.

8. David Kirby, *Grace King* (Boston: Twayne, 1980), 40.

9. Helen Taylor is particularly insightful on the situations of King's female characters (*Gender, Race, and Region, 67–68).*

10. See Robert Bush, *Grace King of New Orleans: A Selection of Her Writings* (Baton Rouge: Louisiana State University Press, 1973), 4.

11. All citations are from Grace King, *Balcony Stories* (New York: Century, 1893). All further references are from this edition and will be given parenthetically in the main text.

12. Grace King, "The Balcony," *Century Illustrated Magazine* 45 (December 1892), 279–80. As was her common practice, the story was reprinted in the collected volume without changes.

13. See my more extensive comments on the iceberg principle in James Nagel, *Anthology of the American Short Story* (Boston: Houghton Mifflin, 2001), 557, 641.

14. The fourteen stories that comprise *Balcony Stories* were all published between December of 1892 and October of 1893. They were included in the volume in the order of publication and without substantive alterations. "A Drama of Three" first appeared in *Century Illustrated Magazine* 45 (December 1892), 280–82.

15. Mary Anne O'Neal, "New Orleans Realists: Grace King, Kate Chopin, and Alice Dunbar Nelson" (dissertation, University of Georgia, 1999), 86.

16. King's "La Grande Demoiselle" was first published in *Century Illustrated Magazine* 45 (January 1893), 323–27.

17. Bush, *Southern Destiny*, 145.

18. For more detailed information about the Freedmen's Bureau educational system, please see Bell Irvin Wiley, *Southern Negroes, 1861–1865* (Baton Rouge: Louisiana State University Press, 1938).

19. Wiley, pp. 271–74.

20. Grace King, "A Southern Educator: Mrs. Mary Humphreys Stamps," *Century Magazine* 78, no. 2 (1909): 271–76.

21. For detailed information on this development, please see Howard Ashley White, "The Freemen's Bureau in Louisiana" (dissertation, Tulane University, 1955).

22. Grace King, "An Old French Teacher of New Orleans," *Yale Review* 11, no. 2 (1922): 380–98.

23. King, *Memories*, 24.

24. I am indebted here to O'Neal, "New Orleans Realists," 88. Her background information on the city is especially useful.

25. The first publication of "The Old Lady's Restoration" was in *Century Illustrated Magazine* 46 (September 1893), 724–27.

26. O'Neal, "New Orleans Realists," 90.

27. "Mimi's Marriage" first appeared in *Century Illustrated Magazine* 45 (February 1893), 493–97.

28. Taylor, *Gender, Race, and Region*, 69.

29. King's "The Miracle Chapel" was originally published in *Century Illustrated Magazine* 45 (February 1893), 497–99.

30. Bush, *Southern Destiny*, 153.

31. King's "The Story of a Day" first appeared in *Century Illustrated Magazine* 46 (June 1893), 230–35. In this version, it carried the subtitle "with pictures by A. E. Sterner." The illustrations were reproduced in the first book edition as well. A few minor changes were made from magazine to published volume but nothing of thematic substance.

32. Kirby, *Grace King*, 42.

33. Bush, *Southern Destiny*, 154–55.

34. King's "Anne Marie and Jeanne Marie" was first published in *Century Illustrated Magazine* 46 (July 1893), 372–74.

35. David Kirby maintains that the theme of the story deals with "the degrading effect of poverty" (*Grace King*, 43). The sisters lead a penurious life, to be sure, but mistrust and betrayal seem much more vital in the story than the rather passive economic background. There is no issue of "need" that necessitates the hiding of the money.

36. King's "A Crippled Hope" was first published in *Century Illustrated Magazine* 46 (July 1893), 374–79. Some paragraph breaks were changed when it appeared in *Balcony Stories*, but otherwise it was reprinted without alteration.

37. Bush is especially insightful on this point and on the lack of colloquial language (*Southern Destiny*, 148–49).

38. Linda S. Coleman, "At Odds: Race and Gender in Grace King's Short Fiction," *Louisiana Women Writers: New Essays and a Comprehensive Bibliography*, ed. Dorothy H. Brown and Barbara Ewell (Baton Rouge: Louisiana State University Press, 1992), 38.

39. Bush, *Southern Destiny*, 148.

40. King's "One of Us" was first published in *Century Illustrated Magazine* 46 (August 1893), 544–46.

41. Kirby, *Grace King*, 44.

42. Kate Chopin's "Desirèe's Baby," was written in November of 1892 and first published in *Vogue* 2 (January 14, 1893), 70–74, under the title "The Father of Desirèe's Baby," putting the emphasis on Armand. It was included in *Bayou Folk* (Boston: Houghton, Mifflin and Company, 1894), 147–58, with a change of title and several minor stylistic alterations. King's "The Little Convent Girl" first appeared in *Century Illustrated Magazine* 46 (August 1893), 547–51.

43. Bush makes a similar point in *Southern Destiny*, 150.

44. O'Neal, "New Orleans Realists," 95.

45. Douglas J. McReynolds, in "Passion Repressed: The Short Fiction of Grace King," *Rocky Mountain Review of Language and Literature* 37, no. 4 (1983): 207–16, argues that there is a sexual meaning to the plunge into the river. My position is that the significance is racial, social, and psychological, not erotic.

46. King's "Grandmother's Grandmother" was first published in *Century Illustrated Magazine* 46 (September 1893), 722–24.

47. King, *Memories*, 183.

48. Kirby, *Grace King*, 44–45.

49. "A Delicate Affair" was first published in *Century Illustrated Magazine* 46 (October 1893), 884–89.

50. Bush, *Southern Destiny*, 146.

51. King's "Pupasse" first appeared in *Century Illustrated Magazine* 46 (October 1893), 889–94, with somewhat different paragraph breaks than in the collected volume.

52. Kirby, *Grace King*, 45–46.

53. Pattee, 324. Taylor, *Gender, Race, and Region*, 69.

54. O'Neal, "New Orleans Realists," 30.

Chapter 3

1. Alice Dunbar-Nelson, *The Goodness of St. Rocque and Other Stories* (New York: Dodd, Mead, 1899). All further references are from this edition and will be given parenthetically in the text.

2. See the letter to Alice in Eugene Wesley Metcalf Jr., "The Letters of Paul

and Alice Dunbar: A Private History" (Ph.D. dissertation, University of California, Irvine, 1973), 110.

3. See Gloria Hull's introduction to *The Works of Alice Dunbar-Nelson*, ed. Gloria Hull, vol. 1 (Oxford: Oxford University Press, 1988), xxxii.

4. See Hamlin Garland, *Crumbling Idols* (Chicago: Stone and Kimball, 1894).

5. Alice Dunbar-Nelson, *Violets and Other Stories* (Boston: Monthly Review, 1895). Later published in *The Works of Alice Dunbar-Nelson*, vol. 1 (Oxford: Oxford University Press, 1988).

6. For a further discussion of this point, see Pamela Glenn Menke, "Behind the 'White Veil': Alice Dunbar-Nelson, Creole Color, and *The Goodness of St. Rocque,*" *Songs of the Reconstructing South: Building Literary Louisiana, 1865–1945*, ed. Suzanne Disheroon-Green and Lisa Abney (Westport: Greenwood, 2002), 82.

7. I am indebted here, as elsewhere, to Mary Anne O'Neal, "New Orleans Realists: Grace King, Kate Chopin, and Alice Dunbar-Nelson" (Ph.D. dissertation, University of Georgia, 1999), 255.

8. Elizabeth Ammons, *Conflicting Stories: American Women Writers at the Turn into the Twentieth Century* (Oxford: Oxford University Press, 1991), 68.

9. See Violet Harrington Bryan, *The Myth of New Orleans in Literature: Dialogues of Race and Gender* (Knoxville: University of Tennessee Press, 1993). She maintains that the myth of the city would have been incomplete without the portrait in this story of a plaçage mistress who was abandoned when her gentleman married a white woman (78).

10. For an extensive discussion of the tragic mulatto theme and the role of this story in it, see Werner Sollors, *Neither Black nor White Yet Both: Thematic Explorations of Interracial Literature* (Oxford: Oxford University Press, 1997), 164.

11. See Sollors, 167–68, 174.

12. See Anna Shannon Elfenbein, *Women on the Color Line: Evolving Stereotypes and the Writings of George Washington Cable, Grace King, Kate Chopin* (Charlottesville: University Press of Virginia, 1989), 1. I am indebted to Elfenbein for her rich discussion of the tradition and detailed historical information.

13. Kristina Brooks, "Alice Dunbar-Nelson's Local Colors of Ethnicity, Class, and Place," *MELUS* 23, no. 2 (1998): 11.

14. Violet Harrington Bryan discusses the mixed-race romantic world of New Orleans but misses the fact that under the *Code Noir* couples of differing races were forbidden to marry. A quadroon could not marry a white man, nor could she marry a black man. That law is what gave rise to the frequency of plaçage relationships. See Bryan's "Race and Gender in the Early Works of Alice Dunbar-Nelson," in *Louisiana Women Writers: New Essays and a Comprehensive Bibliography*, ed. Dorothy H. Brown and Barbara C. Ewell (Baton Rouge: Louisiana State University Press, 1992), 126, 131.

15. See Jordan Stouck, "Identities in Crisis: Alice Dunbar-Nelson's New Orleans Fiction," *Canadian Review of American Studies* 34, no. 3 (2004): 275–76.

16. For Dunbar's letter to Alice Moore, please see Metcalf, "The Letters of Paul and Alice Dunbar," 63.

17. See Robert Whitlow, "Alice Dunbar-Nelson: New Orleans Writer," in *Regionalism and the Female Imagination: A Collection of Essays*, ed. Emily Toth (New York: Human Sciences, 1985), 109–25.

18. Thomas Strychacz, "'You Could Never Be Mistaken': Reading Alice Dunbar-Nelson's Rhetorical Diversions in *The Goodness of St. Rocque and Other Stories*," *Studies in American Fiction* 36 (2008): 78.

19. See O'Neal, "New Orleans Realists," 248.

20. I am indebted to O'Neal ("New Orleans Realists," 267–69) for her insightful observations about this point.

21. Strychacz, "'You Could Never Be Mistaken,'" 77.

22. See Lyle Saxon, *Fabulous New Orleans* (New York: Century, 1928), 289–90.

23. My reading here is in contravention of that offered by Ammons. She argues the supernatural thesis that "both the Wizened One and St. Rocque are responsible" (*Conflicting Stories*, 64). My assessment is more realistic, that any transformation born of these two influences was purely psychological in its effects.

24. I am indebted here to O'Neal ("New Orleans Realists," 270–71) for her overview of the immigrant situation in New Orleans in the 1890s.

25. On this point, see O'Neal, 280.

26. See, for example, Caroline Gebhard, "Inventing a 'Negro Literature': Race, Dialect, and Gender in the Early Work of Paul Lawrence Dunbar, James Weldon Johnson, and Alice Dunbar-Nelson," in *Post-Bellum, Pre-Harlem: African American Literature and Culture*, ed. Barbara McCaskill and Caroline Gebhard (New York: New York University Press, 2006), 173; Jürgen Grant, "Rewriting the Final Adjustment of Affairs: Culture, Race, and Politics in Alice Dunbar-Nelson's New Orleans," *Short Story* 9, no. 1 (2001): 47. There is also the fact that as a general rule, unlike Cable, King, and Chopin, Dunbar-Nelson uses the term "Creole" to refer to people of color.

27. My understanding of the historical background of the strike and resulting violence has been informed by Grant's "Rewriting the Final Adjustment of Affairs," 46–57. He is particularly thorough in exploring the trade organizations involved and the violations of contracts that led up to the strike by the Irish workers.

28. In "Alice Dunbar-Nelson's Local Colors of Ethnicity, Class, and Place," 3–26, Brooks places the labor riots in 1892. It is possible there was more than one strike during this volatile economic time.

29. See Grant, "Rewriting the Final Adjustment of Affairs," 49.

30. See Robert C. Clark, "At the Corner of Bourbon and Toulouse Street: The Historical Context of Alice Dunbar-Nelson's 'M'sieu Fortier's Violin,'" *American Literary Realism* 41, no. 2 (2009): 172–73.

31. Metcalf, "The Letters of Paul and Alice Dunbar," 56.

32. My understanding of the historical context of the French Opera House has been informed by Clark, "At the Corner of Bourbon and Toulouse Street," 163–79.

33. Alice Dunbar-Nelson, "People of Color in Louisiana, Part II," *Journal of Negro History* 2 (1917): 62.

34. See Clark, "At the Corner of Bourbon and Toulouse Street," 172–73.

35. See Clark, 175.

36. I am indebted here to O'Neal, "New Orleans Realists," 278.

37. I am indebted for this account to Clark, "At the Corner of Bourbon and Toulouse Street," 170–71.

38. I am indebted for this point to Clark, 171.

39. Here Whitlow would agree ("Alice Dunbar-Nelson," 121), although he sees the story as having no resolution. I see it as having concluded with the tragic limitations of Fortier's life, which will only decline further over time.

40. See Brooks, "Dunbar-Nelson's Local Colors," 10.

41. See Sister Audrey Marie Detiege, *Henriette Delille, Free Woman of Color: Foundress of the Sisters of the Holy Family* (New Orleans: Sisters of the Holy Family, 1976) for an overview of the life of this remarkable woman.

42. O'Neal compares Odalie to Sister Josepha in her beauty and haughtiness ("New Orleans Realists," 290).

43. Hull, "Introduction," xxix.

44. Menke, "Behind the 'White Veil,'" 87.

Chapter 4

1. Kate Chopin, *Bayou Folk* (Boston: Houghton Mifflin, 1894). All further references are from this edition and will be given parenthetically in the text

2. See "Mrs. Kate Chopin, Author of *Bayou Folk*," *Current Literature* 16, no. 2 (1894): 106.

3. The two most valuable biographies of Kate Chopin are Per Seyersted, *Kate Chopin: A Critical Biography* (Oslo: Universitetsforlaget, 1969), and Emily Toth, *Kate Chopin* (Austin: University of Texas Press, 1990). Both of them cover in detail the marriage and family life of Kate Chopin along with her move back to St. Louis.

4. Hamlin Garland wrote and spoke about the Local-Color movement repeatedly throughout his life, but his clearest and most emphatic statements are in *Crumbling Idols* (Chicago: Stone and Kimball, 1894).

5. Maibelle Justice, "*Bayou Folk* by Kate Chopin," *Godey's* 130 (April 1895): 432.

6. *Kate Chopin's Private Papers*, ed. Emily Toth and Per Seyersted (Bloomington: Indiana University Press, 1998), 187.

7. For the first publication of the story, see Kate Chopin, "A No-Account Creole," *Century Magazine* 47 (January 1894), 382–93. There are only minor changes, such as word division, in *Bayou Folk*.

8. See Nancy A. Walker, *Kate Chopin: A Literary Life* (New York: Palgrave, 2001), 75.

9. Kate Chopin, "A No-Account Creole," *Century Illustrated Magazine* 47 (January 1894), 382–93. It was reprinted in *Bayou Folk* (1–50) with only minor alterations.

10. Chopin, *Private Papers*, 203.

11. O'Neal presents a cogent discussion of the Santien family in the larger context of Chopin's work in her excellent dissertation ("New Orleans Realists," 149).

12. Kate Chopin, "In and Out of Old Natchitoches," *Two Tales* 5 (April 8, 1893): 103–14.

13. Marcia Gaudet provides extensive comments on these free mulattoes in "Kate Chopin and the Lore of Cane River's Creoles of Color," *Xavier Review* 6, no. 1 (1986): 45–52. My understanding of these matters is informed by her article.

14. Indeed, Barbara Ewell contends that this attempt at integration is the key thematic moment in the story. See Ewell's *Kate Chopin* (New York: Ungar, 1986), 57.

15. Allen F. Stein presents an insightful analysis of this point in *Women and Autonomy in Kate Chopin's Short Fiction* (New York: Peter Lang, 2005), 57.

16. Kate Chopin, "At the 'Cadian Ball," *Two Tales* 3 (October 22, 1892): 145–52. Apart from minor changes, "gombo" in *Two Tales* becomes "gumbo" in the volume, the two versions are identical.

17. See Ewell, *Kate Chopin*, 77.

18. See Seyersted, *Critical Biography*, 76.

19. Chopin deleted many sentences from the magazine version as she revised it for inclusion in *Bayou Folk*, removing expository commentary and allowing the importance of many details to be clear by implication. For original publication, see Kate Chopin, "Beyond the Bayou," *Youth's Companion* 66 (June 15, 1893): 302-03.

20. Ewell provides an insightful discussion of this point in *Kate Chopin*, 62–63.

21. See Bonnie James Shaker, *Coloring Locals: Racial Formation in Kate Chopin's* Youth Companion *Stories* (Iowa City: University of Iowa Press, 2003), 72–73.

22. See Kate Chopin, "The Return of Alcibiade," *St. Louis Life* 7 (December 12, 1892), 6–8.

23. The only significant difference in the two texts is that in *St. Louis Life* Robert McFarlane is called Robert McAlpin.

24. Barbara Ewell is insightful on the point of the dual plot (*Kate Chopin*, 63).

25. For original publication, see Kate Chopin, "A Wizard from Gettysburg," *Youth's Companion* 65 (July 7, 1892): 346–47.

26. Ewell, *Kate Chopin*, 63.

27. Shaker argues that he restores the "privilege" of the family, thus restoring their "absolute power" (*Coloring Locals*, 40).

28. See Kate Chopin, "A Lady of Bayou St. John," *Vogue* 2 (September 21, 1893), 154–58. The author altered very little in the later edition, although "Manna-Lulu" in *Vogue* becomes "Manna-Loulou" in the book.

29. See Toth, *Kate Chopin*, 221.

30. For more detailed information, see Hamilton Basso, *Beauregard: The Great Creole* (New York: Charles Scribner's Sons, 1933).

31. I am indebted here to Tonette Bond Inge, "Kate Chopin," in *American Short-Story Writers, 1800–1910, Dictionary of Literary Biography*, vol. 78, ed. Bobby Ellen Kimbel and William E. Grant (Detroit: Gale, 1989), 98.

32. See Kate Chopin, "La Belle Zoraïde," *Vogue* 3 (January 4, 1894), 2–10. As is customary for Chopin, there were few changes in the text, but a sentence was added in the book version to Zoraïde's protestation that she will kill herself if she cannot have Mézor. Her simple statement "I could not help it" in *Vogue* was changed to "but when I heard le beau Mézor say to me, 'Zoraïde, mo l'aime toi,' I could have died, but I could not have helped loving him" (285).

33. See Robert C. Evans, *Kate Chopin's Short Fiction: A Critical Companion* (West Cornwall: Locust Hill Press, 2001), 381. This section of the book is a compilation of comments from a score or more of readers, some of them students.

34. I am indebted here to Evans, 383–84.

35. See Lynn Cothern, "Speech and Authorship in Kate Chopin's 'La Belle Zoraïde'," *Louisiana Literature* 11, no. 1 (1994): 118.

36. For original publication, see Kate Chopin, "The Bênitous' Slave," *Harper's Young People*, 13 (February 16, 1892): 280. There were only minor alterations when the story was included in *Bayou Folk*.

37. Ewell, 67.

38. For the original publication of the story, see Kate Chopin, "Ma'ame Pelagie," *New Orleans Times Democrat* (December 24, 1893), 23.

39. See Seyersted, *Critical Biography*, 94.

40. Ewell, *Kate Chopin*, 65.

41. See Seyersted, *Critical Biography*, 94.

42. The first publication was Kate Chopin, "A Rude Awakening," *Youth's Companion*, 66 (February 2, 1893): 54–55. Chopin deleted two paragraphs from the magazine version for *Bayou Folk*, both of which describe Sylveste as lazy but treating Lolotte with kindness. Joe Duplon in the magazine became Joe Duplan in the book.

43. Seyersted, *Critical Biography*, 78.

44. See Shaker, *Coloring Locals*, 47.

45. See Kate Chopin, *At Fault* (St. Louis, 1890). The novel was privately printed.

46. See Seyersted, *Critical Biography*, 122–23.

47. For original publication, see Kate Chopin, "Love on the Bon-Dieu," *Two Tales* 2 (July 23, 1892): 148–56.

48. Nina Baym, "Introduction" to Kate Chopin, *The Awakening and Selected Stories* (Cambridge: Cambridge University Press, 1981), vii–xi.

49. Linda Wagner-Martin, "Kate Chopin's Fascination with Young Men," in *Critical Essays on Kate Chopin*, ed. Alice Hall Petry (New York: G. K. Hall, 1996), 203.

50. Ewell has commented insightfully on this point (*Kate Chopin*, 76).

51. For first publication, see Kate Chopin, "Désirée's Baby," *Vogue*, 1 (January 14, 1893), 70–71, 74.

52. Per Seyersted offers an informed discussion of these matters (*Critical Biography*, 94).

53. See Fred Lewis Pattee, *A History of American Literature Since 1870* (New York: Century, 1915), 365.

54. Robert Cecil Beale, *The Development of the Short Story in the South* (Charlottesville: Michie, 1911), 63.

55. See Daniel Rankin, *Kate Chopin and Her Creole Stories* (Philadelphia: University of Pennsylvania Press, 1932), 133–34, and Joseph J. Reilly, "Stories by Kate Chopin," *Commonweal*, 25 (March 26, 1937), 73–74.

56. Ewell also discusses Armand in terms of classical tragedy (*Kate Chopin*, 70).

57. Gaudet, "Kate Chopin and the Lore of Cane River's Creoles of Color," 45–52.

58. Mary E. Papke, in *Verging on the Abyss: The Social Fiction of Kate Chopin and Edith Wharton* (New York: Greenwood Press, 1990), 55, discusses Madame Valmondé as the character with the most "liberated consciousness."

59. Elfenbein is insightful in pointing out Madame Valmondé's love for her daughter and Désirée's love for her child, both despite race (*Women on the Color Line*, 126).

60. See Kate Chopin, "The Lover of Mentine," *Vogue*, 1 (January 14, 1893), 74–75.

61. Stein, *Women and Autonomy*, 27.

62. I am indebted here to Stein, 28.

63. For original publication, see Kate Chopin, "Loka," *Youth's Companion*, 65 (December 22, 1892): 670–71.

64. See Ewell, *Kate Chopin*, 69.

65. Shaker, *Coloring Locals*, 64.

66. See Robert Arner, "Kate Chopin," *Louisiana Studies* 14 (1975): 24–25. Arner gives the narrative perspective extended discussion.

67. Inge argues that Loka returns because of her sense of social responsibility ("Kate Chopin," 95). I maintain that it is a matter of psychological change based on love.

68. For original publication see Kate Chopin, "For Marse Chouchoute," *Youth's Companion*, 64 (August 20, 1891): 450–51. There are few changes between the magazine and book versions, but Ma'ame Armand became Ma'ame Verchette in *Bayou Folk*.

69. See Shaker, *Coloring Locals*, 28.

70. See Walker, *Kate Chopin*, 60.

71. Shaker, *Coloring Locals*, 28.

72. For original publication, see Kate Chopin, "A Turkey Hunt," *Harper's Young People* 13 (February 16, 1892): 287.

73. For one such comment, see Ewell, *Kate Chopin*, 68.

74. Peggy Skaggs, *Kate Chopin* (New York: Twayne Publishers, 1985), 13.

75. For original publication see Kate Chopin, "Boulôt and Boulotte," *Harper's Young People* 13 (December 8, 1891): 112.

76. Ewell, *Kate Chopin*, 51–52.

77. For original publication see Kate Chopin, "A Very Fine Fiddle," *Harper's Young People* 13 (November 24, 1891): 79. Cléophat in the magazine is Cléophas in the book.

78. Walker, *Kate Chopin*, 92.

79. I am indebted here to O'Neal, "New Orleans Realists," 163.

80. Kate Chopin, review of Hamlin Garland's *Crumbling Idols*, *St. Louis Life*, 10 (October 6, 1894), 13.

81. Sara deSaussure Davis, "Kate Chopin," in *American Realists and Naturalists*, ed. Donald Pizer and Earl N. Harbert, *Dictionary of Literary Biography*, vol. 12 (Detroit: Gale, 1982), 70.

82. Taylor, *Gender, Race, and Region*, 139.

83. Pattee, *History*, 327.

Conclusion

1. Per Seyersted, *Kate Chopin: A Critical Biography* (Oslo: Universitetsforlaget, 1969), 81.

2. Grace King, *Memories of a Southern Woman of Letters* (New York: Macmillan, 1932), 60.

3. King, *Memories,* 182–83.

4. Mary Anne O'Neal, "New Orleans Realists: Grace King, Kate Chopin, and Alice Dunbar-Nelson" (Ph.D. dissertation, University of Georgia, 1999), 331.

5. For a more detailed analysis of this point, see Violet Harrington Bryan,

"Race and Gender in the Early Works of Alice Dunbar-Nelson," in *Louisiana Women Writers: New Essays and a Comprehensive Bibliography*, ed. Dorothy H. Brown and Barbara C. Ewell (Baton Rouge: Louisiana State University Press, 1992), 121.

6. Seyersted, *Critical Biography*, 81.

7. Seyersted, 80.

8. Bryan, "Race and Gender in the Early Works of Alice Dunbar-Nelson," 44.

Bibliography

Ammons, Elizabeth. *Conflicting Stories: American Women Writers at the Turn into the Twentieth Century*. Oxford: Oxford University Press, 1991.

Ammons, Elizabeth, and Valerie Rohy. *American Local Color Writing, 1880–1920*. New York: Penguin, 1998.

Anderson, James D. *The Education of Blacks in the South, 1860–1935*. Chapel Hill: University of North Carolina Press, 1988.

Anonymous. "*Bayou Folk.*" *Critic* 21 (May 5, 1894): 299–300.

———. "*Bayou Folk.*" *New Orleans Daily Picayune* (April 15, 1894), 14.

———. "Book Reviews." *Public Opinion* 17 (April 12, 1894), 35.

———. "Literary Notices. Recent Fiction." *Hartford Daily Courant*, (April 19, 1894), 10.

———. "*Madame Delphine.*" *Critic* 1 (July 16, 1881), 190.

———. "The New Books." *Review of Reviews* 9 (May, 1894), 625.

Arner, Robert. "Kate Chopin." *Louisiana Studies* 14 (1975), 11–139.

———. "Pride and Prejudice: Kate Chopin's 'Désirée's Baby'." In *Critical Essays on Kate Chopin*, ed. Alice Hall Petry, 139–46. New York: G. K. Hall, 1996.

Asbury, Herbert. *The French Quarter: An Informal History of the New Orleans Underworld*. New York: Alfred A. Knopf, 1936.

Baade, Hans W. "The Law of Slavery in Spanish Luisiana, 1769–1803." In *The Spanish Presence in Louisiana, 1769–1803*, edited by Gilbert C. Din, 366–90. Baton Rouge: Louisiana State University Press, 1983.

Basso, Hamilton. *Beauregard: The Great Creole*. New York: Charles Scribner's Sons, 1933.

Bauer, Margaret D. "Armand Aubigny, Still Passing After All These Years: The Narrative Voice and Historical Context of 'Désirée's Baby.'" In *Critical Essays on Kate Chopin*, ed. Alice Hall Petry, 161–83. New York: G. K. Hall, 1996.

Baym, Nina. Introduction to *The Awakening and Selected Stories,* by Kate Chopin, vii–xi. Cambridge: Cambridge University Press, 1981.

Beale, Robert Cecil. *The Development of the Short Story in the South*. Charlottesville: Michie, 1911.

Benfey, Christopher. *Degas in New Orleans: Encounters in the Creole World of Kate Chopin and George Washington Cable.* New York: Alfred A. Knopf, 1997.

Berlin, Ira. *Many Thousands Gone: The First Two Centuries of Slavery in North America*. Cambridge: Harvard University Press, 1998.

Bikle, Lucy Leffingwell Cable. *George W. Cable: His Life and Letters*. New York: Charles Scribner's Sons, 1928.

Bonner, Thomas. "Kate Chopin's *Bayou Folk* Revisited." *New Laurel Review* 7, no. 2 (1977): 5–14.

Brasseaux, Carl A., Keith P. Fontenot, and Claude F. Oubre. *Creoles of Color of the Bayou Country*. Jackson: University Press of Mississippi, 1994.

Brooks, Kristina. "Alice Dunbar-Nelson's Local Colors of Ethnicity, Class, and Place." *MELUS* 23, no. 2 (1998): 3–26.

Bryan, Violet Harrington. "Creating and Re-creating the Myth of New Orleans: Grace King and Alice Dunbar-Nelson." *Publications of the Mississippi Philological Association* (1987): 185–96.

———. *The Myth of New Orleans in Literature: Dialogues of Race and Gender*. Knoxville: University of Tennessee Press, 1993.

———. "Race and Gender in the Early Works of Alice Dunbar-Nelson." In *Louisiana Women Writers: New Essays and a Comprehensive Bibliography*, ed. Dorothy H. Brown and Barbara C. Ewell, 121–38. Baton Rouge: Louisiana State University Press, 1992.

Bull, Sara Chapman Thorp, *Ole Bull: A Memoir*. Boston: Houghton Mifflin, 1882.

Bush, Robert. "Charles Gayarré and Grace King: Letters of a Louisiana Friendship." *Southern Literary Journal* 7, no. 1 (1974): 100–131.

———. *Grace King: A Southern Destiny*. Baton Rouge: Louisiana State University Press, 1983.

———. "Grace King and Mark Twain." *American Literature* 44, no. 1 (1972): 31–51.

———. *Grace King of New Orleans: A Selection of Her Writings*. Baton Rouge: Louisiana State University Press, 1973.

Butcher, Philip. *George Washington Cable*. New Haven: College and University Press, 1962.

Cable, George Washington. *The Creoles of Louisiana*. New York: Scribner's, 1884.

———. *The Negro Question*. New York: American Missionary Association, 1888.

———. *Old Creole Days*. New York: Scribner's, 1879.

Campanella, Richard. *Bienville's Dilemma: A Historical Geography of New Orleans.* Lafayette: Center for Louisiana Studies, 2008.

Chopin, Kate. *Bayou Folk.* Boston: Houghton Mifflin, 1894.

———. *The Complete Works of Kate Chopin.* Baton Rouge: Louisiana State University Press, 1969.

———. *Kate Chopin's Private Papers.* Edited by Emily Toth and Per Seyersted. Bloomington: Indiana University Press, 1998.

Civil Code of the State of Louisiana. New Orleans: J. C. de St. Romes, 1825.

Clark, Robert C. "At the Corner of Bourbon and Toulouse Street: The Historical Context of Alice Dunbar-Nelson's 'M'sieu Fortier's Violin.'" *American Literary Realism* 41, no. 2 (2009): 163–79.

Clark, William Bedford. "Cable and the Theme of Miscegenation in *Old Creole Days* and *The Grandissimes.*" *Mississippi Quarterly* 30 (Fall 1977): 597–609.

Cleman, John. *George Washington Cable Revisited.* New York: Twayne Publishers, 1996.

Coleman, Linda S. "At Odds: Race and Gender in Grace King's Short Fiction." In *Louisiana Women Writers: New Essays and a Comprehensive Bibliography*, ed. Dorothy H. Brown and Barbara Ewell, 33–55. Baton Rouge: Louisiana State University Press, 1992.

Cothern, Lynn. "Speech and Authorship in Kate Chopin's 'La Belle Zoraïde.'" *Louisiana Literature* 11, no. 1 (1994): 118–25.

Davis, Kenneth. "Racial Designation in Louisiana: One Drop of Black Blood Makes a Negro!" *Hastings Constitutional Law Quarterly* 3, no. 1 (1976): 199–228.

Davis, Sara deSaussure. "Kate Chopin." In *American Realists and Naturalists, Dictionary of Literary Biography*, vol. 12, ed. Donald Pizer and Earl N. Harbert, 59–71. Detroit: Gale, 1982.

Dawdy, Shannon Lee. *Building the Devil's Empire: French Colonial New Orleans.* Chicago: University of Chicago Press, 2008.

Detiege, Sister Audrey Marie. *Henriette Delille, Free Woman of Color: Foundress of the Sisters of the Holy Family.* New Orleans: Sisters of the Holy Family, 1976.

Domínguez, Virginia R. *White by Definition: Social Classification in Creole Louisiana.* New Brunswick: Rutgers University Press, 1986.

Donovan, Josephine. "New England Local-Color Literature: A Colonial Formation." In *A Companion to the American Short Story*, ed. Alfred Bendixen and James Nagel, 91–104. Oxford: Wiley-Blackwell, 2010.

Dunbar-Nelson, Alice. *The Goodness of St. Rocque and Other Stories.* New York: Dodd, Mead, 1899.

———. "People of Color in Louisiana, Part I." *Journal of Negro History* 1 (1916): 361–76.

———. "People of Color in Louisiana, Part II." *Journal of Negro History* 2 (1917): 51–78.

———. *Violets and Other Tales*. Boston: Monthly Review, 1895.

Dunn, Maggie, and Ann Morris. *The Composite Novel: The Short Story Cycle in Transition*. New York: Twayne, 1995.

Ekstrom, Kjell. *George Washington Cable: A Study of His Early Life and Work*. Uppsala: A. B. Lundequistska Bokhandeln, 1950.

Elfenbein, Anna Shannon. *Women on the Color Line: Evolving Stereotypes and the Writings of George Washington Cable, Grace King, Kate Chopin*. Charlottesville: University Press of Virginia, 1989.

Evans, Robert C. *Kate Chopin's Short Fiction: A Critical Companion*. West Cornwall: Locust Hill Press, 2001.

Ewell, Barbara C. *Kate Chopin*. New York: Ungar, 1986.

Fetterley, Judith, and Marjorie Pryse. *American Women Regionalists, 1850–1910*. New York: W. W. Norton, 1992.

Fletcher, Marie. "The Southern Woman in the Fiction of Kate Chopin." *Louisiana History* 7 (Spring, 1966): 117–132.

French, B. F. *Historical Collections of Louisiana: Embracing Translations of Many Rare and Valuable Documents Relating to the Natural, Civil, and Political History of that State*. New York: D. Appleton, 1851.

Fulweiler, Howard W. "Of Time and the River: 'Ancestral Nonsense' vs. Inherited Guilt in Cable's 'Belles Demoiselles Plantation.'" *Midcontinent American Studies Journal* 7 (Fall, 1966): 53–59.

Garland, Hamlin. *Crumbling Idols: Twelve Essays on Art Dealing Chiefly with Literature, Painting, and the Drama*. Chicago: Stone and Kimball, 1894.

———. *Roadside Meetings*. New York: Macmillan, 1930.

Gaudet, Marcia. "Kate Chopin and the Lore of Cane River's Creoles of Color." *Xavier Review* 6, no. 1 (1986): 45–52.

Gebhard, Caroline. "Inventing a 'Negro Literature': Race, Dialect, and Gender in the Early Work of Paul Lawrence Dunbar, James Weldon Johnson, and Alice Dunbar-Nelson." In *Post-Bellum, Pre-Harlem: African American Literature and Culture*, ed. Barbara McCaskill and Caroline Gebhard, 162–68. New York: New York University Press, 2006.

Gosse, Edmund. "*Madame Delphine.*" *Saturday Review* (London), 52 (August 20, 1881): 237–38.

Grant, Jürgen. "Rewriting the Final Adjustment of Affairs: Culture, Race, and Politics in Alice Dunbar-Nelson's New Orleans." *Short Story* 9, no. 1 (2001): 46–57.

Hall, Gwendolyn Midlo. *Africans in Colonial Louisiana: The Development of Afro-Creole Culture in the Eighteenth Century*. Baton Rouge: Louisiana State University Press, 1994.

Hearn, Lafcadio. "The Scenes of Cable's Romances." *Century Magazine*, 27 (November 1883): 40–47.

Howell, Elmo. "Kate Chopin and The Creole Country." *Louisiana History* 20, no. 1 (1979): 209–19.

Hull, Gloria T. "Alice Dunbar-Nelson: A Regional Approach." In *Teaching Women's Literature from a Regional Perspective*, ed. Leonore Hoffman and Deborah Rosenfelt, 64–68. New York: Modern Language Association of America, 1982.

———. Introduction to *The Works of Alice Dunbar-Nelson*, vol. 1, by Alice Dunbar-Nelson, xxix–liv. Oxford: Oxford University Press, 1988.

———. "Researching Alice Dunbar-Nelson: A Personal and Literary Perspective." *Feminist Studies* 6, no. 2 (1980): 314–20.

———. "Shaping Contradictions: Alice Dunbar-Nelson and the Black Creole Experience." *New Orleans Review* 15, no. 1 (1988): 34–37.

Inge, Tonette Bond. "Kate Chopin." In *American Short-Story Writers, 1800–1910, Dictionary of Literary Biography*, vol. 78, ed. Bobby Ellen Kimbel and William E. Grant, 90–110. Detroit: Gale, 1989.

Ingram, Forrest L. *Representative Short Story Cycles of the Twentieth Century*. The Hague: Mouton, 1971.

Johnson, Robert Underwood. "Cable's *Madame Delphine.*" *Scribner's Monthly* 22 (September 1881): 791.

Johnson, Walter. *Soul by Soul: Life Inside the Antebellum Slave Market*. Cambridge: Harvard University Press, 1999.

Justice, Maibelle. "*Bayou Folk* by Kate Chopin." *Godey's* 130 (April 1895): 432.

Kennedy, J. Gerald, ed. *Modern American Short Story Sequences: Composite Fictions and Fictive Communities*. Cambridge: Cambridge University Press, 1995.

Kilbourne, Richard Holcombe, Jr. *A History of the Louisiana Civil Code*. Baton Rouge: Paul Herbert Law Centre Publications Institute, 1987.

King, Grace. *Balcony Stories*. New York: Century, 1893.

———. *Creole Families of New Orleans*. New York: Macmillan, 1921.

———. *A History of Louisiana*, with John R. Ficklen. New Orleans: Graham, 1893.

———. *Memories of a Southern Woman of Letters*. New York: Macmillan, 1932.

———. *New Orleans: The Place and the People*. New York: Macmillan, 1928.

———. "A Southern Educator: Mrs. Mary Humphreys Stamps." *Century* 78 (1909): 271–76.

Kirby, David. *Grace King*. Boston: Twayne, 1980

———. "Grace King." In *American Realists and Naturalists, Dictionary of Literary Biography*, vol. 12, ed. Donald Pizer and Earl N. Harbert, 342–46. Detroit: Gale Research Company, 1982.

Koloski, Bernard. *Kate Chopin: A Study of the Short Fiction*. New York: Twayne, 1996.

Kreyling, Michael. "George Washington Cable." In *American Realists and Naturalists, Dictionary of Literary Biography*, vol. 12, ed. Donald Pizer and Earl N. Harbert, 42–50. Detroit: Gale Research Company, 1982.

LaBarre, Delia, ed. *The New Orleans of Lacadio Hearn*. Baton Rouge: Louisiana State University Press, 2007.

Lundén, Rolf. *The United Stories of America: Studies in the Short Story Composite*. Amsterdam: Rodopi, 1999.

McReynolds, Douglas J. "Passion Repressed: The Short Fiction of Grace King." *Rocky Mountain Review of Language and Literature* 37, no. 4 (1983): 207–16.

Mann, Susan Garland. *The Short Story Cycle: A Genre Companion and Reference Guide*. Westport: Greenwood Press, 1989.

Martin, Joan M. "*Plaçage* and the Louisiana *Gens de Couleur Libre*: How Race and Sex Defined the Lifestyles of Free Women of Color." In *Creole: The History and Legacy of Louisiana's Free People of Color*, ed. Sybil Kein, 57–70. Baton Rouge: Louisiana State University Press, 2000.

Menke, Pamela Glenn. "Behind the 'White Veil': Alice Dunbar-Nelson, Creole Color, and *The Goodness of St. Rocque*." In *Songs of the Reconstructing South: Building Literary Louisiana, 1865–1945*, ed. Suzanne Disheroon-Green and Lisa Abney, 77–88. Westport: Greenwood, 2002.

Metcalf, Eugene Wesley, Jr. "The Letters of Paul and Alice Dunbar: A Private History." Dissertation, University of California, Irvine, 1973.

Mills, Gary B. *The Forgotten People: Cane River's Creoles of Color*. Baton Rouge: Louisiana State University Press, 1977.

"Mrs. Kate Chopin, Author of *Bayou Folk*." *Current Literature* 16, no. 2 (1894): 106.

Nagel, James. "The American Short-Story Cycle." In *The Columbia Companion to the Twentieth-Century American Short Story*, ed. Blanche Gelfant, 9–14. New York: Columbia University Press, 2001.

———. *The Contemporary American Short-Story Cycle*. Baton Rouge: Louisiana State University Press, 2001.

———, ed. *Anthology of the American Short Story*. Boston: Houghton Mifflin, 2001.

O'Neal, Mary Anne. "New Orleans Realists: Grace King, Kate Chopin, and Alice Dunbar-Nelson." dissertation, University of Georgia, 1999.

Papke, Mary E. *Verging on the Abyss: The Social Fiction of Kate Chopin and Edith Wharton*. New York: Greenwood Press, 1990.

Pattee, Fred Lewis. *The Development of the American Short Story*. New York: Harper and Brothers, 1923.

———. *A History of American Literature Since 1870*. New York: Century, 1915.

Petry, Alice Hall. *A Genius in His Way: The Art of Cable's* Old Creole Days. Rutherford: Fairleigh Dickinson University Press, 1988.

———, ed. *Critical Essays on Kate Chopin*. New York: G. K. Hall, 1996.

Powell, Lawrence N. *The Accidental City: Improvising New Orleans.* Cambridge: Harvard University Press, 2012.

Rankin, Daniel. *Kate Chopin and Her Creole Stories*. Philadelphia: University of Pennsylvania Press, 1932.

Reilly, Joseph J. "Stories by Kate Chopin." *Commonweal*, 25 (March 26, 1937): 71–74.

Rhode, Robert D. *Setting in the American Short Story of Local Color, 1865–1900*. The Hague: Mouton, 1975.

Ringe, Donald A. "Cane River World: Kate Chopin's *At Fault* and Related Stories." *Studies in American Fiction* 3, no. 1 (1975): 157–66.

———. "The Moral World of Cable's 'Belles Demoiselles Plantation'." *Mississippi Quarterly* 29 (Winter 1975–76): 83–90.

Rubin, Louis D., Jr. *George W. Cable: The Life and Times of a Southern Heretic*. New York: Pegasus, 1969.

Saxon, Lyle. *Fabulous New Orleans*. New York: Century, 1928.

Seyersted, Per. *Kate Chopin: A Critical Biography*. Oslo: Universitetsforlaget, 1969.

Shaker, Bonnie James. *Coloring Locals: Racial Formation in Kate Chopin's* Youth Companion *Stories*. Iowa City: University of Iowa Press, 2003.

Shurbutt, Sylvia Bailey. "The Cane River Characters and Revisionist Mythmaking in the Work of Kate Chopin." *Southern Literary Journal* 25, no. 2 (1993): 14–23.

Simpson, Claude M., ed. *The Local Colorists: American Short Stories, 1837–1900*. New York: Harper and Brothers, 1960.

Skaggs, Peggy. *Kate Chopin*. New York: Twayne, 1985.

Sollors, Werner. *Neither Black nor White Yet Both: Thematic Explorations of Interracial Literature*. Oxford: Oxford University Press, 1997.

Stampp, Kenneth M. *The Era of Reconstruction, 1865–1877*. New York: Alfred A. Knopf, 1975.

Steiling, David. "Multi-cultural Aesthetic in Kate Chopin's 'A Gentleman of Bayou Teche.'" *Mississippi Quarterly* 47 (Spring 1994): 197–200.

Stein, Allen F. *Women and Autonomy in Kate Chopin's Short Fiction*. New York: Peter Lang, 2005.

Stouck, Jordan. "Identities in Crisis: Alice Dunbar-Nelson's New Orleans Fiction." *Canadian Review of American Studies* 34, no. 3 (2004): 269–89.

Strychacz, Thomas. "'You . . . Could Never Be Mistaken': Reading Alice Dunbar-Nelson's Rhetorical Diversions in *The Goodness of St. Rocque and Other Stories*." *Studies in American Fiction* 36 (2008): 77–94.

Sublette, Ned. *The World That Made New Orleans: From Spanish Silver to Congo Square.* Chicago: Lawrence Hill Books, 2008.

Taylor, Helen. *Gender, Race, and Region in the Writings of Grace King, Ruth McEnery Stuart, and Kate Chopin*. Baton Rouge: Louisiana State University Press, 1989.

Toth, Emily. *Kate Chopin*. Austin: University of Texas Press, 1990.

Turner, Arlin. *Critical Essays on George W. Cable.* Boston: G. K. Hall, 1980.

———. *George W. Cable: A Biography*. Baton Rouge: Louisiana State University Press, 1966.

———. "A Novelist Discovers a Novelist: The Correspondence of H. H. Boyesen and George W. Cable." *Western Humanities Review* 5 (1951): 343–72.

Wagner-Martin, Linda. "Kate Chopin's Fascination with Young Men." In *Critical Essays on Kate Chopin*, edited by Alice Hall Petry, 197–206. New York: G. K. Hall, 1996.

Walker, Nancy A. *Kate Chopin: A Literary Life*. New York: Palgrave, 2001.

White, Howard Ashley. "The Freemen's Bureau in Louisiana." Dissertation, Tulane University, 1955.

Whitlow, Robert. "Alice Dunbar-Nelson: New Orleans Writer." In *Regionalism and the Female Imagination: A Collection of Essays*, ed. Emily Toth, 109–25. New York: Human Sciences, 1985.

Wiley, Bell Irvin. *Southern Negroes, 1861–1865*. Baton Rouge: Louisiana State University Press, 1938.

Williams, Ora. "Alice Moore Dunbar Nelson." In *Afro-American Writers before the Harlem Renaissance, Dictionary of Literary Biography*, vol. 50, ed. Trudier Harris and Thadious M. Davis, 225–33. Detroit: Gale Research Company, 1986.

Wilson, Edmund. "Mr. Hemingway's Dry-Points." *Dial* 77 (October 1924): 340–41.

Wilson, Theodore B. *The Black Codes of the South*. Tuscaloosa: University of Alabama Press, 1965.

Index